CREATIVE WEEKENDS

23½ Ready-to-Use Events for Single Adult Ministry

Compiled by Paul Petersen

Cook Ministry Resources
a division of Cook Communications Ministries
Colorado Springs, Colorado—Paris, Ontario

SINGLES MINISTRY RESOURCES is a division of Cook Communications
Ministries International (CCMI). In fulfilling its mission to encourage the acceptance of Jesus Christ as personal Savior and to contribute to the teaching and putting into practice of His two great
commandments, CCMI creates and disseminates Christian communication materials and services to people throughout the
world. SINGLES MINISTRY RESOURCES provides training seminars, a
national convention, a journal, and resource materials to assist
churches in developing a ministry with single adults that will
encourage growth in loving God and each other.

Creative Weekends
Compiled by Paul Petersen

Cover illustration by Randy Lyhus
Cover design by Helen Lannis
Interior design by Paula Grocke
Edited by Ardith Bradford, Jerry Jones, Jean Stephens,
    Cathy Walker, and Jeffery Wallace

Printed in the United States of America

ISBN 0-7814-5060-8

10   9   8   7   6   5   4   3   2

TABLE OF CONTENTS

ICEBREAKERS AND TEAM-BUILDING EXERCISES

ACKNOWLEDGMENTS

The Network of Single Adult Leaders provides many avenues for involvement and leadership in single adult ministries nationally. This book is the result of that involvement and leadership. Many thanks to all who have contributed to this book, not only those whose names appear, but also to the others who submitted excellent ideas, but could not be included due to space limitations or topical balance.

From the time I was in the fifth grade, I've been going on retreats and other special weekend events. They have changed my life. I am thankful to Woody Strodel, who took me on that first fifth grade getaway, and has remained a friend and mentor.

Foundational to the events presented in this book are concepts, ideas, job descriptions, and timelines. I am grateful to Paul Clough of Single Point Ministries and John Splinter of Single Life Ministries for many of these basic resources. But I am most grateful for the Bridges Singles Class of Highland Park Presbyterian Church in Dallas, Texas. Not only did they provide many of the background or support materials, but also my inspirational material. Jesus said, "I am the Bread of Life" (John 6:48). We ate richly for many years together.

It is my prayer that as you use this book it will be a resource that draws you and your single adults closer to Christ and enhances your ministry to all that He brings to you.

—*Paul M. Petersen*

INTRODUCTION: HOW TO USE THIS BOOK

**Nearly Five Years of Creative Weekend Ideas
for Your Singles Ministry**

That's right. Depending on how many special events per year you want, this book has from two years (one per month) to eleven years (two per year) of ideas. And every one has been used and recommended by your peers. Try every idea in the book. Or select only a few that seem to most effectively fit your needs. Adapt and improve these ideas to best accomplish your ministry objectives.

WHY A BOOK ON CREATIVE WEEKENDS?

You may notice that we did not use the title *Creative Retreats*. This book is not just about retreats, although there are many excellent ones included. This is a book about a variety of special weekend events.

As we looked across the country at strong, growing ministries with single adults, one common fact was that their annual programming included a special weekend event two, three, four, or more times each year. These weekends generated special energy and excitement or provided a concentrated opportunity for personal and spiritual growth.

One of the most important aspects of building a healthy single-adult ministry is developing quality relationships. And weekend events can be one of the best ways to stimulate camaraderie and deepen relationships. Think back in your own life. If you are like most of us, you can remember at least one special weekend event—a conference, a getaway, a retreat, an outdoor adventure—when you solidified your relationship with God; deepened a relationship with a friend; were inspired, motivated, encouraged, or challenged; began a new significant relationship; or found some quiet and peace that helped you gain a new perspective on life. Such events are often high points in our lives.

Weekends will offer the same benefits for your ministry. Due to their more concentrated nature, they are one of the best relationship-building, growth-nurturing, community-developing things you can do in your ministry. Whether a social function, a camping trip, a leadership training event, or a community service project, weekend events bring people together for fun, fellowship, and personal growth.

The weekend events in this book provide single adults with opportunities for getting acquainted, playing, reflecting, discussing issues, studying God's Word, singing, praying, interacting, resting, and enjoying God's great outdoors. This book provides you with hands-on, step-by-step instructions for weekend ideas that have been submitted by other singles ministry leaders. Their prayer is that your ministry will be enriched—as theirs have been—by the ideas in this book.

If you are already involved in planning weekend events, we want to give you some new, fresh ideas to consider. There will be a decline in interest if your singles begin to notice that the activities and events are the same old thing year after year. Nothing stays the same in our constantly changing culture. For example, during the past several years much of the singles ministry focus has been on baby boomers. But now a growing number of the singles in our groups are baby busters. In many ways they are responding differently, often seeking more condensed weekend events.

Furthermore, nearly everyone today expects more choices, more options. Remember that in a short period of time we have gone from three network television channels to at least fifty cable stations. People expect a tremendous range of choice in almost every area of life. There are many changes taking place in the church and in our world. And there are new groups to reach.

We have to constantly find ways to make what we do relevant and practical for those we are trying to reach. That effort includes developing new traditions. That's why this book explores a variety of weekend ideas to help stimulate and explore some new ways to bring freshness to your weekend planning.

BUILD YOUR OWN EVENT

This book promises twenty-three and one-half weekend events for single adults. What's the half idea? It's actually a list of ideas to use in building your own creative event. Using the "Basic Steps: How to Create a Successful Event," the resource pages in the appendix, and the outline on page 224, you can create your own event or adapt any of the ideas in this book for use with your own single-adult group.

HOW TO USE THIS BOOK

Remember that the material in this book is to be seen as a helpful guide. Adapt, change, and add to this information as needed to meet your specific planning needs.

As Your Event Planning Guide

After selecting an event, photocopy the Planning Timeline pages for that event, along with the appropriate checklists and resources on pages 225-255, for each member of your Planning Team.

As an Idea Starter

Use this book to get your creative juices flowing. As you look through the ideas, let your mind imagine and dream. What new, innovative ideas can this book stimulate? Encourage your leadership team to look through this book, too. Then have a brainstorming session about weekend events that will be especially meaningful for your church and community.

As a Source for Icebreakers and Team-Building Exercises

This book includes many activities. Refer to the Table of Contents for a list of ideas that can be used in a variety of settings.

REPRODUCIBLE RESOURCES

Many pages in this book are reproducible. Whenever you see this icon you have permission to copy the page or resource.

BASIC STEPS: HOW TO CREATE A SUCCESSFUL EVENT

Follow these basic steps as you move from the dreaming stage to planning, implementing, and evaluating your event.

1. RECRUIT A PLANNING TEAM—AND GIVE THEM OWNERSHIP.

Developing an effective leadership team is how a successful event begins, so the first and most important step is praying about who should be a part of that team. An effective singles weekend event needs a team of people who own it, lead it, and develop the schedule of events. Recruit volunteers who work well with others and who have the skills for completing the tasks to be done. Also, choose leaders who represent every group within the single-adult community—people who are new and those who have been around for a long time; men and women; those with a variety of backgrounds and gifts. Be sure to select leaders who delegate and get others involved.

As you will find, each event in this book has been designed to involve as many people as possible. Although this may make the process more time-consuming and less controlled, it will give your single adults needed ownership in the event, a sense of belonging, and an opportunity to grow and serve. Getting singles involved in the planning process also encourages relationship building and offers varied ministry opportunities—always a plus for a healthy, growing ministry. Furthermore, everyone on the Planning Team is sure to attend the event—another good reason to encourage many people to get involved.

However, if you must assign more than one task to an individual, be careful not to use the same person in too many roles. Though the singles ministry leader may take on all or part of the Event Director's responsibilities, all other tasks should be assigned to volunteers if possible.

2. PRAY.

Encourage each person on the Planning Team to prepare for the event with prayer. Ask for God's guidance each step of the way as you each seek to make this event one that will help single adults come to know Him better and to bring honor to His name.

3. MAKE SURE EACH PERSON'S RESPONSIBILITIES AND DEADLINES ARE CLEAR.

Have accountability in each area of responsibility. Agree on a timetable and deadlines. Go over the specific areas of responsibility with the members of the Planning Team. Equip and train them as necessary. Help them all plan for success.

In this book there are reproducible step-by-step guides, suggestions, and checklists for the following areas of responsibility:

Event Director (see page 226)

Assistant Event Director (see page 227)

Audio/Visual Coordinator (see page 228)

Budget Coordinator (see page 229)

Bus Captains Coordinator (see page 231)

Children's Coordinator (see page 232)

Drama Coach (see page 232)

Equipment/Supplies Coordinator (see page 233)

Event Materials Coordinator (see page 233)

Event Site Coordinator (see page 234)

Food Coordinator (see page 236)

Hospitality Coordinator (see page 227)

Music Coordinator (see page 237)

Publicity Coordinator (see page 238)

Recreation Coordinator (see page 240)

Registration Coordinator (see page 241)

Retreat Leader (see page 240)

Small-Group Coordinator (see page 247)

Speaker/Workshop Leaders Coordinator (see page 250)

Transportation Coordinator (see page 252)

Worship Coordinator (see page 251)

4. SET GOAL(S).

Once your Planning Team has been selected, meet to brainstorm and explore ideas. Discuss the question, "What do we want to accomplish?" Be specific. Determine your goals and write them down. You may include: "To provide a quiet, meditative time that allows people to focus on God. To build people up. To have fun." All the ensuing decisions hinge on the Planning Team's goals for the event.

5. FIND A PLACE AND SET A TIME.

Finding the best time to hold your event is a daunting but important task. Consider the lead time needed to schedule and plan the event, the best time of year for this type of event, and other possible conflicting activities on the church or community calendar. Once you've settled on a date, CLAIM IT! Make sure the date appears on all of the appropriate church calendars, and announce it to your group.

6. PLAN THE PROGRAM.

Refer to the many program ideas and activities in this book. Or develop your own. What are the elements of the event that will work best in your situation? What are the topics or issues to address? And what would be the best way to address them?

Most of the events in this book do not require a special outside speaker, but if you choose to have one, what kind of speaker do you need? What do you want your participants to leave with, and how can you best accomplish that?

Whatever type of program you plan, make it lively and enjoyable. Consider including icebreakers and games where appropriate. (See Table of Contents for suggestions.)

7. WORK OUT THE DETAILS.

Do a pre-event walk-through, asking yourself questions from the perspective of someone who will be attending one of your events for the first time. (Always be sensitive to newcomers.) This will help you identify and take care of details that can make the event run smoothly and efficiently. The following walk-through can be modified for use in planning your event.

Pre-Event Walk-Through

❖ Participants are at work or at home and are ready to leave for the event. Do they know what to bring along? How did they get this information? Do they have maps? How did they get them?

❖ The speaker/musician(s) must get to the event location. How are they coming—by car, bus, plane? Who's picking them up? Does that person have all necessary travel information (flight numbers, arrival times, etc.)? Who's attending to the lodging reservations and paying the honorarium? Who's taking care of the travel needs of the speaker/musician(s) after the retreat?

❖ Participants arrive at a pickup point or final destination. Do they know what to do with their cars? How do they know? What do they do when they arrive? Where do they find their name tags and room assignments? How and when will all of this be communicated?

❖ Participants go to their rooms, freshen up, and then go to the hospitality area. How are room assignments being handled? Who's responsible? How do people know about the hospitality area? What will be included in the hospitality area? When will it be open? Who will run it?

Continue this process for each activity scheduled. Anticipate questions that might come up or things that might go wrong: someone has a flat tire while bringing the musician or the speaker; a workshop leader calls in sick at the last moment; the sound system isn't set up properly. Create a rough game plan should problems like these occur.

The Event Director or a delegated person should lead in this exercise. As you do it, each Planning Team member should be thinking of his/her area(s) of responsibility, and making note of items that need attention. No detail should be left unassigned.

End the exercise at the point where people get into their cars or onto the bus and go home.

After doing this exercise three or four times for the event, the Planning Team gains a clear idea of what's planned, when it should happen, and who's in charge. This exercise gives them a good idea of what to do if problems arise.

8. DO IT!

9. EVALUATE THE EVENT AND THANK THE PEOPLE RESPONSIBLE.

Meet with the Planning Team within two weeks after the event to evaluate it and make recommendations for planning future events. Be sure to thank all leaders—in person or in writing—for their contributions to the event's success. (See page 255 for a sample evaluation form. See page 254 for suggested ways to follow up each event.)

HOW TO FIND THE RIGHT EVENT

Use this handy guide to locate a specific type of event. Adapt these events as needed to fit your particular needs.

DISCOVERY WEEKEND

An Interactive "Come-and-Go" Event

Event Summary: A unique "come-and-go" event that combines a number of traditional ideas: a Friday night banquet, a Saturday morning clinic, a Saturday night talk show feature, and Sunday school, using one Discovery theme, and possibly one or two guest speakers.

Length of Event: Flexible schedule from Friday evening through Sunday morning

Suggested Theme Verse: Varies with Discovery topic selected

Ideal Number of Participants: 75+

Estimated Cost Per Person: $3–$30

Facility Requirements: Church and/or banquet meeting room

Recommended Planning Team: 12–15 people

Advance Planning Needed: 6–9 months

INTRODUCTION

by Doug Fagerstrom, Minister with Single Adults
Calvary Church, Grand Rapids, Michigan

For most single adults, deciding whether or not to attend a special event is fourfold. The first concern or question asked is, What is this weekend going to cost me in time and money? The second question soon follows: What is the topic, and is it relevant for my life today? Next, Who will be there to address the issues? The fourth concern is, Will anyone I know be there?

After ongoing dialogue with single adults, including their concerns about time, money, and personal issues, we developed Discovery Weekends. During a Discovery Weekend, each participant becomes a learner who takes a journey into uncharted territory. Questions need answers. Feelings need resolution. Actions need change. Some aspects of the journey may be painful, others bring moments of celebration.

We carefully chose the word *discovery* to represent the overall approach and understanding of how adults learn and make meaningful choices. We do not want to just tell single adults what to do, nor do we believe that just giving answers to their questions facilitates effective learning. We do believe that adults need to decide for themselves what to believe and do. The participants are given an opportunity to discover truth through the speaker, the Bible, and dialogue with others. Our role is to help them through the process of discovery.

A Discovery Weekend is a series of events or gatherings with a single focus and topic. The schedule for Friday night through Sunday morning or evening is very flexible. People can come and go throughout the weekend as they wish. Cost is minimal. Interpersonal dynamics and opportunities are non-threatening. Topics are presented in a way that encourages interaction during the dinner on Friday, the breaks, and the small groups. These discovery weekends provide a variety of options for single adults. The flexible schedule allows them to attend one or two sessions, or all the sessions if they choose. We've found these weekends to be very successful for our ministry.

OBJECTIVES

- ❖ To provide single adult participants an opportunity to seek, learn, grow, and be challenged in a particular area of need, concern, or biblical imperative.
- ❖ To build relationships and community.
- ❖ Depending upon the topic, to provide a tool for outreach to unchurched single adults.

THE BIG EVENT

SCHEDULE

Friday

❖ *Get as many people as possible involved in the planning of this event.*

6:30 P.M.—Registration table opens
7:30 or 8:00 P.M.—Banquet with speaker (Session 1)

Saturday

8:30 A.M.—Registration table opens (new participants only)
9:00 A.M.—Speaker (Session 2)
9:30 A.M.—Break/refreshments
10:00 A.M.—Clinics/workshops (Session 3)
11:30 A.M.—Speaker (Session 4)
12:30 P.M.—Leadership luncheon
1:00–7:00 P.M.—Free time (for participants to accomplish weekend chores and for personal time)
6:30 P.M.—Registration table opens (new participants only)
7:00 P.M.—Singles Viewpoint Saturday Night (Session 5)

Sunday

9:30 A.M.—Registration table opens (optional)
9:45 A.M.—Speaker during Sunday school (Session 6)
11:00 A.M.—(Optional) Worship with main speaker (Session 7)

PROGRAM IDEAS AND SUGGESTIONS

ICEBREAKERS

❖ *For more icebreakers, see the Table of Contents.*

We attempt to have an opening icebreaker at each session so that community can be built. These icebreakers are simple and non-threatening questions. We ask one person to stand and greet two or three people, asking them one or more questions like the following:

- "What is your favorite pizza topping?"
- "What type of car do you drive? What would you prefer to drive?"
- "Where are you from originally?"
- "What is your favorite ice cream flavor?"

FRIDAY NIGHT BANQUET

Begin with a Friday night banquet that features a nice meal. An alternative for the Friday dinner is a "bring-your-favorite-dish" event. Of course, pizza is always a winner, and sometimes "desserts only" will work well.

A guest speaker addresses the topic for the weekend. Some topics we have used are "Discovering Your Spiritual Gifts," "Discovering Your Faith," "Discovering Your Dreams," "Discovering Healthy Relationships," and "Discovering Life after Forty." There are all kinds of options. Be creative, as the needs of people are diverse.

SATURDAY MORNING CLINIC

Continue to concentrate on the weekend theme by providing several clinic sessions (or workshops), including one or two by the guest speaker. For example, he or she might give an introductory session followed by a coffee break. Then have some workshop sessions led by various members of the group on the weekend theme. Everyone then comes back for another general session with the keynote speaker just before noon.

If possible, seat people at round tables for the clinic sessions. During or following each session, provide an opportunity for participants to discuss the topic. Each person should have the opportunity to be heard or at least hear what their peers are thinking and feeling. This happens best in the small groups. It is best if each small group has a facilitator to guide the discussion.

LEADERSHIP LUNCHEON

At noon have an informal leadership luncheon exclusively for your singles ministry leaders. This gives them an opportunity to visit with the guest speaker, to ask questions, or to discuss issues pertaining to singles ministry. If the speaker is from out of town, he or she can share what's happening in another part of the country. Discuss the topic of the morning and its specific implications for your ministry: Where do we go from here? How do we as leaders responsibly act concerning the topic?

SINGLES VIEWPOINT SATURDAY NIGHT

Come back together on Saturday night for this special event. Singles Viewpoint is a talk-show format where people are encouraged to ask questions of a panel of guests (including the special speaker) as well as respond to other audience members. The host and one or more assistants circulate out in the audience with wireless microphones to encourage and stimulate audience participation. Ask the panel members to keep their comments and answers short and crisp. They may also talk to other panel members or ask the audience questions.

Because this format often touches on hot topics, encourage and allow provocative statements. Some of the topics that might be addressed include compulsive behaviors, workaholism, sexual addiction, and abortion. Attempt to find people for the panel who represent both sides of an issue, such as abortion. If we can't deal openly in the church with these hot topics, we're in big trouble.

The focus of this night is not the church's viewpoint, but the singles' viewpoint. It's a chance to "discover" what others think and feel about various issues. This is a natural tie-in for the discovery weekend idea, providing a special program on Saturday night that does not involve a meal. There is no cost. And this again opens up the weekend to another group of people. Many people who attended Friday night and/or Saturday morning are going to return on Saturday night. And they may bring someone else with them.

If possible, have everyone sit around circular tables for a warmer, friendlier atmosphere during Singles Viewpoint night. Serve light refreshments. You will find that this evening creates fellowship. People will hang around or go out to a restaurant afterwards, often continuing with the topic of discussion.

SUNDAY SCHOOL

Discovery Weekend wraps up on Sunday morning with the speaker as the teacher. When possible, also have that person preach in the main service—Sunday morning and/or Sunday night—for the entire congregation. This option usually doesn't exist when you have a speaker at a traditional retreat setting. There is great benefit for the singles ministry and the church at large when the entire congregation gets to hear a person address specific needs and issues, or simply speak from the single adult perspective.

❖ *The more people who have owner-ship and involvement in the planning, the greater success you will have.*

EQUIPMENT/SUPPLIES (To be furnished by the event leaders)

☐ Name tags
☐ Overhead projector (if needed)
☐ Sound equipment
☐ Round tables, chairs, table decorations
☐ Light refreshments
☐ Handouts

WHAT TO BRING (To be provided by participants)

☐ Bible
☐ Notebook
☐ Pen/pencil
☐ Casual clothes
☐ Dressy or semi-formal attire for the banquet

PLANNING THE EVENT

PLANNING TEAM

For this event you will need an Event Director and, if your group is large, an Assistant Event Director, as well as volunteers to take responsibility for the event site, speaker, budget, registration, hospitality, publicity, small groups, audio/visual needs, food, materials, and equipment/supplies.

Planning Timeline

Event: *Discovery Weekend*   **Date of event:** _____

Event Director: _____   **Phone:** _____

Thanks for agreeing to serve on our Planning Team. Please check over this timeline for the task(s) assigned to you. Adapt as needed. Supplement this timeline with the generic job descriptions found on pages 225-252. Highlight your tasks (and due dates) each time they appear. Mark your calendar accordingly.

Date: _____	6 TO 9 MONTHS IN ADVANCE

Event Director (page 226)

☐ Recruit a Planning Team for this event. As a team, brainstorm ideas and adapt this weekend event to fit your particular ministry goals and objectives. Select a relevant and interesting theme to be addressed. Discuss possible speakers.

☐ Make sure each team member understands his or her responsibilities.

☐ Determine if this timeline will work and make adjustments accordingly.

Event Site Coordinator (page 234)

☐ With the Planning Team's input, carefully choose one or more facilities for the weekend. (Your church may be the best place for this event.) The site will set the tone for the event. Ask for a written confirmation that includes price, dates, payment arrangements, etc.

☐ Put the dates on the church calendar.

Speaker/Workshop Leaders Coordinator (page 250)

☐ With input from the Planning Team, begin searching for a speaker to address the Discovery Weekend theme. The key is having a qualified person who can clearly address the assigned topic, and can motivate and challenge participants.

Budget Coordinator (page 229)

☐ Begin developing a budget proposal for the event.

Registration Coordinator (page 241)

☐ Work with the Publicity Coordinator to develop a registration form. Include boxes for people to check which weekend sessions they plan to attend.

☐ Set all registration deadlines and encourage signing up early.

☐ If scholarship funds are available, provide the necessary application forms, including a deadline. (See example on page 246.)

Publicity Coordinator (page 238)

☐ Begin developing a promotional strategy.

Date: _____	5 MONTHS IN ADVANCE

Event Director

☐ Meet with the Planning Team. Discuss progress.

Budget Coordinator

☐ With the Planning Team, finalize the budget.

Publicity Coordinator

☐ Once the speaker, event site, dates, theme/topic, and registration fees have been confirmed, complete brochures and or flyers and begin promotion.

Speaker/Workshop Coordinator

☐ Confirm the speaker's plans in writing.

☐ Send a deposit, if necessary.

❖ *For more ideas and help, refer to job description beginning on page 225.*

Event Director

☐ Meet with the Planning Team to discuss the program schedule, progress of plans, possible small-group facilitators, and other details.

☐ Pray for those who will be attending the event.

Event Site Coordinator

☐ Be sure a signed contract is on file at the event site and at the church.

☐ Make sure all details are correct.

☐ Verify that a deposit has been paid.

Small-Group Coordinator (page 247)

☐ With input from the Planning Team, begin contacting individuals to facilitate small groups during this event. Plan for a facilitator for every six to ten people.

☐ Inform facilitators that a mandatory training session is provided one month before the event.

Speaker/Workshop Coordinator

☐ Send the speaker a schedule.

☐ Ask the speaker to send any outlines, handouts, and discussion questions at least one month prior to the event. These are needed to help train small-group facilitators.

☐ If any travel arrangements are needed, make the reservations.

Audio/Visual Equipment Coordinator (page 228)

☐ Determine the audio/visual needs of the speaker and small-group facilitators.

☐ Write for permission to tape the speaker.

Food Coordinator (page 236)

☐ Make arrangements for the Friday evening banquet and refreshments for the remainder of the weekend.

Date:	2 MONTHS
_____	IN ADVANCE

Event Director

☐ Meet with the Planning Team to discuss the progress of plans, possible small-group facilitators, and other details. Pray for those who will be attending the event.

Publicity Coordinator

☐ Continue promotions.

Registration Coordinator

☐ Continue registration of those who wish to attend.

☐ Remind applicants that scholarship forms are due. Send them to the person responsible for approving them.

☐ Once approved, inform the recipients.

☐ Order blank name tags.

☐ Find someone who will prepare the name tags one week before the event.

Speaker/Workshop Coordinator

☐ If the speaker has not sent the material, remind him or her to send an outline, suggested questions, and other information that will assist small-group facilitators.

Date:	1 MONTH
_____	IN ADVANCE

Event Director

☐ Meet with the Planning Team to discuss all the plans for the event. Make sure everything is on schedule.

Event Site Coordinator

☐ Confirm all plans with the event site.

☐ Send a program schedule to contact person.

☐ Check details of the payment plan.

☐ With the help of the Planning Team, create and maintain a list of all items/services needed while at the facility. Coordinate these needs with the facility management.

Small-Group Coordinator

☐ Meet with all facilitators to provide basic training. Use material on pages 248-249.

Speaker/Workshop Coordinator

☐ Confirm all arrangements for the speaker.

Food Coordinator

☐ Finalize plans for the Friday evening banquet and for refreshments throughout the weekend.
☐ Be sure you have adequate teams of servers and clean-up crews.
☐ Purchase the nonperishable items.

Registration Coordinator

☐ Continue registration.
☐ Begin preparing a confirmation letter to registrants. (Adapt the sample letter on page 244 for your group and event.)
☐ Finalize plans for on-site registration. Because this is a come-and-go event, a registration table should be open at the beginning of each session. Recruit capable, friendly, helpful people to assist since they will make the first impression as participants arrive. Have extra materials on hand for walk-ins.

Event Materials Coordinator (page 233)

☐ Working with the Registration Coordinator, have the event schedule, materials for small groups, maps, confirmation letter to registrants, literature about your ministry, and any other materials ready for mailing.

Equipment/Supplies Coordinator (page 233)

☐ Locate and/or gather all the supplies that will be needed for activities and atmosphere.

Hospitality Coordinator (page 227)

☐ Visually impact the participants with banners and other interesting decorations.
☐ Place information signs at various locations throughout the facility. Don't assume people know where anything is located, even in your church building.

| Date: _____ | **10 DAYS IN ADVANCE** |

Registration Coordinator

☐ Mail the confirmation letter to all who have preregistered.

| Date: _____ | **1 WEEK IN ADVANCE** |

Event Director

☐ Meet with the entire Planning Team to discuss all plans and cover any last-minute details.

Event Site Coordinator

☐ Send to the facility an update on the number of participants expected. Confirm reservations.

Registration Coordinator

☐ Give the numbers of those preregistered for each part to all members of the Planning Team so they can prepare accordingly.
☐ Prepare the name tags.

Food Coordinator

☐ Confirm meal counts, refreshment plans, meal times, and so on.

| Date: _____ | **2 TO 4 WEEKS AFTER THE EVENT** |

☐ See "Followup Guidelines" on page 254.

2 TRAIN TRIP ADVENTURE

An Enchanting Ride on the Rails

Event Summary: A creative, nostalgic weekend train trip that combines play, relationship building, and small-group study with a variety of optional activities at the destination city.

Length of Event: 1–3 days

Suggested Theme Verse: "This is the day the Lord has made; let us rejoice and be glad in it." Psalm 118:24

Ideal Number of Participants: 10+

Estimated Cost Per Person: Depends on cost of train ticket and length of event

Facility Requirements: Train and a destination point

Recommended Planning Team: 5–7 people

Advance Planning Needed: 6 months

INTRODUCTION

by Dr. Paul M. Petersen
Senior Pastor
Westminster Presbyterian Church
Aurora, Illinois

Ready for something creative, romantic, and adventuresome? Consider a one- or two-day train trip. In this day of air travel, many singles have not ridden trains. Yet there is still something enchanting and appealing to most of us about such travel.

Depending on the part of the country you live in, Amtrak provides some great weekend packages, sometimes even including sleeper cars. The purpose of such a trip is primarily for friendship, fellowship, and adventure. Often times there's just something special—a camaraderie—that happens on a train (or even a bus) trip.

You hop on the train Friday evening or Saturday morning, getting off at some scenic sites along the way, if so desired, returning home by Sunday night. Trains can provide great opportunity and freedom for talking, sightseeing, and games. (I remember a game that lasted twenty-six hours.) Keep the teaching on the lighter side and the fun, relaxation, and vacation frame of mind more predominant.

This event has been a real memory maker and friendship builder for several single adult groups. I'd encourage you to consider such a trip as you plan your annual events calendar. I'm confident that this getaway will be a welcome break from the stress of everyday living and will provide the circumstances that often recharge our faith in God.

OBJECTIVES

❖ To spend extended time together in an enclosed space for relationship building.
❖ To travel together at "see level."
❖ (Optional) To spend time with a host church in the destination city.

THE BIG EVENT

SCHEDULE FOR ONE-DAY TRIP

Obviously, many details of this event hinge on the train schedules available in your area. Make this a Saturday trip, taking three or four hours to go somewhere and then coming home the same day. If the schedule allows, do some sightseeing at the destination before returning home.

Saturday

6:00 A.M.—Meet at train station.
7:00 A.M.—Depart and enjoy breakfast on train.
10:30 A.M.—Arrive at destination.
11:00 A.M.—Begin sightseeing or other plans.
5:00 P.M.—Return to train station.
6:00 P.M.—Depart.
9:30 P.M.—Arrive at station.

SCHEDULE FOR TWO-DAY/ WEEKEND TRIP

Leave on a Friday evening or Saturday morning and return Sunday evening. This allows you to go a longer distance if so desired. It also includes more opportunities at the destination city. For example:

❖ Take in a sports event, visit museums, or go sightseeing. Explore all the possibilities at your destination city.

❖ Combine the train trip with a work project. Find a church, an organization, or an older person who could use some help such as painting, cleaning, or repairs for an afternoon. This could be done with the help of another singles group in the destination city.

❖ Combine the trip with a Leadership Vision Trip (see page 161).

❖ Make this a leadership training event, having only your current and prospective leaders participate. Upon arrival at your destination, provide some leadership training sessions, possibly at a local church.

Friday

7:00 P.M.—Meet at train station.
8:00 P.M.—Depart.

Saturday

6:00 A.M.—Arrive at destination point.
7:00 A.M.—Eat breakfast.
8:30 A.M.—Take part in sightseeing, a sporting event, a work project, time with host church, or other activity.
5:00 P.M.—Have dinner.
7:30 P.M.—Again choose an activity such as sightseeing, a sporting event, a work project, or time with host church.
10:30 P.M.—Arrive at sleeping location.

Sunday

10:00 A.M.—Attend host church singles group and worship service.
12:30 P.M.—Have lunch.
2:00 P.M.—Arrive at train station.
3:00 P.M.—Depart for home.
11:00 P.M.—Arrive at train station.

OVERNIGHT HOUSING

On a two-day trip, there will be at least one night in the destination city. You could stay in a hotel. But also consider staying at a retreat center, a resort, or even a convent or monastery if one is available. Or stay in the homes of singles group members of the host church. Make the decision that works best for your particular needs and interests.

PROGRAM IDEAS AND SUGGESTIONS

ICEBREAKERS

Consider using one or more of the following icebreakers on this trip.

• **A Sketch in the Dark.** In a dark place, and with eyes tightly closed, make a pencil drawing of a scene that is described verbally: Draw a house. Place a tree to the

❖
For more icebreakers see the Table of Contents.

left of the house. Draw a car in the driveway. Draw your friends on the lawn. Vote on the best picture in your group of four. The best picture of your four then goes up against the winners of the other groups to declare a grand champion.

• **Spelling around the Circle.** Play a spelling game. Usually it is played as a whole group, but on the train it may have to be played in groups of four or eight (foursomes across the aisle).

One person begins by naming a letter. Moving around the circle, each person adds one letter at a time to the previous letter(s). The object is to avoid completing a word. Someone who accidentally, or without recourse must finish a word, loses.

For example:

> Person 1 says "A"
> Person 2 says "P"
> Person 3 says "P"
> Person 4 says "L"

If Person 5 says "E," thus spelling "apple," he or she is out of the game. But if Person 5 says "I," then Person 6 needs to add a letter that can lead to a word. If Person 5 says "I," the others, thinking "apple" is the only possibility, can challenge the letter "I." Person 5 can defend the letter by saying "application," and is still in the game. This continues until only one person remains, who is the "winner."

BIBLE STUDY/DEVOTIONAL TIME

• **Small Groups on the Train.** Given the dynamics of the layout of the train car and the noise of the train in motion, the best way to accomplish any teaching is to use a short book (preferably with study questions) on a topic of interest or a Bible study booklet. This eliminates any need for an outside speaker. See the reproducible discussion starter called "The Station" on page 25.

In most cases a train car is arranged so people sit either in pairs or in fours, allowing for groups of two or four to share together. There will be ample time for sharing and rela-

tionship building while on the train. Consider having each small group do a short study/discussion sometime on the trip, while allowing plenty of time for games, too. If desired, occasionally have the small groups switch members to facilitate getting to know a greater number of people. (Possibly even make this a game.)

There is no need to read this study material in advance as there is time on the train. Depending on the length of the train trip, modify or choose certain sessions from a study booklet to fit the time available. For example, if you use *My Heart, Christ's Home* study of six sessions, but you have only four small-group times on the trip, select the four sessions that you think will be most beneficial for your group (and challenge the group to do the remaining sessions on their own once they return home).

• **Larger Group Times.** If your number of participants allows, try to reserve an entire car for your group only! (Each car seats approximately forty-eight people.) This would allow the Event Director or some other person to lead a short devotional or discussion for the entire group. Keep in mind that the noise of the train's movement may make large-group presentations difficult. The speaker may be able to present at the very beginning, while the train is standing still or moving slowly out of the city, setting up the context for the small-group discussions.

• **Devotionals at Destination City Only.** Another possible alternative is to do Bible study or teaching only at the destination city, once you are off the train and at your hotel or the host church.

RECOMMENDED RESOURCES

There are a number of books in print that can provide great discussion starters. Here are some examples from *201 Great Questions* by Jerry Jones (Colorado Springs, CO: NavPress, 1988):

#10. What is one thing you never did in high school that you wish you had done?

#109. Does God like to have fun? If so, how would you describe the fun-loving side of God? If not, why not?

#168. What kind of people bring out the best in you? What two or three people in particular?

The Book of Questions, by Gregory Stock (New York: Workman Publishing, 1987), includes the following:

#33. What is the greatest accomplishment of your life? Is there anything you hope to do that is even better?

#199. You are given $1,000,000 to give away to charity or a stranger. How would you dispose of it?

#217. If you were guaranteed an honest answer to any three questions, who would you question and what would you ask?

And from *Would You Rather . . . ?,* by Doug Fields (El Cajon, CA: Youth Specialties, 1994) there are discussion starters such as:

Would you rather ...

Be guilty or feel guilty?

Be a famous athlete or a famous rock musician?

Be known for your intelligence or your personality?

❖ A suggested booklet that can have a great impact on personal holiness is *My Heart, Christ's Home,* from InterVarsity Press, P.O. Box 1400, Downers Grove, IL 60515. It is now available in a six-session Bible study format. InterVarsity also has several other studies to consider.

❖ Several excellent Bible studies and discussions come from Serendipity House, Littleton, CO, 800-525-9563, and NavPress, Colorado Springs, CO, 800-366-7788.

Contact either of the following for the location of possible churches to visit: The Network of Single Adult Leaders, P.O. Box 1600, Grand Rapids, MI 49501, 616-956-9377; Singles Ministry Resources, P.O. Box 60430, Colorado Springs, CO 80960, 719-635-6020.

EQUIPMENT/SUPPLIES (To be furnished by the event leaders)

- ☐ Materials for studies/discussions
- ☐ Materials for icebreakers/mixers

WHAT TO BRING (To be provided by participants)

- ☐ Games that can easily be played on the train
- ☐ Casual clothes
- ☐ Bible, notebook, pen/pencil
- ☐ Overnight toiletries
- ☐ (Optional) sack lunch, drinks, and snacks; food can be quite expensive on the train!
- ☐ Money for meals and sightseeing not included in the registration fee

---

PLANNING THE EVENT

PLANNING TEAM

For this retreat, you will need an Event Director (possibly an Assistant Event Director) and volunteers to take responsibility for the destination site, registration, budget, transportation, food, and speaker (optional).

❖ *The more people who have ownership and involvement in the planning, the greater success you will have.*

Planning Timeline

Event: *Train Trip Adventure*   **Date of event:** _____

Event Director: _____   **Phone:** _____

Thanks for agreeing to serve on our Planning Team. Please check over this timeline for the task(s) assigned to you. Adapt as needed. Supplement this timeline with information on the reproducible, generic job descriptions found on pages 225-252. Highlight your tasks (and due dates) each time they appear. Mark your calendar accordingly.

Date: _____	**6 MONTHS IN ADVANCE**

Event Director (page 226)

☐ Recruit a Planning Team. Brainstorm ideas, and adapt this event to fit your particular ministry goals and objectives.
☐ Make sure each team member understands his or her assigned tasks and responsibilities. Determine if this timeline will work for your area and make adjustments accordingly.
☐ Discuss possible host locations, studies/discussions, and/or guest speakers. If you desire one, determine who will act as the Speaker Coordinator.

Transportation Coordinator (page 252)

☐ Call Amtrak (1-800-USA-RAIL) or a travel agent and check train schedules to some potential destinations. Check prices and group rates. Also check the option of renting an entire train car for your group.

Event Site Coordinator (page 234)

☐ If requested by the Planning Team, call singles ministry hosts in the destination city. Discuss the possibility of them hosting your group overnight, if your schedule calls for such arrangements.

Budget Coordinator (page 229)

☐ Begin developing a budget proposal.

Publicity Coordinator (page 238)

☐ Begin developing a promotional strategy.

Date: _____	**5 MONTHS IN ADVANCE**

Event Director

☐ Hold another Planning Team meeting and check on progress.
☐ Determine what studies/discussions will be done on this event. Coordinate with Small-Group Coordinator.

Transportation Coordinator

☐ Once the destination city has been determined, arrange for any needed transportation in the host city. Your group may want to rent one or more vans or a bus. Or consider public transportation where appropriate. If you visit a church group, they may also be able to help you with transportation.

Registration Coordinator (page 241)

☐ Choose a registration deadline.
☐ Also, since train tickets must be purchased in advance, determine the amount of deposit required to register.

Budget Coordinator

☐ Finalize the budget.

Publicity Coordinator

☐ Prepare promotional materials.

❖ *For more ideas and help, refer to job descriptions beginning on page 225.*

<table>
<tr><td>

Date:
_____

</td><td>

4 MONTHS IN ADVANCE

</td></tr>
</table>

Date: _____

4 MONTHS IN ADVANCE

Publicity Coordinator

☐ Begin promotion.

Registration Coordinator

☐ Begin to preregister attendees.
☐ If scholarship funds are available, provide the application forms and the deadline for returning the forms. (See samples on pages 245 and 246.)

Event Site Coordinator

☐ Determine what attractions are available in the host city. Gather pricing information and make any necessary reservations. Some attractions offer group rates.
☐ If the group is staying overnight, continue to finalize all arrangements.

Small-Group Coordinator (page 247)

☐ Prepare for small-group study/discussion materials. Order materials if needed.

Date: _____

2 MONTHS IN ADVANCE

Event Director

☐ Check on the Planning Team's progress.

Publicity Coordinator

☐ Continue to promote the event.

Registration Coordinator

☐ Continue to register people until space available on the train is filled.

Transportation Coordinator

☐ Confirm all transportation, including that in the host city.

Date: _____

2 TO 4 WEEKS IN ADVANCE

Event Director

☐ Meet with the Planning Team to make sure they are on schedule.
☐ Finalize details pertaining to the program schedule.

Transportation Coordinator

☐ Contact the train service to confirm reservations and time of departure.
☐ Check on when tickets must be purchased and/or when deposit is due.

Event Site Coordinator

☐ Check with the host group to confirm all arrangements and schedules.
☐ Finalize any sightseeing details.

Registration Coordinator

☐ Continue to register people.
☐ Send a confirmation letter to registrants. (See sample on page 244.)
☐ Order name tags and name tag jackets.
☐ Scholarship forms should be due. Have them approved. Inform recipients of available funds.
☐ Recruit someone to make name tags.

Small-Group Coordinator

☐ All study/discussion group materials should be ready.
☐ Coordinate any study/discussion times with the Event Director.
☐ If recruiting small-group facilitators to help lead each group, do so now.

Budget Coordinator

☐ Prepare any checks that need to be paid.

Date: _____

2 TO 4 WEEKS AFTER THE EVENT

☐ See "Followup Guidelines" on page 254.

"The Station" Small Group Discussion

Read the following short item and then discuss it in your small group.

Tucked away in our subconscious minds is an idyllic vision in which we see ourselves on a long [train trip] that spans an entire continent. . . . From the window, we drink in the passing scenes of cars on nearby highways, of children waving at crossings, of cattle grazing in distant pastures, of smoke pouring from power plants, of row upon row of cotton and corn and wheat, of flatlands and valleys, of city skylines and village halls.

But uppermost in our minds is our final destination—for at a certain hour and on a given day, our train will finally pull into the station.

"Yes, when we reach the station, that will be it!" we promise ourselves. "When we're eighteen . . . win that promotion . . . put the last kid through college . . . buy that 450SL Mercedes Benz . . . pay off the mortgage . . . have a next egg for retirement."

From that day on we will all live happily ever after.

Sooner or later, however, we must realize there is no station in this life, no earthly place to arrive at once and for all. The journey is the joy. The station is an illusion—it constantly outdistances us. . . .

"Relish the moment" is a good motto. Psalm 118:24 [says], "This is the day the Lord has make; let us rejoice and be glad in it."

So stop pacing the aisles and counting the miles. Instead, . . . climb more mountains, kiss more babies, count more stars. Laugh more and cry less. Go barefoot oftener. Eat more ice cream. . . . Watch more sunsets. Life must be lived as we go along.

Excerpted with permission from "When Joy Abounds" by Robert J. Hastings, *Reader's Digest*, June 1988.

Questions for discussion:

1. What does this story say to you personally?
2. In your life right now do you spend more time thinking about the "trip" or the "destination"? Explain.
3. What are the two or three destinations you are pursuing most at this time in your life? Are they attainable? How do you think your life will be different once you have reached your destinations?
4. What are you waiting for in life?
5. If you were to stop waiting, how would your life be different?
6. There's a line in the story that says, "The station is only a dream that constantly outdistances us." What does this mean to you? Do you agree or disagree with the statement? Why?
7. Describe what happiness means to you.
8. What is it that often causes us to become more preoccupied with the "destination" than with enjoying the "trip"?
9. Do you agree with this statement: "The true joy of life is the trip"? Why or why not? If you were to totally live your life as if the joy is in the trip, how would you live your life differently this next week? This next month? This next year?
10. What does Psalm 118:24 mean to you? What needs to change to make this verse more a part of how you live your daily life?

3 SINGLES DRAMA RETREAT

"Here Am I . . . Send Me!"

Event Summary: A weekend opportunity for participants to let the little child in them come out to play; to discover hidden talents and to grow in new ways, much like Moses did after Horeb, the mountain of God. Encourages development of individual speaking skills, group interaction techniques and team building through drama—and could be the stimulus that launches your own group drama ministry.

Length of Event: Friday–Sunday

Suggested Theme Verse: "When the Lord saw that he [Moses] had gone over to look, God called to him from with the bush, 'Moses! Moses!' And Moses said 'Here I am.' " Exodus 3:4

Ideal Number of Participants: 20+ (To make this retreat work well, there need to be at least four groups of five people each.)

Estimated Cost Per Person: $50–$90, depending on facility

Facility Requirements: Retreat center, conference center, or hotel

Recommended Planning Team: 10 people plus a Drama Coach

Advance Planning Needed: Approximately 6–9 months

INTRODUCTION

by Pat VanDyke Souza, Associate Director
Singles and Stepfamilies Ministry
Roswell United Methodist Church, Roswell, Georgia

OBJECTIVES

❖ To help participants release the child within who has forgotten how to play as an adult.
❖ To enhance leadership abilities by nurturing individual speaking skills, group interaction techniques, and team building through drama.
❖ To provide single adults with an opportunity to discover unique gifts and talents, and increase feelings of accomplishment and self-esteem.
❖ To encourage participants to hear the "voice of the Lord" by helping them be part of a creative event.

When Moses stood at the mountaintop doubting his ability to do as the Lord had asked, he was at a turning point in his life. When Moses first left Egypt, he had experienced an "identity crisis" and now his life in Midian as a sheep herder and family man seemed safe and peaceful. But Moses was called to do more than he had ever imagined possible. God's plan was unfolding. The stage was set.

The Bible is rich with drama, and for centuries, life's stories have been played out on the world stage. Through a fresh, innovative drama weekend retreat, single adults have an opportunity to play and laugh together, learn new skills, and experience teamwork and group interaction. Many singles who are fearful of speaking in public often gain confidence and develop into group leaders after having the opportunity to express themselves through drama.

Clearly, every member of your group will not be interested in a drama weekend. But for those who have such an interest, I've found this retreat to be a wonderful way to encourage and nurture leadership confidence and to tap into gifts and talents that often go unnoticed in our churches.

Furthermore, spiritual growth takes place when people are able to identify with a biblical character. This drama retreat can be a turning point for anyone who dares to come back down the mountain . . . with Moses!

THE BIG EVENT

SCHEDULE

Friday

7:30 P.M.—Sign-in, greetings, and name tags
   "People Bingo" (or some other icebreaker)
8:00 P.M.—Official welcome
   Introduction of retreat leaders
   Overview of schedule/activities
   Music and devotions
   Monologue by Drama Coach
   "Machine Performance" by all participants
9:00 P.M.—Drama group assignments
   "Children's Story" skit
10:00 P.M.—Snacks and games
11:00 P.M.—Bedtime

❖ **Get as many people as possible involved in the planning of this event.**

Saturday

8:00 A.M.—Breakfast
8:45 A.M.—Personal devotions
9:15 A.M.—Playtime Topic 1:
   IMPROVISATION
10:00 A.M.—Ten-minute break
10:10 A.M.—One-act play
   assignments
12:00 P.M.—Lunch

1:00 P.M.—Playtime Topic 2:
   CHARACTERIZATION TECHNIQUES
3:00 P.M.—Fifteen-minute break
3:15 P.M.—Playtime Topic 3:
   RELAXATION TECHNIQUES
4:00 P.M.—Free time: hiking, volleyball, basketball, tennis, etc.
6:00 P.M.—Dinner
7:00 P.M.—Playtime Topic 4:
   PRESENTATION TECHNIQUES
8:00 P.M.—Drama group rehearsals
9:00 P.M.—Music and devotional
9:30 P.M.—Fellowship, refreshments, games
10:30 P.M.—Bedtime

Sunday

7:45 A.M.—Breakfast
8:30 A.M.—Music and devotional
9:00 A.M.—Drama team performances
11:00 A.M.—Morning break
11:15 A.M.—Drama team performances

12:00 P.M.—Lunch
1:00 P.M.—Drama team performances
3:00 P.M.—Closing session, prayer
3:30 P.M.—Head home

PROGRAM IDEAS AND SUGGESTIONS

ICEBREAKERS

• Let's Play "Machine" (Friday, 8 P.M.)

The Drama Coach directs participants to combine motions and noises to make up one large whirring, buzzing, chugging, clanging machine! First, the coach chooses one person to kneel, and one person to stand in the center of the room. (These two should be close enough to each other to be touching.) The coach then asks them each to invent a motion that would overlap with the other motions.

Example: The first person stands and moves one arm back and forth, making a noise that matches the movement. The second person, on knees, will thrust one arm upward between the motion of the other person's arm.

Add another person and movement with noise, and then another. Each time a person is added, have the "machine" practice motions and sounds. After there are six to eight people making up the machine, start it up and enjoy the "performance." The end result is a collective overlapping, buzzing machine, with arms, heads, legs, and hands going every which way.

• Let's Play "Baby-sitter" (Friday, 9 P.M.)

The Drama Coach will help participants begin to work as teams by dividing them into five small "drama" groups (four or five people per group). One person in each group is assigned the role of baby-sitter, while the others are children. Each group is given a "story setting" to act out. Allow five minutes for each group to plan their "skit" and then three minutes to act it out. Some sample story settings:

1. Baby-sitter is trying to order a pizza on the telephone, while children "help" her.

2. Children are breaking in a new sitter.

3. The dog is having puppies and the children ask all sorts of questions.

• **Games (Friday, 10:00 P.M.)**

Encourage participants to play a few fun, childlike games that mix the group and help people feel comfortable with one another. Possible games could be: (1) Musical Chairs; (2) Simon Says; (3) Blowing Bubbles (biggest, highest, etc.); (4) Charades.

❖ *For more icebreakers, see the Table of Contents.*

FRIDAY, 7:30 P.M., ARRIVAL

• **People Bingo**

As participants arrive they receive name tags (to be worn all weekend) and a "People Bingo" game sheet. "People Bingo" is an 8 $^1/2$- by 11-inch sheet of paper divided into twenty squares. The top of the sheet says: FIND SOMEONE WHO . . . Each square has room for a person's signature and a few words like:

(1) . . . has performed in a play
(2) . . . has attended a Broadway play.
(3) . . . was in a play in grade school.
(4) . . . has traveled to Europe.
(5) . . . has the same birth month as you.
(6) . . . has the same middle name as you.

FRIDAY, 8:00 P.M., DEVOTIONS

Read selected verses from Exodus 3 and 4. Challenge the singles to discover how God could use their talents after this retreat. Point out how God uses hidden talents and even self-doubts as He unfolds His plan.

Following devotions, the Drama Coach should perform a brief monologue or dramatic reading of his/her choice to demonstrate techniques that will be covered over the weekend. (For example, one drama coach acted out King Arthur from a scene in Camelot.) This also helps establish credibility with the Coach.

SATURDAY, 8:45 A.M., PERSONAL DEVOTIONS/TIME ALONE

Ask each participant to read and reflect on Exodus 3 and 4. In what ways was Moses about to learn improvisation? What were the props used in this "drama"? Do you ever feel inadequate when speaking to an audience? Can you relate to Moses? If so, in what way? What is God trying to communicate to Moses? What is one personal application for your own life from this reading?

SATURDAY, 9:15 A.M., PLAYTIME TOPIC 1: IMPROVISATION

Improvisation is playing "let's pretend." It is acting out a character or situation as you see it. It's being part of a make-believe machine. Children use improvisation all the time.

Put each scene on a card, then draw some out of a hat to determine which ones you use. Request the help of "volunteers." Read the scene to the whole group. Ask the volunteers to use simple props (chair, table, etc.) and act out or "improv" the scene as they see it. Give them one or two minutes to discuss the scene and three minutes to act it out.

Sample Improv Scenes

SCENE I: A man and a woman are on a date at an expensive restaurant. The man really wants to make a good impression, but when the check comes, he discovers he has forgotten his credit cards and doesn't have enough cash. Does he ask the woman for help? How does she respond? [*Props: two chairs and small table. Extra: Man as waiter (optional)*]

SCENE II: Repeat the above scene with new volunteers and one change: the couple has been married for twenty years!

SCENE III: A newlywed couple is dressed and ready to leave for a party. The wife doesn't like what her husband is wearing. She doesn't want to hurt his feelings, so how does she sweetly convince him to change his shirt?

SCENE IV: Same story, except (you got it) the couple has been married for twenty years!

SCENE V: Two couples are on a blind date.

However, the wrong persons are attracted to each other! What happens? *[Props: four chairs arranged like a car or at a table]*

SCENE VI: A single mom is going on her first date in years. Teen daughters are "helping" her get ready. Do they help or hinder?

Create scenes your single adults can relate to, for instance, the date of a single parent meeting the children. These scenes allow singles to laugh at things that may have once reduced them to tears.

After the group has enjoyed the freedom of exploring improvisation, the Drama Coach gives some additional instruction on improvisational theater techniques. (Remember, keep it fun. No one is getting grades here.) ·

SATURDAY, 10:10 A.M., PLAY ASSIGNMENTS

1. Choose the small-group leaders. (You will need a leader for each team of four or five people.) Give each leader a one-act play book—or predetermined script—for their group. Each play should be no longer than thirty or forty minutes. (Find sources for one-act plays and scripts on page 30.) Divide groups based on the number of characters needed in each short play. (Most one-act plays are limited to four or five parts.) Each group will prepare one short play, determining how to do the play as best as possible. Talk about the character each person will play and how to make that character come alive. (It is not necessary to memorize all the lines. The key is to put enough personality into each role to make the character come alive.)

2. These groups will work together as a cast for the remainder of the retreat.

3. Dismiss groups to go read through their play (away from the other small groups if possible) until lunch time.

SATURDAY, 1:00 P.M., PLAYTIME TOPIC 2: CHARACTERIZATION TECHNIQUES

Key verse: Exodus 4:10: Oh Lord, I have never

been eloquent, . . . I am slow of speech and tongue. (Like some of us, Moses felt insecure about his abilities.)

Characterization is bringing a person to life. The goal is to give the character a personality through voice, facial expressions, and gestures. During this time, each small group will work on character development as the coach gives pointers. This is best done in one large room with groups apart from each other.

SATURDAY, 3:15 P.M., PLAYTIME TOPIC 3: RELAXATION TECHNIQUES

Key verse: Exodus 4:13: Oh Lord, please send someone else. . . . (Moses felt anxiety.)

Exercises are taught in breathing, stretching, and focusing before a performance. Groups continue to work together on their one-act plays until the afternoon free-time period.

SATURDAY, 7:00 P.M., PLAYTIME TOPIC 4: PRESENTATION TECHNIQUES

The Drama Coach provides pointers and examples of voice projection, speech volume, physical expression, and delivery techniques.

At this time, participants in each group continue to rehearse their play, focusing on the presentation techniques just explained by the Drama Coach.

SATURDAY, 8:00 P.M., PLAY REHEARSALS

Small groups rehearse their one-act plays. The Drama Coach offers pointers and advice.

SATURDAY, 9:00 P.M., GROUP DEVOTIONS

Exodus 4:15: You shall speak to him [Aaron] and put words in his mouth; I will help both of you speak and will teach you what to do. (Teamwork! Moses and Aaron take their show on the road.)

SUNDAY, 8:30 A.M., DEVOTIONS

Exodus 4:21: The Lord said to Moses, "When you return to Egypt, see that you perform before Pharaoh all the wonders I have given you the power to do . . ." (The Lord gives us the strength and power to do all that He asks of us, just as He did with Moses.)

SUNDAY, 9:00 A.M., SHOW TIME

Under the direction of the Drama Coach, each group will present their one-act play. The Coach will gently critique and offer some advice at the end of each performance, which takes approximately thirty to forty minutes. The others watch (and applaud!).

If possible, have someone use a video camera to record the final performances and other activities of the retreat to show to the entire group back home. Also, have this person take a still photo of each drama team.

SUNDAY, 3:00 P.M., CLOSING SESSION

How will each person use what has been discovered on the walk back down the mountain with Moses? Brainstorm as a group possible future ministry opportunities using drama. (See suggestions on page 32.)

EQUIPMENT/SUPPLIES (To be furnished by the event leaders)

- ☐ Stopwatch (to time skits)
- ☐ A few quick, simple props (such as a scarf or bandanna, wig, hat, old clothes, etc.)
- ☐ Volleyball and net (if needed); basketball
- ☐ One-act plays
- ☐ Evaluation form
- ☐ Two or three extra Bibles (for participants who may forget to bring one)

WHAT TO BRING (To be provided by participants)

- ☐ Bible, pen, and note paper
- ☐ Casual, comfortable clothes, walking shoes, tennis gear
- ☐ Snack to share on Saturday evening
- ☐ Guitars and favorite songs
- ☐ Change for vending machines
- ☐ Camera (video and/or still)

RECOMMENDED RESOURCES

Plays and Musicals for All Theaters. I. E. Clark, Inc., (409) 743-3232
Baker's Plays, (617) 482-1280
Dramatic Publishing Co., (800) 448-7469
Basic Catalogue of Plays. Samuel French, Inc., (212) 206-8990

PLANNING THE EVENT

PLANNING TEAM

For this event, you need an Event Director and coordinators for the event site, publicity, budget, music, transportation, food, registration, worship, and equipment/supplies.

In addition to the above Planning Team, you will need a Drama Coach. Ideally you will be able to find a Drama Coach who is also a Christian and able to lead the devotional times. However, if that is not possible, find the best Drama Coach available in your community—even if the person is not a Christian— who would be comfortable in a retreat setting with your group. Discuss fees or honorarium. Possible persons to contact regarding the position of Drama Coach:

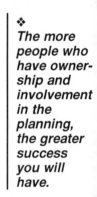

❖ *The more people who have ownership and involvement in the planning, the greater success you will have.*

1. Someone you know of who has a history of participation in theater, perhaps as an actor or director.
2. A teacher of drama in your local high school or college.
3. Someone in your church family (with good experience in theater) who is committed to helping your singles drama group.
4. A faculty member from a Christian college or seminary in the area.

Planning Timeline

Event: *Singles Drama Retreat*   **Date of event:** _____

Event Director: _____   **Phone:** _____

Thanks for agreeing to serve on our retreat Planning Team. Please check over this timeline for the task(s) assigned to you. Adapt as needed. Supplement this timeline with information on the job descriptions found on pages 225-252. Highlight your tasks (and due dates) each time they appear. Mark your calendar accordingly.

Date: _____ | **6 TO 9 MONTHS IN ADVANCE**

Event Director (page 226)

- ☐ Recruit a Planning Team to brainstorm ideas. Adapt this weekend event to fit your particular ministry goals and objectives.
- ☐ Make sure each team member understands his or her assigned tasks and responsibilities. Determine if this timeline will work and make adjustments accordingly.
- ☐ Recruit the Drama Coach.

Event Site Coordinator (page 234)

- ☐ Select and reserve an event site.
- ☐ Put event on the church calendar.

Budget Coordinator (page 229)

- ☐ Begin estimating costs for the event.

Publicity Coordinator (page 238)

- ☐ Begin developing a promotional plan.

Date: _____ | **3 MONTHS IN ADVANCE**

Drama Coach (page 232)

- ☐ Select short one-act plays, each involving three to five people.
- ☐ Begin to prepare four workshops.

Budget Coordinator

- ☐ With the help of the Planning Team, finalize a budget.
- ☐ Begin a scholarship fund, if necessary.

Music Coordinator (page 237)

- ☐ (The Event Director or Assistant Event Director may take this responsibility.)
- ☐ Recruit one or more people to share their musical abilities via piano or guitar. Musicians could lead singing during devotional times and at other times as the schedule allows.

Worship Coordinator (page 251)

- ☐ (If appropriate, the Drama Coach may take this responsibility.)
- ☐ Prepare to lead devotions throughout the retreat.

Publicity Coordinator

- ☐ Once costs, location, and other pertinent details are confirmed, have promotional flyers and posters prepared and printed.
- ☐ Begin promotion.

Audio/Visual Equipment Coordinator (page 228)

- ☐ Make arrangements for needed equipment such as microphones, sound system, and video camera.

Transportation Coordinator (page 252)

- ☐ If group transportation to the event site is needed, begin making arrangements.
- ☐ In addition, make arrangements for Bus Captains if needed (see page 231).

❖ *For more ideas and help, refer to job descriptions beginning on page 225.*

Food Coordinator (page 236)

☐ Work with the Event Director in planning a menu, the number of meals needed, and location of meals during the weekend event.

☐ Make arrangements for refreshments on Friday and Saturday evening.

Registration Coordinator (page 241)

☐ Begin taking registrations.

Equipment/Supplies Coordinator (page 233)

☐ Work with the Drama Coach and Event Director to determine needed supplies for this event.

Date: _____ | **6 WEEKS IN ADVANCE**

Event Director

☐ Meet with the Planning Team to be sure each committee member is on schedule.

Date: _____ | **1 TO 2 WEEKS IN ADVANCE**

Event Director

☐ Meet with the Planning Team to tie up loose ends and be sure each committee member is on schedule.

Registration Coordinator

☐ Send out information letter to all registrants (see sample on page 244).

Date: _____ | **2 TO 4 WEEKS AFTER THE EVENT**

All Interested Participants

☐ Plan various ministry opportunities with drama in which participants can use their new skills. Program possibilities are many:
1. Develop a singles ministry drama team that gives class announcements and/or skits that could be used as discussion starters or as an introduction to the teacher's material.
2. Begin a "street drama evangelism team" to perform in public areas on weekends.
3. Put together a major drama production to be performed for the entire church.
4. Invite people from a local community theater to visit your singles group. Discuss why they act and how they do it.
5. Invite local community players to perform a brief one-act play.
6. A few participants from the group may prepare monologues and "try them out" as part of a program. Monologues may be dramatic or comical. Often others are motivated by these deliveries and wish to become involved in future drama events. Encourage members to use their newly acquired skills in future ministry programs.
7. Ask a Drama Coach to perform some improvisational pieces for the singles group. Choose a situation or personality and ask the coach to act it out.
8. A few of the more outgoing members may participate in an "improv program" directed by a guest Drama Coach. The coach asks for two volunteers to come forward to be the actors. (You may want to "plant" the first two volunteers and prepare them beforehand. This plant becomes the opening act on improv night.)

☐ See "Followup Guidelines" on page 254.

A GREAT WAY TO KILL AN EVENING

A Murder Mystery Dinner

Event Summary: An out of the ordinary, fun, adventuresome, "guess-who-done-it" murder mystery evening that has appeal to non-Christian singles, too—making it a very effective, non-threatening outreach event .

Length of Event: 4–6 hours

Ideal Number of Participants: 75+

Estimated Cost Per Person: $20–$35

Facility Requirements: Banquet hall, gymnasium, or retreat center

Recommended Planning Team: 6–10

Advance Planning Needed: 5 months

INTRODUCTION

by Pam Harper Dodge, Director of Young Adult Ministries and Maureen Kelly, Fellowship Administrator

Ward Church

Livonia, Michigan

Single adults—both Christian and non—are looking for "good-time-together" opportunities. They also enjoy something out of the ordinary, a new experience, some excitement and adventure. This evening offers all of that and more— an alternative event that can be very appealing to non-Christian singles, too.

In fact, we consider this one of the best outreach ministries we do. Because of the positive reputation and wide exposure generated by this event, it has become something everyone wants to attend, including many unchurched singles in our community. Because everyone is sitting around small tables, it allows our own people to comfortably mix and mingle with the newcomers. In addition, planning and preparing this adventurous evening helps develop greater unity and momentum within our ministry.

If well planned, this event can become one of the highlights of your yearly program calendar, with people looking forward to attending and bringing their friends. It can become a first point of contact with many singles who will eventually become a part of your group.

This event could work well almost any time of the year. We have chosen to schedule this each year as our New Year's Eve event, providing a safe, fun, non-alcoholic alternative. We include a dinner and the murder mystery theater, followed by an optional New Year's Eve service at our church. If this is done on New Year's Eve, plan a safe, active event following the Mystery dinner (such as ice skating, bowling, sleigh rides, etc.) to help keep people involved, alert—and off the roads. Be sensitive to the needs of your audience. If your church has a midnight service for the New Year, be sure it will appeal to the non-churched you are hoping to attract before you make it a part of your official evening. You may want to have a point in the evening that allows those who wish to leave to do so.

OBJECTIVES

❖ To provide a first-class, wholesome, and unique evening of fun and fellowship.

❖ To raise awareness in the community about our singles ministry.

❖ To provide a great opportunity for singles to bring their non-Christian friends to an entertaining and non-threatening event.

THE BIG EVENT

SCHEDULE

❖
Get as many people as possible involved in the planning of this event.

6:00-6:30 P.M.—Registration
6:15-7:00 P.M.—Hors d'oeuvres
7:00 P.M.—Murder Mystery Dinner
10:30 P.M.—(Optional) New Year's Eve service

PROGRAM IDEAS AND SUGGESTIONS

THEME

Suggest a theme, such as a mobster and '20s theme, a '50s theme, or a western theme. If desired, ask people to come dressed in costume for the evening.

DINNER

Have the meal included in the price of the evening and provided by the hotel or facility where you are having this event (or a catering service, if necessary).

TABLE HOSTS

Since this is an outreach event, it is important to help everyone feel welcome as they arrive. Because this event requires preregistration for the total number of meals needed, name tags should be preprinted and available as people arrive. Assign a host to each table to welcome people and strike up a conversation. We use our ministry's small-group leaders. Use someone who is trained and comfortable in talking to others they don't know. It is best if each table host is knowledgeable about your ministry so he or she will know who is new and can answer questions. Be sure to have literature about your ministry at each table.

If you are concerned that newcomers might be left standing in a corner, consider offering a prize to the three hosts who get their tables filled first. In general, however, people are free to sit wherever they like.

THE MYSTERY THEATER SCRIPT

A script is needed for the murder mystery. See "Recommended Resources" on page 35 for possible sources of a script.

If your budget is bountiful, consider having the script written specifically for your murder mystery dinner. Hire a local agency that specializes in interactive dinner theater murder mysteries. Many of these agencies advertise strictly by word-of-mouth, but a shuffle through the Yellow Pages and calls to theatrical agents or entertainers might provide leads.

Ask the agency to write the script with your ministry and needs in mind. Oversee the writing of the script to make certain the play is appropriate for your purposes and audience, since the agency may not have the same Christian standards as your group. If possible, assist the scriptwriter in incorporating specific "high profile" members of your group. For example, if one of your single adults is a banker, accuse him or her of laundering money. Include many people from the group that you know will be in attendance. Some agencies may be willing to provide the actors and actresses to play out the mystery. This script should be completed one month prior to the event.

PROGRAM

As the people arrive, they are given a brochure that contains the schedule (see above) and the background to the murder mystery plot for the evening. On page 39 you will find an example of what one single adult ministry used. To keep the evening entertaining and non-threatening, presentations or talks are discouraged. Open the event by welcoming everyone, briefly explaining your singles ministries, going over the evening schedule, and praying for the meal.

The type of murder mystery you use will dictate whether the group is involved in the mystery or only observing the actors and actresses play it out. If your mur-

❖
For a list of icebreakers, see the Table of Contents.

der mystery is the interactive type, then at the beginning of the meal, before the mystery begins, instructions need to be given to the tables to ask questions of the actors/actresses in order for each table to solve the mystery. It might be necessary, especially if your group is new to the murder mystery idea, for the Mystery Coordinator to "plant" someone at each table who has been briefed on what is going on (see below under Planning Team). The "plant" may be the table host.

PRIZES

Award three or four sleuths that solve or come closest to solving the murder mystery. These can be inexpensive gag gifts. Do not worry about expensive prizes.

EQUIPMENT/SUPPLIES (To be furnished by the event leaders)

☐ The Murder Mystery script that you have purchased or had written
☐ Props for murder mystery
☐ Banquet decorations
☐ Sound equipment, if needed
☐ Prizes for winning sleuths

WHAT TO BRING (To be provided by participants)

☐ Costumes to fit the theme
☐ An adventurous attitude

RECOMMENDED RESOURCES

A game called "How to Host a Murder Mystery" is available in the adult section of most toy and department stores (there should be a variety of games to choose from). The game provides a suggested script, characters and other directions, and is generally less than $50. Waldenbooks carries in their game section at least four different titles from Decipher Inc. (P.O. Box 56, Norfolk, VA 23501, 804-623-3600), each costing between $28 and $30.

PLANNING THE EVENT

PLANNING TEAM

For this event you need an Event Director (and possibly an Assistant Director), plus volunteers to take responsibility for the facilities, food, budget, publicity, registration, hospitality, audio/visual needs, equipment/supplies, and materials (including prizes).

In addition, you will need someone to coordinate the murder mystery performance, either working with the scriptwriters or buying a mystery "off the shelf." If the murder mystery is to be interactive, the Mystery Coordinator will brief the Hospitality Coordinator and table hosts on the procedures and processes for the Murder Mystery portion of the evening so they will be able to assist their table, if necessary, in solving the crime.

❖ *The more people who have ownership and involvement in the planning, the greater success you will have.*

Planning Timeline

Event: *A Great Way to Kill an Evening*　　**Date of event:** _____

Event Director: _____　　**Phone:** _____

Thanks for agreeing to serve on our retreat Planning Team. Please check over this timeline for the task(s) assigned to you. Adapt as needed. Supplement this timeline with information on the reproducible, generic job descriptions found on pages 225-252. Highlight your tasks (and due dates) each time they appear. Mark your calendar accordingly.

Date: _____	**6 TO 9 MONTHS IN ADVANCE**

Event Director (page 226)

☐ Recruit a Planning Team. Brainstorm ideas and adapt this weekend event to fit your particular ministry goals and objectives.

☐ Make sure each team member understands his or her assigned tasks and responsibilities. Determine if this timeline will work and make adjustments accordingly.

☐ Put the event date on the church calendar.

Event Site Coordinator (page 234)

☐ Secure a large banquet facility to hold the approximate number of people expected. If the event is planned for New Year's Eve, secure the facilities as early in the year as possible since the best locations fill quickly. Also, many banquet hall managers are reluctant to rent halls on New Year's Eve without the guarantee of a contract for high-profit items such as alcoholic beverages. Have participants drive as little as possible because it could be hazardous.

☐ Confirm this in writing.

Budget Coordinator (page 229)

☐ Begin developing a budget proposal.

Food Coordinator (page 236)

☐ Discuss various menus. With the help of the Planning Team, settle on a selection.

☐ Be sure meal arrangements are included in the facilities contract.

Date: _____	**5 MONTHS IN ADVANCE**

Budget Coordinator

☐ Finalize the budget.

Publicity Coordinator (page 238)

☐ Once the date, location, and costs have been determined, begin developing all promotional materials.

Date: _____	**4 MONTHS IN ADVANCE**

Publicity Coordinator

☐ Begin promoting the event. Keep unchurced singles in mind.

Registration Coordinator (page 241)

☐ Begin registering people.

☐ Require a preregistration deposit at the time of registration.

Hospitality Coordinator (page 227)

☐ Recruit key leaders and active members to serve as Table Hosts, one for each table.

Mystery Theater Coordinator

☐ Arrange for the murder mystery. See pages 34, 35 for information and script ideas.

☐ Purchase the game or hire a scriptwriter and talent agency.

❖ *For more ideas and help, refer to job descriptions beginning on page 225.*

Publicity Coordinator

☐ Continue to promote the event.
☐ Encourage people from your group to invite their friends.

Audio/Visual Equipment Coordinator (page 228)

☐ Determine audio/visual needs for the event and locate equipment as needed.
☐ Arrange for appropriate background music to fit the theme of the event.

Hospitality Coordinator

☐ Continue recruiting Table Hosts.

Mystery Theater Coordinator

☐ Check on all details pertaining to the script and actors.

Date: _____ | **2 MONTHS IN ADVANCE**

Event Director

☐ Meet with the Planning Team to be sure all details are on schedule.
☐ Recruit an emcee. The Event Director can be the emcee if he or she has good up-front skills. This person awards the prizes.

Event Site Coordinator

☐ Confirm that a signed contract is on file at the event facility and at the church. Make sure all details are correct.
☐ Be sure the deposit is paid.
☐ Meet with the Planning Team to determine the program schedule and communicate this to the facility contact.

Equipment/Supplies Coordinator (page 233)

☐ Begin gathering small prizes to award to three or four sleuths. If someone in your group is able to secure higher valued gifts (such as a free night at a resort, a free meal coupon, free limousine service), go for it. In general, things such as gift certificates to a Christian bookstore, a tape of a Christian recording artist, or a Christian book are great. Gifts that follow the theme for the night are excellent. A murder mystery might have as a prize a "Groucho Marx" glasses/nose/mustache. A '50s theme might have a hula hoop for a prize.

Publicity Coordinator

☐ Continue to promote the event.
☐ Recruit a photographer to capture the event on film and/or video.

Registration Coordinator

☐ Continue registration.
☐ Order name tags. Recruit someone to prepare them one week prior to the event.

Hospitality Coordinator

☐ Continue recruiting Table Hosts.

Mystery Theater Coordinator

☐ Have the script finalized at this time.

Date: _____ | **1 MONTH IN ADVANCE**

Event Director

☐ Meet with the Planning Team to be sure all details are on schedule.

Event Site Coordinator

☐ Check with the contact person at the event site to confirm reservations for the facility and meal arrangements. Provide the latest registration numbers.
☐ With input from the Planning Team, create and maintain a list of all items/services needed while at the facility. Coordinate these needs with the facility.

Mystery Theater Coordinator

☐ Confirm all murder mystery details.

Publicity Coordinator

☐ Dress in costume and promote the event at singles functions or in classes, as is appropriate for your church.

Registration Coordinator

☐ Continue to register people.
☐ Begin preparing a confirmation letter to registrants. (A sample letter is found on page 244. Adapt it for your event.)
☐ Recruit two or three assistants to help with registration at the event.

Equipment/Supplies Coordinator

☐ Have all supplies needed to decorate the banquet area. Check with the contact person at the event site to determine what is supplied by the facility, what you are allowed to bring, and if there are fees.
☐ Recruit a few individuals to help decorate the facility and remove all decorations following the event.

| Date: _____ | **10 DAYS IN ADVANCE** |

Event Director

☐ Meet with the Planning Team to cover any last-minute details.

Registration Coordinator

☐ Close registration.
☐ Send the confirmation letter to registrants.
☐ Inform the Event Director of the final number of registrants.
☐ In case you do not already have them, get every attendee's name, address, and phone number as people arrive. This will allow your ministry to follow up all newcomers.

Hospitality Coordinator

☐ Confirm and meet with all Table Hosts. Brief them on the importance of their role, which includes helping people find their way to a table, and making everyone feel welcome and comfortable.
☐ Have the Mystery Theater Coordinator meet with the Table Hosts to instruct them on the role they can play, if any, in helping solve the mystery.

Event Site Coordinator

☐ Send a copy of the final event schedule to the contact person at the event site. Include the current number of registrants.

Food Coordinator

☐ Confirm all meal arrangements.
☐ Check details of the payment plan. Communicate the payment plan to the Budget Coordinator.

Budget Coordinator

☐ Prepare checks for payment as needed.

| Date: _____ | **1 TO 2 WEEKS AFTER EVENT** |

Event Director and All Ministry Leaders

☐ This is an outreach event, so it is critical that all visitors are sent a letter thanking them for their attendance and inviting them to your regular meetings. Include a calendar of events with the letter. Within a week after the event, make sure each newcomer also receives a phone call, thanking them for their participation and inviting them to upcoming activities. This helps increase the likelihood of a repeat visit.
☐ See "Followup Guidelines" on page 254.

Plot Background for the Murder Mystery

It's New Year's Eve 1925 and gangsters and the Charleston are all the rage. Louie and Fanny are former members of Ma Baker's gang and have just been paroled from federal prison to the custody of our singles group. Thanks to their attorney, "Big Mike," they did time for "Possession of a Weapon," a lesser offense than the original count of "Bank Heist." As former members of Ma Baker's gang, Louie and Fanny had been caught the first time they tried to rob a bank without Ma's help.

But that's all behind them now. Louie and Fanny, fresh out of prison, want a fresh start with a clean slate. With the help of "Big Mike," who is very adept at money laundering, they have purchased a banquet hall through which they hope to earn a living by catering parties. In celebration of going straight, they've decided to ring in the New Year with a party to which our singles group is invited.

The trouble begins, however, when the guest list includes their shady, former friends from Ma Baker's gang. Also, Fanny, who's not wrapped too tightly anyway, inadvertently included Ma Baker in the invitations.

Will Ma still hold a grudge because Louie and Fanny left the gang? Animosity burns as the evening begins. Ma still thinks she has claim on Louie, her expert safecracker. To make matters worse, Ma's escort turns out to be the notorious "Rooster," the gang's heavy. "Big Mike" and his wife, "Lil," the gang flirt, are also invited. Suspense rises, rumors run, and tempers flare!

Given the players in this deadly game of "Murder and Intrigue," it's only reasonable to expect at least one of them to be eliminated before the party is over. So be careful who you sit next to. Your dinner partner could be a murderer. You will have the opportunity to talk with the characters, dine with them, and ask any questions that might help you solve . . . the murder.

5 UNITED WE STAND

A Cross-Cultural Single-Adult Weekend

Event Summary: An opportunity for two different singles groups—representing predominantly different ethnic backgrounds—to spend a weekend together to fellowship, do a community service project, discuss racial issues and concerns, and learn more about what it means to be brothers and sisters in Christ.

Length of Event: Friday evening to Sunday noon

Suggested Theme Verse: "For you are all one in Christ Jesus." Galatians 3:28

Ideal Number of Participants: 10+ from each of two churches of predominantly different ethnic backgrounds

Estimated Cost Per Person: $15 (plus cost of eating out and/or group entertainment)

Facility Requirements: Church building (plus community service project)

Recommended Planning Team: 5–7 people from each church

Advance Planning Needed: Approximately 6 months

INTRODUCTION

by Chris Eaton
Founder, Single Purpose Ministries
St. Petersburg, Florida

Are the members of your singles group primarily from one ethnic background? Do they have few opportunities to interact with singles from other racial groups? If so, this event may be just what you need to help your group—as it did ours—move toward real Christian community, uniting races by taking part in meaningful interaction and helpful Christian service.

Prior to this event, members of our group, Single Purpose, were feeling the need to improve interaction between themselves and other races, but had few opportunities to do so—especially within the church.

I had been reading about the struggle of African-Americans in America and the civil rights movement. Many accounts told of heroic people who had acted against the norm. After reading, I knew we, a predominantly Caucasian group, could do one less-than-heroic act. The "act" we selected was to join with members of an African-American congregation (which became our host) in cleaning the house and yard of an ill member of their congregation. The event combined a work project, worship services, shared meals and lodging, and discussion times. The experience was eye-opening for both groups, helping us experience what unity in Christ really means!

Whatever racial background is predominant in your singles group, you can adapt this weekend idea for a truly exciting cross-cultural experience.

OBJECTIVES

❖ To promote better interaction between people of various races in the community.
❖ To promote growth and awareness of race-related issues within the church.
❖ To join two (or more) groups from different ethnic backgrounds for one weekend of community service.

THE BIG EVENT

SCHEDULE

Friday

7:00 P.M.—Arrival at host church

7:30 P.M.—Get-acquainted activities

> *8:30 P.M.*—Worship service
>
> ❖ *9:30 P.M.*—Video (optional); facilitated small-group discussion on cross-culture issues
>
> *11:00 P.M.*—Refreshments
>
> *11:30 P.M.*—Lights out

Get as many people as possible involved in the planning of this event.

Saturday

7:00 A.M.—Breakfast

8:00 A.M.—Begin work project

10:30 A.M.—Snack break

12:30 P.M.—Complete work project

1:00 P.M.—Lunch

3:30 P.M.—Facilitated small-group discussion: "How Can We Help Improve Race Relations?"

6:00 P.M.—Dinner at a favorite restaurant of the host church group

7:00 P.M.—Bible study/small-group discussions

9:30 P.M.—Refreshments

11:00 P.M.—Lights out

Sunday

8:30 A.M.—Breakfast (and distribution of evaluation forms)

10:00 A.M.—Worship service

12:00 P.M.—Lunch at a favorite restaurant of the visiting church group (and collection of completed evaluation forms)

A SCHEDULE OPTION

Depending on the interests and desires of your group, you may want to consider having the Bible study on Saturday afternoon and then spending Saturday evening having fun (for example, volleyball, roller skating, bowling, attending a sports event).

HOUSING

Part of the success of this weekend is to have the participants staying together. Much of the relationship building takes place when people are relaxing together during unstructured time. Here are three options to consider:

1. All participants "camp out" at the host church, sleeping on the floor or in the pews.

2. The visiting group participants stay in the homes of the host group.

3. If the travel distance is not too great, have one half of the visiting group stay in host church homes and one half of the host group stay in visiting group homes.

PROGRAM IDEAS AND SUGGESTIONS

GET-ACQUAINTED ACTIVITIES FRIDAY, 7:30 P.M.

The first phase of your time together needs to be spent in getting acquainted. Try some non-threatening, get-acquainted questions.

❖ **For a list of icebreakers, see the Table of Contents.**

WORSHIP SERVICE FRIDAY, 8:30 P.M.

Briefly introduce the Bible study topic that will be addressed more thoroughly on Saturday evening.

Be intentional about reflecting the cultures of both groups and learning forms of worship from each other. This can often be done best through music. Participate with both a teachable and worshipful attitude.

OPTIONAL VIDEO, FRIDAY, 9:30 P.M.

Consider using a videotape on racial issues as a springboard for the opening night discussion. Check local libraries or bookstores for suggestions on documentaries, biographies of key persons in race relations, or commercial releases such as *Do the Right Thing, Boyz 'N' the*

Hood, Guess Who's Coming to Dinner, and *Raisin in the Sun.* (Be sure to preview any movie or video before choosing to use it.)

Have a time of small-group discussion about the messages, feelings, and impressions stimulated by the video. What cross-cultural issues were addressed?

SMALL-GROUP DISCUSSION TIME SATURDAY, 3:30 P.M.

For discussion times, divide the participants into smaller groups of four to six people (some from each church) and provide a sheet of discussion questions for each group to use. Afterward, have the groups summarize their insights for the whole group.

The focus of this session is to explore ways to improve race relations. See Resource 1 on page 46 for discussion starters.

BIBLE STUDY, SATURDAY, 7:00 P.M.

See Resource 2 on page 46.

WORSHIP SERVICE, SUNDAY, 10:00 A.M.

Here are two options to consider.

1. Have the visiting group attend the host church's worship service, possibly participating in it with a song, testimony, or group presentation, and a report on the weekend event.

2. Divide the participants into two groups. One stays at the host church and one goes to the church of the visiting group. Each church would then have the benefit of hearing about the events and things learned during the weekend

---

EQUIPMENT/SUPPLIES (To be furnished by the event leaders)

☐ Needs determined by the work project
☐ Items needed for activities
☐ (Optional) Video to watch on Friday night
☐ Copy of questions for each participant

WHAT TO BRING (To be provided by participants)

☐ Sleeping bag and toiletries
☐ Work clothes, boots, and gloves
☐ Clothing for 2 1/2 days
☐ Bible, notebook, pen or pencil
☐ (Optional) Guitar or other musical instrument(s)

PLANNING THE EVENT

PLANNING TEAM

Once you find a participating church, expand the Planning Team by getting volunteers from both churches involved, using the following timeline as a guide.

You will need two of each: Event Directors, Small-Group Facilitators, Food Coordinators, Worship Coordinators, Work Project Coordinators, and Registration Coordinators (one from each church). In addition, you will need one Budget Coordinator, one Publicity Coordinator, and one Transportation Coordinator.

❖ *The more people who have ownership and involvement in the planning, the greater success you will have.*

Planning Timeline

Event: *United We Stand*   **Date of event:** _____

Event Director: _____   **Phone:** _____

Thanks for agreeing to serve on our Planning Team. Please check over this timeline for the task(s) assigned to you. Adapt as needed. Supplement this timeline with information on the reproducible, generic job descriptions found on pages 225-252. Highlight your tasks (and due dates) each time they appear. Mark your calendar accordingly.

| Date: | **6 MONTHS** |
| _____ | **IN ADVANCE** |

Event Director (from visiting church) (page 226)

☐ Recruit a Planning Team. Brainstorm ideas and adapt this weekend event to fit your particular ministry goals and objectives.

☐ Make sure each team member understands his or her assigned tasks and responsibilities. Determine if this timeline will work and make adjustments accordingly.

☐ Contact the church you've chosen to join in this event, clearly communicating the goals for the weekend. It is important to establish a partnership between churches. Once a church agrees to participate, it should appoint an Event Director.

Event Directors (from both churches)

☐ Establish a Planning Team from the second church to assist with details.

☐ Agree on dates for the event and mark both church calendars.

| Date: | **5 MONTHS** |
| _____ | **IN ADVANCE** |

Event Directors

☐ Meet with the Planning Teams from both churches to determine a schedule of events for the weekend. To insure success of this event, do not over plan. Allow for some spontaneity and free time.

☐ Determine lodging accommodations. Eating and sleeping in either group's church helps build community. The church where the groups sleep, eat, and worship together becomes the "host" church.

Work Project Coordinators

☐ Decide on a suitable work project for Saturday morning. The project must be large enough for both groups to work hard together, yet small enough that it can be completed in a half day.

☐ Begin a list of necessary supplies and make arrangements for borrowing or purchasing them.

❖ *For more ideas and help, refer to job descriptions beginning on page 225.*

Budget Coordinator (page 229)

☐ Determine per-person costs for the weekend. Include food and, if needed, miscellaneous materials for the work project.

Registration Coordinators (page 241)

☐ Set a deadline for registration and payment.

☐ Communicate information to the Publicity Coordinator.

Publicity Coordinator (page 238)

☐ Begin preparing brochures and flyers to promote the event.

<table>
<tr><td>**Date:**
_____</td><td>**3 MONTHS**
IN ADVANCE</td></tr>
</table>

Publicity Coordinator

☐ Begin distributing promotional materials to both groups.

Registration Coordinators

☐ Start to register those from both churches who wish to participate in the event. Try to get at least twelve participants from each church.

Worship Coordinators (page 251)

☐ Plan the Friday night worship service together. It should reflect the worship experience and culture of both groups.

<table>
<tr><td>**Date:**
_____</td><td>**2 MONTHS**
IN ADVANCE</td></tr>
</table>

Food Coordinators (page 236)

☐ Plan the snacks and menus together. At least one meal should include typical ethnic foods prepared by members of one or both of the groups.
☐ Contact individuals to prepare this meal.

Publicity Coordinator

☐ Continue promoting the event to each church's singles group.

Registration Coordinators

☐ Continue registering those who wish to attend.
☐ Order name tags and name tag jackets.
☐ Find someone to prepare name tags one week prior to the event.

Transportation Coordinator (page 252)

☐ Determine the best means of transportation to the host church and work site. Be sure to arrange transportation for both church groups.
☐ Make necessary arrangements.

☐ Provide maps for all drivers.

<table>
<tr><td>**Date:**
_____</td><td>**1 MONTH**
IN ADVANCE</td></tr>
</table>

Event Directors

☐ Meet with the Planning Teams from both groups to finalize the program.

Work Project Coordinators

☐ Finalize plans for the work project and gather needed supplies, or delegate this responsibility to other participants from each church.

Small-Group Coordinators

☐ Work together to develop the content and discussion questions that will help both groups benefit from the time together.
☐ Be sure the movie or videotape you choose will be available when needed.
☐ Arrange to have a TV and VCR available.

Publicity Coordinator

☐ Continue to promote the event. Attend singles functions at both churches to make announcements and generate enthusiasm for the weekend.

Registration Coordinators

☐ As space allows, continue registration.
☐ Begin preparing a letter to be sent to all registrants. (A sample letter is found on page 244. Adapt as needed for your group and event.)

<table>
<tr><td>**Date:**
_____</td><td>**2 WEEKS**
IN ADVANCE</td></tr>
</table>

Registration Coordinators

☐ Send the confirmation letter to all those registered.
☐ Provide names and needed materials to person(s) responsible for preparing name tags.

Date:	**1 WEEK**		Date:	**2 TO 4 WEEKS**
-----	----------		-----	----------------
_____	**IN ADVANCE**		_____	**AFTER EVENT**

1 WEEK IN ADVANCE

Event Directors

☐ With the Planning Team, finalize the schedule, accommodations, meal preparation, worship plans, and work project.

☐ At the final Planning Team meeting, review logistics and discuss participants' expectations for the weekend.

☐ As an exercise, have each person list the stereotypes often ascribed to the other group, and to his or her own group. Then answer the questions: Are these fair categorizations? How did they arise? Why do they persist? How are they harmful?

☐ Prepare evaluation forms to be distributed near the end of the event. (See sample on page 255.)

☐ Pray for the weekend and for the members of the other group.

Work Project Coordinators

☐ Confirm plans to be at the work project on the given date.

☐ Be certain of time and expectations.

Food Coordinators

☐ Finalize arrangements for all meals.

☐ Contact those individuals who are responsible for providing Saturday's lunch.

Transportation Coordinator

☐ Confirm all transportation arrangements.

Worship Coordinators

☐ Confirm plans for the worship sessions.

2 TO 4 WEEKS AFTER EVENT

Event Directors

☐ Meet individually with your own group to discuss the results of the weekend. What did you learn about the other group as a result of this experience? What did you learn about yourself? How did you feel about working with this group on a service project? What might we do in the future to continue building bridges with groups from other cultures? If we were to do this event again, what would we do differently and why?

☐ See the "Followup Guidelines" on page 254.

Improving Race Relations

1. Recall the first time you met someone of a different ethnic group. What was that experience like?

2. What were the racial prejudices in your family/community/church as a child?

3. "Racial differences" to me means . . .

4. A key to understanding racial differences for me is . . .

5. Do you have friends (people you socialize with) who are members of a different racial or ethnic group? If so, how did that come about? If not, why do you think you don't?

6. The hardest aspect about having "friends" from a different ethnic group is . . .

7. The one thing I would like to understand better about others this weekend is . . .

8. The one thing I plan to do to help improve racial relations is . . .

Bible Study Guide

Colossians 3:11: Here there is no Greek or Jew, circumcised or uncircumcised, barbarian, Scythian, slave or free, but Christ is all, and is in all.

Galatians 3:28: There is neither Jew nor Greek, slave nor free, male nor female, for you are all one in Christ Jesus.

Using these two verses, discuss why Paul wrote this to the church at that time. What was his intent? What was his goal for the church then? Did he mean for people to forget their cultural background? To ignore their skin color? Or was it something more?

Then bring it to the present. What is God's desire for the church today, based on these verses? What does it mean to you that there are no differences in Christ? Why, then, do these differences separate us so? What factors highlight differences so much that we isolate from or avoid others?

How can we live out this challenge? What steps could we take to live in a way that says in Christ there is no black or white?

THE URBAN PLUNGE

Living "Homeless" for a Weekend in the Inner City

Event Summary: A unique opportunity for a small group of your singles to gain some first-hand exposure to the people of the inner city, and to see what it's like to survive the weekend on only $2. An excellent way for your group to become more aware of the needs of "the least of these" among us.

Length of Event: Friday night through Sunday evening dinner

Suggested Theme Verse: "Whatever you did not do for one of these least of these, you did not do for me." Matthew 25:45

Ideal Number of Participants: 9–12 people (plus 2–3 saftey team members)

Estimated Cost Per Person: Approximately $25–$40

Facility Requirements: Eating and sleeping facilities provided by an inner-city church or mission

Recommended Planning Team: 4–6 people

Advance Planning Needed: Approximately 3 months

Special Instructions: Safety precautions for event participants

INTRODUCTION

by Kim Hurst and J.D. Ward
University Presbyterian Church
Seattle, Washington

What's it like to be homeless, poverty-stricken, or at risk of violence? Let your group find out for themselves through Urban Plunge—an intensive exposure to inner-city streets. This event helps participants learn about issues surrounding urban communities, and reminds them of how Jesus showed compassion for the downtrodden.

Here's how it works: Allow each participant only two dollars, the clothes on his or her back, a sleeping bag, and necessary toiletries for the entire weekend. Divide participants into Plunge Teams of three people each (at least one man per group).

From Friday to Sunday, participants live, eat, and sleep in downtown facilities—and not the Hilton! During the day and evening, Plunge Teams explore the streets, rescue missions, welfare offices, and places where people live outside. Just before bedtime each night, everyone records personal experiences and impressions in his or her own journal.

(Note: This weekend event also benefited greatly from the ideas and leadership at Campus Ministries, Urban Involvement, Seattle Pacific University, Seattle.)

OBJECTIVES

❖ To gain a new awareness of and exposure to "the least of these."

❖ To give participants exposure to the tremendous contrasts and needs of the inner city.

❖ To learn about and critique the church's response to the city's needs.

❖ To develop a heart for those who live and/or work in the inner city.

THE BIG EVENT

SCHEDULE

❖ **Get as many people as possible involved in the planning of this event.**

One Week before Event

Mandatory preparatory meeting for all participants

Friday

5:00 P.M.—Meet at location where participants can safely leave cars for the weekend. All money and valuables are collected for safekeeping. Two dollars are distributed to each participant. Take public transportation (preferably) or van to mission 1.

5:30 P.M.—Arrive at mission 1 for introductory talk by mission personnel. Then the Urban Plungers will join the street population and eat dinner at the mission.

8:30 P.M.—Group is divided into teams of three. (Remember to have at least one man in each group.) These teams then disperse to walk the downtown streets as observers.

10:00 P.M.—Arrive at mission lodging facility for group debriefing and personal journaling. If debriefing with your group cannot be done in private, be careful not to discuss anything that would offend others who are staying at the mission. (Note: Missions often have strict rules about check-in time. Be sure to discuss your schedule with mission personnel and be prepared to make adjustments.)

11:00 P.M.—Lights out.

Saturday

6:00 A.M.—Wake up.

6:45 A.M.—Teams go to various soup kitchens for breakfast.

10:30 A.M.—Teams spend time walking the streets. (Note: Teams must use this time to begin researching options for the evening meal.)

2:00 P.M.—Meet at mission 2 for discussion.

4:00 P.M.—Teams disperse to find an evening meal and other evening activities common to street people.

10:00 P.M.—Arrive at mission for group debriefing and personal journaling.

11:00 P.M.—Lights out.

Sunday

6:00 A.M.—Wake up.

6:45 A.M.—Teams go to various soup kitchens for breakfast.

8:00 A.M.—Teams find a downtown church service to attend.

12:00 P.M.—Teams find a way to get lunch.

4:30 P.M.—Participants arrive back where cars are parked.

5:00 P.M.—All participants meet for dinner and debriefing.

PROGRAM IDEAS AND SUGGESTIONS

THE ROLE OF SERVER OR RECEIVER

Throughout the weekend it is important to remember one guideline: Choose the role of either server or receiver, then maintain that role for the entire weekend. For example, do not serve meals on Friday night, then receive a meal the next night as though you were homeless. This is confusing, and potentially offensive, to the street people.

❖ **For a list of icebreakers, see the Table of Contents.**

DRESSING FOR THE EVENT

It won't take long to pack. Those taking part will wear the same clothing all weekend! Wear old clothing and try to dress so you will blend in with the others in the shelters. Avoid clothing that might provoke certain groups, such as clothing with the name of a sports team, name-brand athletic shoes, colors associated with a particular gang, or bandannas. Avoid jewelry, perfume, or cologne. If this event is done in colder weather, dress in layers.

SOME THINGS TO DO

See the list of objectives (Resource 1 on page 52) to accomplish as you walk the streets.

SAFETY PROCEDURES

Establish a saftey team *that is not a part of the inner-city group.* The safety team consists of the Assistant Event Director and one or more persons who will agree to carry cellular phones or voice pagers throughout the weekend. The safety team members can stay at home throughout the weekend if they so choose. If any problem arises, the urban plungers should contact the safety team for help. (A digital pager is not effective because many inner-city pay phones will not accept calls. Therefore, if a team member dials the beeper and punches in the number of the pay phone, the safety team has no way to return the call.)

A list of safety precautions is found on page 53 (Resource 2).

RECOMMENDED RESOURCES

Find additional ideas and suggested discussion starters in *Vacations with a Purpose* by Kim Hurst and Chris Eaton (Elgin, IL: David C. Cook Church Ministries, 1992).

EQUIPMENT/SUPPLIES (To be furnished by the event leaders)

☐ Cellular phones or voice pagers for the safety team.
☐ List of participants and phone numbers of friends or family members to call in case of an emergency.

WHAT TO BRING (To be provided by participants)

☐ One piece of identification
☐ Sleeping bag
☐ Toothbrush and toothpaste
☐ Bible and journal
☐ (Optional) Small pocket notebook and pen for jotting down notes during the day

Please do not bring anything else on the Urban Plunge. Leave all valuables and credit cards at home. Participants will be provided with $2.00 for meals, transportation, and other necessities.

PLANNING THE EVENT

PLANNING TEAM

For this event you need an Event Director, an Assistant Event Director, and volunteers for transportation, budget, registration, speaker(s), transportation, and publicity.

The Assistant Event Director will attend to any minor details, such as collecting and storing group member valuables and arranging for the Sunday night dinner and debriefing. During the Urban Plunge, this person will not be a part of a plunge team, but will be available at a central location as the safety team captain to respond to emergency situations.

> ❖
> *The more people who have ownership and involvement in the planning, the greater success you will have.*

Planning Timeline

Event: *The Urban Plunge*   **Date of event:** _____

Event Director: _____   **Phone:** _____

Thanks for agreeing to serve on our Planning Team. Please check over this timeline for the task(s) assigned to you. Adapt as needed. Supplement this timeline with information on the reproducible, generic job descriptions found on pages 225-252. Highlight your tasks (and due dates) each time they appear. Mark your calendar accordingly.

| Date: _____ | **3 MONTHS IN ADVANCE** |

Event Director (page 226)

❖ *For more ideas and help, refer to job descriptions beginning on page 225.*

☐ Recruit a Planning Team. Brainstorm ideas, and adapt this event to fit your particular ministry goals and objectives.

☐ Make sure each team member understands his or her assigned tasks and responsibilities. Determine if this timeline will work and make adjustments accordingly.

☐ Contact inner-city missions organizations. Explain your goals and ask for the opportunity to have the group visit and possibly lodge in (or near) their facility.

Plan to work with at least four missions if possible: one for lodging and storage of your sleeping bags, Bibles, and journals (mission 1); one for Friday night's introduction and meal (mission 2); one for breakfasts (mission 3); and one for Saturday afternoon's discussion (mission 4). To strengthen the educational experience, arrange for Plunge teams to eat or serve in several missions.

☐ On Friday evening and Saturday afternoon, the group will hear presentations by the director or other personnel of two missions (2 and 4). Make these arrangements, including paying the speaker an honorarium or making a donation to the mission. Possible topics: How the mission serves the downtown population; homelessness in America; how the mission personnel got involved in working at the mission; what it's like to work at a mission; helping people understand their heart and sense of calling; how they see God at work through their mission; some of the biggest frustrations and joys in the life of the mission.

☐ Confirm dates and times with the organizations that wish to participate.

Publicity Coordinator (page 238)

☐ Prepare flyers and brochures to promote the event.

Budget Coordinator (page 229)

☐ Determine per-person costs for the weekend. The cost is based on donations you will make to the participating missions, Sunday's debriefing dinner, transportation to downtown, honoraria for speakers, and $2.00 spending money for each participant.

| Date: _____ | **2 MONTHS IN ADVANCE** |

Event Director

☐ Work with the Publicity Coordinator and other Planning Team members to recruit participants.

☐ As people sign up, have them sign a liability release form (sample on page 253).

Assistant Event Director (page 227)

☐ Organize a safety team (consisting of the Assistant Event Director and one or more persons not on the Urban Plunge teams) who will carry cellular phones or voice pagers throughout the weekend.

☐ The safety team must have a plan of action for any emergency that might arise. (Contact the local fire or police department for a recommended plan of action.)

Transportation Coordinator (page 252)

☐ Arrange transportation to and from downtown. If possible, travel in a church or group member's van. Contact a church located near the downtown core to see if it can provide safe parking for the van from Friday through Sunday. If a church van is available, reserve it and complete any necessary forms.

☐ If a van is not the best mode of transportation or safe parking cannot be found, consider using public transportation to the inner city. (This fare is not part of the $2.00 allocation.)

Date: _____	**1 MONTH** **IN ADVANCE**

Event Director

☐ Continue to recruit if space is available.

Assistant Event Director

☐ Arrange for the Sunday night dinner. Keep in mind that the participants will be dirty and tired. If possible, meet at your own church and have food prepared in the kitchen or brought in.

Date: _____	**2 WEEKS** **IN ADVANCE**

Event Director

☐ Finalize and divide the list of participants into teams of three, appointing one person on each team as the leader. Make sure there is at least one man per team.

☐ Send a confirmation letter to participants. (Adapt the sample letter on page 244 to meet your needs.)

Assistant Event Director

☐ Develop discussion material for the preparatory meeting and Sunday debriefing dinner. Before the plunge you might explore peoples' attitudes toward the homeless, runaways, immigrants, prostitutes, and others. Give people a chance to voice fears and concerns. (Optional) Provide a list of Bible verses for each team member to study prior to the Urban Plunge. These verses could include Matthew 25:42-46; Ezekial 16:49; Proverbs 21:13; Proverbs 14:31.

Date: _____	**1 WEEK** **IN ADVANCE**

Event Director

☐ Work with the Assistant Event Director to hold a mandatory preparatory meeting for all participants. Use this time to distribute materials, talk about fears, expectations, guidelines, and safety precautions.

☐ Confirm all mission speakers and arrangements for sleeping, eating, and parking.

Budget Coordinator

☐ Collect and distribute funds as needed.

Date: _____	**2 TO 4 WEEKS** **AFTER EVENT**

Event Director

☐ Hold one follow-up meeting with all participants. This is a good chance to further debrief the team and to develop a plan for members to follow up on the experience.

All Participants

☐ Plan a presentation to the entire singles group (and/or church congregation) about the experiences of this Urban Plunge.

☐ See the "Followup Guidelines" on page 254.

Objectives

1. Locate as many bathrooms as possible. Be brave; go inside and report on the condition to other participants.

2. Discover where people can go to take free showers.

3. Locate where people hang out. Depending on your city, look for Native Americans, immigrants, youth, elderly, women with children, and prostitutes. What other groups do you see? How do these people pass time?

4. Draw a mental map of downtown, then write it down in your journal. Mark the locations where people tend to gather.

5. Discover through observation and appropriate conversation what the philosophies of different agencies are in serving the street population.

6. Look for God in unexpected places. Where did He meet you? Where does He meet people on the streets? Who represents God on the streets?

7. When you visit church on Sunday morning, looking yourself like a street person, observe how you are greeted and treated—and how you feel.

8. Look for answers to the following questions:

• You are all alone and bored. It is pouring rain and very stormy. How could you spend three or four hours of your time inside (legitimately) where it is warm and dry, and perhaps learn something as well?

• You are fourteen years old and a runaway. Your situation back home is worse than the prospects on the street. You can't go home, but you want to get off the streets. Where could you go for help?

• You are wheelchair-bound. Of the various agencies you visit this weekend, which are accessible to you? In general, how easy is it to get around?

Safety Precautions

1

Schedule at least two check-ins per day. Meet with the Event Director either in person or by phone to report your location and any problems that may need to be addressed.

2

Remember you are entering another culture. Observe and respect the rules. Assimilate! Try not to become too noticeable.

3

Do not give last names, phone numbers, or addresses. And absolutely no hitchhiking or panhandling.

4

Do not lie about your identity. You may choose to be forthcoming or vague, but do not lie. In the future, you may need to rely on having established credibility.

5

Always stay in groups of three, with at least one man in each group. When walking down the streets, keep the man on the outside. Never go off, even as a group, with people you don't know.

6

In case of problems, stay calm. If you observe a fight, get out of the way. If someone is injured, call 911 first. If it is an Urban Plunge participant, call the Safety Team.

7

Do not bring anyone you meet back to the lodging site to spend the night. As guests, that is not your option.

7 A VACATION WITH A PURPOSE

Cross-Cultural Service Mission Weekend

Event Summary: An energizing, beyond-the-comfort-level Service Mission Weekend where your single adults get involved in serving a neighbor or someone in need. This event also helps build deeper relationships among the participants and raises up new leaders in your singles ministry.

Length of Event: 2–4 days (or longer)

Suggested Theme Verse: ". . . If anyone wants to be first, he must be the very last, and the servant of all." Mark 9:35

Ideal Number of Participants: 8+

Estimated Cost Per Person: Variable, depending on project and location

Facility Requirements: A cross-cultural setting

Recommended Planning Team: 4–6 people

Advance Planning Needed: Approximately 7–9 months

INTRODUCTION

by Scot Sorensen
Pastor, Zion Lutheran Church
San Antonio, Texas

If you are interested in energizing your single adults and raising up ministry leaders, this is one of the best things you can do. Here are five reasons this event has benefited our singles ministry.

First, by serving a neighbor we understand what it means to "carry each other's burdens, and in this way you will fulfill the law of Christ" (Gal. 6:2). But the real beauty of this event is in what God teaches those involved about themselves, about their relationships with fellow teammates, and about what it means to care for others.

Second, this type of event has been one of the best ways I've found to raise up leaders for our ministry. People discover skills that they had not previously realized. Spiritual gifts are displayed in action. Several participants will eventually become some of your key ministry (and spiritual) leaders.

Third, a dynamic sense of community is discovered when a group is challenged through demanding work within the context of an unfamiliar culture. By unfamiliar culture I mean going beyond the comfort level and social setting which is standard for the majority of participants of any given single adult ministry.

Fourth, this event can be condensed into a weekend to give those reluctant to sign up for a more extended, seven- to fourteen-day trip a taste of what happens on service or mission trips. These weekend excursions serve as interest stimulators and recruiting tools for the longer, more commitment-intensive project trips, as well as being a self-contained experience.

Fifth, it builds bridges within the larger Christian community by breaking down stereotypes which exist between various ethnic groups and differing cultural communities.

OBJECTIVES

❖ To provide the participants with the opportunity to put feet to their faith.
❖ To live out the call to serve Christ by serving others.
❖ To build community among leadership teammates.

THE BIG EVENT

Schedule this trip as a three-day event (Friday night through Sunday) or a four-day event (Thursday night through Sunday, or Friday night through a holiday Monday), depending on how far you will travel and on participants' ability and willingness to miss a day of work.

SCHEDULE FOR 3-DAY EVENT

❖ *Get as many people as possible involved in the planning of this event.*

Friday

7:00 P.M.—Leave for destination
9:00 P.M.—Arrive and settle in
9:30 P.M.—Team meeting

Saturday

8:00 A.M.—Breakfast
8:30 A.M.—Team devotions
9:00 A.M.—Begin work for local church/agency/work site
12:00 P.M.—Lunch
1:00–4:30 P.M.—Complete work and return to "home base"
5:00 P.M.—Shower and cleanup
6:00 P.M.—Team devotions/Bible study
7:00 P.M.—Dinner and "Tourist Time" (local culture, sights, etc.)
10:30 P.M.—Personal devotions

Sunday

8:30 A.M.—Breakfast
10:00 A.M.—Worship (at the host site to be enriched by the diversity of worship styles)
1:00 P.M.—Lunch
2:30 P.M.—Travel back home/"Tourist Time"

SCHEDULE FOR 4-DAY EVENT

Thursday or Friday

7:00 P.M.—Leave for destination
9:00 P.M.—Arrive and settle in
9:30 P.M.—Team meeting

Friday and/or Saturday

8:00 A.M.—Breakfast
8:30 A.M.—Team devotions
9:00 A.M.—Begin work for local church/agency/work site

12:00 P.M.—Lunch
1:00–4:30 P.M.—Complete day's work and return to "home base"
5:00 P.M.—Shower and cleanup
6:00 P.M.—Team devotions/Bible study
7:00 P.M.—Dinner and "Tourist Time" (local culture, sights, etc.)
10:30 P.M.—Personal devotions

Sunday

8:30 A.M.—Breakfast
9:30 A.M.—Worship (at the host site, to be enriched by the diversity of worship styles)
1:00 P.M.—Lunch
2:00–4:00 P.M.—Finish day's work as needed (If this is day four, travel back home and "Tourist Time")
5:00 P.M.—Dinner and "Tourist Time"
10:30 P.M.—Personal or team devotions

Sunday or Holiday Monday

9:00 A.M.—Breakfast
10:00 A.M.—Closing worship and Bible study
11:30 A.M.—Complete project work or "Tourist Time" (local culture, sights, etc.)
6:00 P.M.—Back home

PROGRAM IDEAS AND SUGGESTIONS

HOW TO SELECT A PROJECT

There are many ways to find a project that fits your group's needs, skills, time, and interests:

1. Denominational leadership. Most denominations have suggested projects and resource people to call for more information.

2. Senior pastor.

3. Bridge Builders, 833 Oak Street N E, St. Petersburg, FL 33701, 813-898-4152—an organization that helps coordinate short-term mission projects for single adult ministries.

4. Habitat for Humanity, 121 Habitat Street, Americus, GA 31709-3498.

5. Area inner-city missions or social services.

   Project sites could include:
   ❖ an inner-city church/mission/home
   ❖ an Indian reservation

❖ an elderly person's home
❖ an orphanage or "troubled youth"
facility
❖ an impoverished rural area
❖ another country (if geographic location,
travel time, and budget allow)

Some of the types of projects that usually
work best over a weekend include:
❖ helping build/repair a building
❖ cleaning, painting, and refurbishing
❖ feeding the homeless/working in a soup
kitchen
❖ door knocking/making cold calls for a
church/ministry
❖ working with children in an orphanage
❖ yard work

Physical projects like these are usually less
threatening, require less emotional commitment, and are easier to make short-term commitments to (on both the giving and receiving
end). It is also easier to see the results of the
effort expended. Such projects help whet a
person's appetite and open up a world of
longer-commitment projects.

How to Select Participants

With most of your events, you want to get
everyone possible to participate—the more the
better. However, when undertaking a short-
term mission project, you may need to be
somewhat selective in who can participate. For
that reason, it is recommended that you use an
application process rather than an open registration process. Anyone can apply to participate, but due to the specific skills and abilities
needed with your project, and because of possible limited numbers that can be involved,
the application process will usually work best.

Some of what you may want to watch for
on the applications include:
❖ Medical conditions that could create a
problem or concern on the trip.
❖ Wrong motivations for participating.
Does the person seem to understand and agree
with the primary goal and purpose of the trip?
❖ Financial difficulties. Depending on the
costs and fund-raising needs of the trip, can

the person handle it without undue stress on
his/her personal finances?
❖ Has the person had a negative experience on a previous project trip?
❖ Emotional or psychological problems.
Is the person able to handle stressful situations
well? Is he or she sensitive to other racial or
cultural groups?

These are some of the things you want to
consider as you prayerfully select and approve
applicants for this trip.

Growing As a Team before the Trip

Once the participants are determined, begin
developing this group of individuals as a
"team." There are three particular ways to help
accomplish this. First, spend time as a team
planning, studying, and praying together.
Second, have some team-building exercises.
Third, have several team preparation meetings.

Planning, Studying, and Praying

If schedules allow, it can be a tremendous
asset to meet weekly as a team for four to six
weeks before the trip. This provides an opportunity to discuss the project, location, how to
prepare, etc. It is also a great opportunity to
begin studying and praying together about
what it means to be a servant. (An excellent
six-part pre-trip study is available in the Team
Member's Manual of *Vacations With a Purpose*
[VWAP] by Kim Hurst and Chris Eaton, published by David C. Cook Church Ministry
Resources, 1993.)

Team-Building Exercises

These are best done two or three weeks prior
to the event itself. Remember, what develops
among group members during this weekend—
intimacy, trust, conflict resolution, spiritual
growth, lifestyle and ministry priorities—is
often as important as the project they do.
What happened *in* me today is more important than what happened *to* me today. Times of
team building and studying together can be
crucial to the success of this event. Here are
some suggested team-building exercises.

• **All about Me.** Break the team into pairs and have each pair try to learn at least three things about each other without using any verbal communication (e.g., draw pictures or use sign language). Then come together as a group and have partners share what they learned about each other. This is a great way for the team to experience the frustration they may feel on the field when they can't easily communicate with the host community. (Contributed by Doug and Adele Calhoun and published in *VWAP*, Leader's Manual, p. 91.)

• **Teamwork Factor.** Distribute copies of Resources 1 and 2 (pages 64-65). Going around the room one at a time, have team members give a definition or example of the words that make the acronym "Teamwork Factor." Then have them compile their own list of traits of a person who is not a team player. (For example, you might start with **N**oncooperative, **E**litist, **S**tubborn.) Without revealing the solution, see if they can figure it out. (Send Me Home!) (*VWAP*, Leader's Manual, p. 91.)

❖ *For more icebreakers, see the Table of Contents.*

• **World Hunger Meal.** This is an excellent way to raise awareness among just the event participants or your entire singles group about how others live. Divide everyone into people groups roughly representing the world population (50% from developing countries, 30% from semi-developed countries, and 20% from highly developed countries). Each person will receive a color-coded dinner ticket as he or she enters the room. Do not explain the differences between the tickets, simply serve the meal as follows:
Developing countries—only rice and water.
Semi-developed nations—salad, rice, meat, and choice of beverage.
Highly-developed countries—all of the above plus rolls and dessert.
If you use this idea, make arrangements for those who may have special health situa-

tions and need to eat regularly.
After eating, lead a short discussion with these questions:
❖ How did you feel about your dinner?
❖ How did you feel about what your neighbor was served?
❖ Did those at your table accept their dinners without questions? share? ask to share?
❖ What thoughts do you have about the "haves" and "have nots?"

Team Preparation Meetings

The purpose for weekly team meetings is:
To develop team goals and ownership.
To create a sense of community.
To prepare each participant for the event and all they will be involved with on-site.

GROWING AS A TEAM DURING THE TRIP

Ideas in this section have been adapted from *VWAP*, Leader's Manual, pages 144 and 145.

Team Journal

Have a notebook or blank book specified as the "Team Journal" and accessible during the entire event. Throughout the trip, participants slip by to jot down thoughts and prayers. When complete, this journal can be copied and distributed to the entire group.

Daily Prayer Partners

Other teams have *daily prayer partners*. Besides ensuring that team members spend time one-on-one with all other participants, praying together enhances the sense of community. Before departure and each morning, put all the team members' names into a hat and draw them out in pairs. Encourage each pair to meet once that day to talk and pray.

Devotions

Team devotions can be handled any number of ways. The nature of your particular team will determine how your devotions operate. Three suggestions are listed here.

• **Buddy System.** Before departure choose devotion teams of two or three. Pair new Christians and non-Christians with more mature Christians. Each devotion team is responsible for organizing either a morning's team devotions or an evening's group Bible study (sharing, prayer, and praise). They are to bring thought-provoking questions for discussion, and then keep the group from digressing, complaining, or gossiping. The delightful benefit of team-led devotions is the diversity that each devotion team can bring. This is also a great way to give the quieter members a real sense of their importance to the team.

• **Rotation.** This format is the same as above, except that, instead of teams, different individuals lead each devotion or Bible study time. Use this alternative when pairs of team members do not have a chance to prepare and coordinate a devotional. When something is weighing heavily on the collective heart of the group, one team member may be asked to lead a spontaneous sharing time. Diversity can be wonderful. Devotions are a time to see the gifts of the Body at work.

• **Team Pastor.** This format works well when the "pastor" is thoroughly prepared. One person is chosen well ahead of time to prepare a series to be taught during the trip. Any member of the team who has Christian maturity, the will to do the preparation, and a good teaching style can be chosen. This person should choose a series that will relate directly to the experiences of the trip and provide ample fuel for discussion. The Bible study portion should help team members see how they can integrate their new experiences into their everyday lives as Christians.

• **Special Guests.** While time alone as a team is important, so is taking advantage of what your hosts can teach you. Some teams have invited the host missionary or pastor to join them for one of their team meetings so they could hear the pastor's testimony or the missionary's dreams. Keep an eye out for opportunities to invite a special guest to one of your meetings.

Bible Study

Remember that the heart of this event is serving others, so Bible studies and devotions should reflect service themes such as being sent, Christian service, servanthood, following Christ, unity, and oneness in Christ.

Another option is to select one or more of the following passages to study together during the trip and/or before the trip.

❖ Jesus sends out the seventy-two—Luke 10:1-12

❖ The great judgment—Matthew 25:31-46

❖ The good Samaritan—Luke 10:25-37

❖ Jesus washes the disciples' feet—John 13:1-9

❖ Bear one another's burdens—Galatians 6:1-10

❖ True greatness—Mark 9:33-37; Mark 10:35-45

❖ Unity of the Body of Christ—I Corinthians 12

(Consult the *Serendipity Bible for Study Groups* for possible outlines for group discussions on these and other texts.)

This form of study offers the participants an opportunity to reflect on their serving others, their relationship with the team, and the things God is showing and teaching them in the process.

EQUIPMENT/SUPPLIES (To be furnished by the event leaders)

- ☐ First aid medical kit
- ☐ Food and cooking utensils (if needed)
- ☐ Drinking water container
- ☐ Large flashlight with extra batteries
- ☐ Camping gear (if needed)
- ☐ Recreational items (softball, soccer ball, Frisbee, etc.)
- ☐ All other items will be determined by the type of project you select. Make a careful list of the tools and other items needed to best accomplish your chosen task.

WHAT TO BRING (To be provided by participants)

- ☐ Adapt the list on Resource 2, page 65.

RECOMMENDED RESOURCES

Vacations With a Purpose by Kim Hurst and Chris Eaton (David C. Cook Church Ministry Resources, Colorado Springs, 1993)

This resource is available in both a Leader's Manual and a Team Member's Manual and it covers topics such as planning the mission project, recruiting the team, raising the funds, dealing with conflict on the team, things to study together as a team, etc. It is the most practical, helpful resource available for a short-term mission trip.

Serendipity Bible for Groups by Lyman Coleman, Richard Peace, and Denny Rydberg (Serendipity House, Littleton, CO, 1988)

This is an excellent resource for use in your team Bible study times.

For participants to read when preparing for this trip:

The Wounded Healer by Henri Nouwen (Doubleday & Company, New York, 1979)

Out of Solitude by Henri Nouwen (Ave Maria, Notre Dame, 1974)

PLANNING THE EVENT

PLANNING TEAM

For this event, you need an Event Director (possibly an Assistant Event Director) and volunteers to take responsibilities for the event site, budget, publicity, printed materials, registration, food, worship, transportation, and equipment/supplies. Detailed, though generic, task descriptions for these coordinators are found on pages 225-252 and are cross-referenced on the following timeline. Glean information from these descriptions that relate to this particular event.

❖ *The more people who have ownership and involvement in the planning, the greater success you will have.*

The position of Event Director requires at least a seven- to nine-month commitment. (See page 226 for more information regarding this responsibility.) It will require about two hours a week for the first two months of work. At least one hour a week is needed from nine months to three months prior to the event. The last three months before the event will require from two to five hours a week.

The Event Director will develop managerial skills in delegating responsibilities and insuring that those responsibilities are fulfilled. He or she must also be able to motivate people. A commitment to service/mission ministry is essential. Such a commitment on behalf of the Event Director will help expand the mission vision of the members of this ministry and support the host congregation or service/mission/ministry agency.

Planning Team members will work with the entire single adult group and others as needed to fulfill each assignment. A love for the Church and a genuine concern for people is essential.

Planning Timeline

Event: *A Vacation with a Purpose*   **Date of event:** _____

Event Director: _____   **Phone:** _____

Thanks for agreeing to serve on our mission Planning Team. Please check over this timeline for your assigned task(s). Adapt as needed and supplement with information in the generic job descriptions. Highlight your tasks (and due dates) and mark your calendar accordingly.

Date: _____   7 TO 9 MONTHS IN ADVANCE

Event Director (page 226)

- ☐ Recruit a Planning Team.
- ☐ Brainstorm ideas and adapt this event to fit your ministry goals and objectives.
- ☐ Distribute copies of this timeline and related job descriptions. Make sure team members understand their assigned tasks and responsibilities.
- ☐ Determine if this timeline will work for your area and make any adjustments.
- ☐ Decide what type of setting/project will provide growth for your people.
- ☐ Determine the length of the event. Thursday through Sunday? Friday through Sunday? Or Friday through Monday holiday weekend?
- ☐ (Optional) Order copies of *Vacations With a Purpose* (one copy of the Leader's Manual for each member of the Planning Team; one copy of the Team Member's Manual for the remaining participants). Order through your local Christian bookstore or by calling 1-800-323-7543.

Event Site Coordinator (page 234)

- ☐ Explore various cities or locations with interest and appeal to your people.
- ☐ Through your denomination, pastor, or service organizations such as Habitat for Humanity, make contact with a sister congregation or organizational site which will meet your desired project goals. Begin negotiating a time when your group can work at their site. Discuss various needed projects they have that might fit the skills/interests of your people.
- ☐ Explore options for housing, meals, on-site transportation, and team R & R.
- ☐ Place tentative dates on church calendar.

Transportation Coordinator (page 252)

- ☐ Determine best method of travel to site.

Budget Coordinator (page 229)

- ☐ Begin estimating total costs (and cost per person) for this event.

Date: _____   6 MONTHS IN ADVANCE

❖ *For ideas and help, refer to job descriptions beginning on page 225.*

Event Director

- ☐ Meet with the Planning Team to discuss each person's area of responsibility.
- ☐ Plan tentative itinerary.

Event Site Coordinator

- ☐ With Planning Team input, finalize project location and related details.
- ☐ Confirm the dates with the Planning Team and on the church calendar.
- ☐ If traveling to a foreign country, check into necessary shots and preventive medication.
- ☐ Determine any possible funds needed to accomplish the project.

Transportation Coordinator

- ☐ Finalize travel plans and costs.

Budget Coordinator

- ☐ With the Planning Team, finalize the trip budget and per-person costs.

- [ ] Set payment dates and amount of deposit.
- [ ] If additional funds will be needed to accomplish the selected project, propose fund-raising ideas.
- [ ] Contact church treasurer regarding the handling of funds.

Publicity Coordinator (page 238)

- [ ] Develop a game plan for advertising this event and recruiting participants, including announcements in the church bulletin and in the single adult class(es).
- [ ] Emphasize the type of service work and the destination as key ingredients in designing promotional materials.

Date:	**5 MONTHS**
_____	**IN ADVANCE**

Event Director

- [ ] Meet with the Planning Team to go over progress and areas that need attention.
- [ ] Schedule the first informational meeting where interested participants can learn more about this special event.

Publicity Coordinator

- [ ] Once a site and dates have been confirmed, prepare publicity materials and begin promotion.

Registration Coordinator (page 241)

- [ ] Determine the deadline for registration and also the number of spaces available for this event.
- [ ] Prepare and distribute application forms. Begin taking applications.
- [ ] If scholarship funds will be awarded, provide the forms now (see page 246).

Date:	**4 MONTHS**
_____	**IN ADVANCE**

Event Director

- [ ] Meet with the Planning Team to discuss progress and areas that need attention.

- [ ] Schedule weekly team preparation sessions and their locations.
- [ ] Schedule a commissioning service with the church.
- [ ] Hold the first informational meeting with interested participants. Be prepared to share the goals, schedule, location and date, number of participants, and expectations for this event.

Publicity Coordinator

- [ ] Continue promoting the event.

Registration Coordinator

- [ ] Continue taking applications and deposits.

Date:	**3 MONTHS**
_____	**IN ADVANCE**

Event Director

- [ ] Meet with the Planning Team to go over progress and areas that need attention.
- [ ] If needed, hold the second informational meeting with interested participants.

Publicity Coordinator

- [ ] Continue promoting the event.

Registration Coordinator

- [ ] Continue taking applications and deposits.
- [ ] With the assistance of the Event Director, go over applications to determine eligibility for participation.

Event Site Coordinator

- [ ] Be in contact with your host site and finalize, as needed, the expected number of participants and probable service activities (house building, general maintenance and clean-up, community outreach).
- [ ] Discuss possible recreational activities and local sights and attractions.
- [ ] Sign a contract or letter of agreement if necessary and be sure a copy is on file at the church.

<table>
<tr><td>

Date:

_____

</td><td>

2 MONTHS
IN ADVANCE

</td></tr>
</table>

Event Director

- ☐ Discuss the Planning Team's progress.
- ☐ With the Registration Coordinator interview applicants and make your final selection. The event Planning Team now expands to include all team members.
- ☐ Inform team members of team preparation meetings, team policies, necessary documentation, and financial obligations.

Registration Coordinator

- ☐ Close the registration/application process.
- ☐ Assist the Event Director in meeting with applicants and selecting the team.
- ☐ Distribute "Liability Release Forms" to all team members (see page 253).
- ☐ Give scholarship forms to the right person.
- ☐ Inform recipients of available funds.

Budget Coordinator

- ☐ With the team, plan needed fund-raising.

Transportation Coordinator

- ☐ Confirm all final travel arrangements.

Food Coordinator (page 236)

- ☐ Work with the Event Site Coordinator to determine available food services.
- ☐ Make any necessary arrangements.

Equipment/Supplies Coordinator (page 233)

- ☐ In cooperation with the team, compile a list of all needed equipment and supplies.
- ☐ Begin locating needed items.

<table>
<tr><td>

Date:

_____

</td><td>

6 WEEKS
IN ADVANCE

</td></tr>
</table>

Event Director

- ☐ Begin first of the weekly team preparation meetings. (Optional: Use the team prepa-

ration materials in the *Vacations With a Purpose,* Leader's Manual.)

Team Members

- ☐ Begin identifying people who will pray for team members (be prayer partners) during this project trip.
- ☐ Make financial preparation as needed.

Worship Coordinator (page 251)

- ☐ With the Event Director, decide how the devotionals/Bible studies will be conducted (see ideas on pages 57 and 58).
- ☐ If needed, prepare Bible study and devotional materials for use on the trip. (See pages 57 and 58 for ideas.) Or use ideas found in the *Vacations With a Purpose Team,* Member Manual. This material is designed especially for those involved in a short-term missions project.

<table>
<tr><td>

Date:

_____

</td><td>

4 WEEKS
IN ADVANCE

</td></tr>
</table>

Event Director

- ☐ Meet with the team to discuss final plans for the event.
- ☐ Check on team finances.
- ☐ Be certain everything is on schedule and being completed in an organized manner.
- ☐ Continue the weekly team meetings, including team-building activities (see pages 56-57).
- ☐ Schedule post-trip follow-up meetings and presentation to the congregation.

Team Members

- ☐ Continue with fund-raising as needed.

Registration Coordinator

- ☐ Collect all "Liability Release Forms."

Publicity Coordinator

- ☐ Recruit one or two team members to be official team photographer/videographers.

Transportation Coordinator

☐ Prepare a map to the site and make available to any drivers as needed.

Equipment/Supplies Coordinator

☐ Put together a first aid medical kit.

Budget Coordinator

☐ Determine procedure for obtaining necessary cash for team trip.
☐ Provide funds as needed for those purchasing supplies prior to trip.

Event Site Coordinator

☐ Be sure all details and schedules for the event are covered at the facility.
☐ Obtain emergency contact phone number for the destination site.

| Date: _____ | **3 WEEKS IN ADVANCE** |

Event Director

☐ Continue the weekly team meetings.

Transportation Coordinator

☐ Finalize all travel arrangements.

Equipment/Supplies Coordinator

☐ Purchase any necessary supplies.

Registration Coordinator

☐ All team member trip funds should be due at this time.
☐ Send a letter (or distribute at team meeting) to all registrants informing them of the place, time, and date to meet. Include an emergency phone number at the facility, an itinerary, and what-to-bring list.

| Date: _____ | **1 WEEK IN ADVANCE** |

Event Director

☐ Hold final pre-trip team meeting and discuss any last minute details.
☐ Be certain the church staff have phone numbers and addresses for the event site.

Event Site Coordinator

☐ Discuss final arrangements with the contact person at the host facility.
☐ Confirm all lodging arrangements and estimated arrival times.

Transportation Coordinator

☐ Confirm plans for all travel arrangements.

Budget Coordinator

☐ Obtain traveler's checks/funds as needed.

Team Members

☐ Participate in team commissioning service with church congregation.

| Date: _____ | **2 TO 4 WEEKS AFTER EVENT** |

☐ Spend time debriefing as a team. What did you learn on this project? What new or different perspectives did you bring back? How has it changed you, if at all? Where should we go from here?
☐ As a team, plan presentation(s) you could make to the entire singles group and/or church congregation. What do you want them to know about this trip? What challenge do you have for them?
☐ Discuss ways to begin recruiting the next special mission team.
☐ Send thank-yous to all financial supporters and prayer partners.
☐ See "Followup Guidelines" on page 254.

The Teamwork Factor

Just what does teamwork mean? What are the traits of a team player? We have come up with fourteen words that form the basis of what we call the "Teamwork Factor," the traits exhibited by those who are pitching in to do their part for the good of the group.

T is for Teachable Spirit
A teachable spirit helps create a noncompetitive environment in which learning and sharing come naturally. Teachability gives all members the freedom to make mistakes as they learn.

E is for Encouraging
Think of how encouraging words enhance the development of a community. What difference do they make?

A is for Appreciative
What things can we appreciate in others on the team? How can we show our appreciation?

M is for Motivated
Take initiative! Do all things as unto the Lord! (Colossians 3:17, 23).

W is for Willing
Team members may have different levels of strength, skill, and health, but each should be willing to work to the best of his or her capabilities. Willingness also includes accepting uncomfortable conditions in the host location. Willingly take on the heat, food, bugs, and germs.

O is for Open
Be open with what you are learning, experiencing, feeling, thinking, etc. Express both the positive and negative. Your vulnerability with others builds community.

R is for Refreshing
The times may be tough—heat, sickness, exhaustion, physical labor, emotion drain, and so on. In those times it will be incredibly refreshing to have another team member help pick up your spirits! Think about how you can be replenishers to each other on a daily basis.

K is for the Kindred Spirit
There's a sense of camaraderie as we pursue this together. We are all part of the Christian family and we're all in this together!

F is for Flexible
Anything can change from day to day. A flexible team member will learn to accept the unexpected as the norm.

A is for Agreeable
Living together in close quarters, sharing crowded bathing facilities, and every other aspect of group travel requires everyone to be gracious.

C is for Cooperative
Share with one another, help and assist one another. Instead of grumbling about problems, propose solutions!

T is for Thoughtful
What can you do to make a teammate's day a little easier?

O is for Obedient
There will be times when the team leader has to "pull rank" and make unpopular decisions. A team player will respect the leader's authority and encourage others to do the same.

R is for Relational
Get to know the others on your team. Go out of your way to learn about their hopes, their dreams, their history.

(Continued)

"The Teamwork Factor" is reprinted with permission from *Vacations With a Purpose*, Leader's Manual, by Chris Eaton and Kim Hurst. © David C. Cook Publishing, Colorado Springs, 1993. pp. 91-93.

Creative Weekends © 1995 David C. Cook Publishing Co. You may photocopy this form for ministry use in your local church.

Get the picture? The "TEAMWORK FACTOR" spells out the difference between a group of isolated individuals and a team of interconnected members.

Now it's your turn to compile your own list of negative traits, using the first letter shown in each space below. Think of words that work against community and destroy team spirit.

N

E

S

E

M

H

E

M

O

D

Now rearrange the letters to find out what you're saying when you exhibit these traits:

— — — — — — — — — — — !

What to Bring

(To be provided by participants)

- ☐ Work clothes
- ☐ Casual clothes
- ☐ Coat/raincoat
- ☐ Sweatshirt/sweater
- ☐ Work gloves/shoes
- ☐ Cotton socks
- ☐ Hat and/or bandannas
- ☐ Swimming clothes (if needed)
- ☐ Sleeping bag/pillow (or equivalent)
- ☐ Air mattress (optional)
- ☐ Toiletries/soap/towel
- ☐ Towelette packets
- ☐ Insect repellent/lotion
- ☐ Sunscreen/sunglasses

- ☐ Beach towel
- ☐ Servant's attitude
- ☐ Flashlight/batteries
- ☐ Bible, 2-3 pens or pencils, and journal
- ☐ Spending money (for souvenirs, gifts, snacks, etc.)
- ☐ Large water squeeze bottle
- ☐ Camera/film
- ☐ Positive, flexible spirit
- ☐ Passport/birth certificate/driver's license (if needed)
- ☐ Carpenter's belt (if doing any kind of construction work)
- ☐ Cheap watch (maybe to give away when you leave)
- ☐ Small, simple gifts for hosts/children

8 HOLE-IN-ONE GOLF TOURNAMENT

(. . . and a Chance to Win a Free Car!)

Event Summary: A one-day golf tournament and dinner designed as an enjoyable outing as well as an opportunity for outreach (especially with men) and raising awareness about your ministry in the community.

Length of Event: Saturday afternoon and evening

Ideal Number of Participants: Approximately 70–150. (For the smaller church, consider doing this event in conjunction with two or three other area churches.)

Estimated Cost Per Person: $35–$65

Facility Requirements: Golf course and dining facility (or catering service)

Recommended Planning Team: 8–14 people

Advance Planning Needed: Approximately 4–7 months

Special Instructions: Make arrangements to provide the opportunity to win a free car on a specific hole-in-one.

INTRODUCTION

by Timm Jackson
Senior Pastor
Canyon Creek Community Church
Chandler, Arizona

Over the past ten years (in Michigan, Tennessee, and now in Arizona), this has been one of our most popular events. It's a great way to provide fun and fellowship for our single adults, and at the same time it serves as a catalyst to attract new people to the singles group. Golfing foursomes compete to win prizes, all the while having a wonderful day on the links.

OBJECTIVES

❖ To provide a fun activity for your singles.
❖ To reach out into the community with an event that will appeal to the unchurched.
❖ (Optional) To raise money for some special project such as a missions trip or single-parent scholarship fund.

Non-golfers are invited to join the outdoor cookout/awards dinner at the end of the day and can also register for door prizes and raffle items.

The key benefits to doing an event like this include the following:

❖ It serves as a wonderful icebreaker for those who might not normally attend church. For the single golfers in your community (and there are probably thousands of them), this event says to them, "Here's a church that might appeal to me."

❖ Since it is fairly easy to publicize (especially in light of the fact that someone might win a free car), this event provides an excellent opportunity for media coverage and exposure throughout your community.

❖ This event also gives you the option to raise a significant amount of money. We have raised as much as $20,000 from this one-day event for our short-term missions teams. (As you do this event time and again over several years, it can become an even more successful fund-raiser.)

THE BIG EVENT
SCHEDULE

Saturday

❖

Get as many people as possible involved in the planning of this event.

11:30 A.M.—Set up registration tables; display car/prizes

12:30 P.M.—Registration and practice range open

1:30 P.M.—Opening comments and starting gun

6:00 P.M.—Registration for dinner-only participants

6:30 P.M.—Awards Banquet/Cookout

8:00 P.M.—Event ends

PROGRAM IDEAS AND SUGGESTIONS

SCRAMBLE FORMAT GOLF

To get more people involved in the tournament, move the players quickly through the course by using a scramble format. After all players from a foursome tee off, each player takes his or her next shot from the position of the best ball played. This scramble format also makes it easier for the less-experienced golfers to participate equally in the tournament. (If you are a non-golfer, the scramble format can be more fully explained by an experienced golfer in your group or by a staff member at a golf course in your area.)

TOURNAMENT AWARDS AND PRIZES

(Note: If this is a fund-raising event, you'll be able to offer more and better prizes since more sponsors will be willing to participate.)

The Tournament Director, along with the Planning Team, should determine what tournament events will be awarded prizes. The prizes offered, except for the free car, will be determined to a large extent by the type of products and services that area businesses donate. Here are some ideas to consider:

"Best of . . ." Prizes

Here's where you can let your creativity flow. What prizes would you like to give out at the closing dinner? Examples include prizes for:

- hitting the longest drive on hole 6;
- hitting closest to the pin on hole 12;
- hitting the longest putt on hole 18; and
- the top three foursomes.

In addition, you could establish the above prizes by category: men, women, under 40, over 40, etc.

For ease of judging, it may be best to limit all prizes to only two or three holes (i.e., hole 6, hole 12, and hole 18). This makes it easier for the judge to concentrate time and energy on just two or three places rather than on the entire golf course.

"Best of . . ." prize items could include such things as a new golf bag, a putter, a weekend stay at an area resort, or an evening of limo service. These prizes could be announced well in advance of the event and given out at the evening dinner.

For fun, consider also presenting some "spoof" awards to participants. These awards might include prizes for:

- the best-dressed golfer;
- the worst-dressed golfer;
- the golfer with the funniest-looking swing; and
- the golfer losing the most balls.

Grab Bag Prizes

Have everyone attending the evening dinner put his or her name on a card. During the evening meal, draw cards at random for various prizes that have been donated by area businesses. Grab bag items could include T-shirts, cases of soft drinks, a dinner for two, golf balls, etc. (A good goal to set would be to have enough prizes so that at least one-half of those at the dinner will leave with some sort of prize.)

❖

For a list of icebreakers, see the Table of Contents.

Free Car Prize

This prize will increase interest and help get people more excited about participating in the event. Some insurance companies specialize in offering such prizes for a hole-in-one. Acquire the names of such insurance companies through professional golf courses in your area or call 1-800-Hole-in-One for more information. The insurance company will write a policy that promises to buy a specific car for the person who hits a hole-in-one on a pre-designated hole during the tournament. (If specified in the policy, the person can also opt for cash instead of the car.)

Part of the fee that each tournament participant pays to play in this tournament goes toward covering the insurance policy. It is crucial that all details pertaining to this insurance be carefully followed to assure that the policy is in fact payable should someone hit a hole-in-one. Further details are provided later pertaining to this free car prize.

AWARDS BANQUET/COOKOUT

Since the day will be long and tiring for many participants, try to hold the awards dinner at the golf course club house and limit it to an hour or an hour and a half. For example, your schedule might look like this:

Hors d'oeuvres (15-20 minutes). This allows those from your church to mix and mingle with the newcomers. Take advantage of this time to meet new people.

Dinner (30-45 minutes). Consider having appropriate background music during this time.

Awards Presentation (5-10 minutes).

Speaker (Optional) (10-15 minutes). Invite a Christian athlete to briefly share a personal testimony that is upbeat, direct, but non-threatening to unbelievers.

EQUIPMENT/SUPPLIES (To be furnished by the event leaders)

☐ Registration tables, name tags, and related supplies
☐ Prizes, grab bag items, and related supplies
☐ Sponsor signs, posters, etc.

WHAT TO BRING (To be provided by participants)

☐ Golfing equipment

PLANNING THE EVENT

PLANNING TEAM

For this event, you need a Tournament Director (and possibly an Assistant Tournament Director) and volunteers to take responsibilities for the event site, budget, publicity, printed materials, registration, speaker, and equipment and supplies. Detailed (though generic) task descriptions for these coordinators are found on pages 225-252 and are cross-referenced on the following timeline. Glean information from these descriptions that relate to this particular event.

In addition, you will need a Prize Coordinator, Sponsor Coordinator, Hole-in-One Coordinator, "Best of . . ." Judge, Photographer, and Sign-maker (optional). The hole-in-one car prize coordinator must be very detail-oriented, with keen negotiating skills. The Judge needs to be fair and impartial.

> ❖ *The more people who have ownership and involvement in the planning, the greater success you will have.*

Planning Timeline

Event: *Hole-in-One Golf Tournament*   **Date of event:** _____

Event Director: _____   **Phone:** _____

Thanks for agreeing to serve on our tournament Planning Team. Please check over this timeline for the task(s) assigned to you. Adapt as needed. Supplement this timeline with information on the reproducible, generic job descriptions found on pages 225-252. Highlight your tasks (and due dates) each time they appear. Please mark your calendar accordingly.

Date: _____   ## 6 OR 7 MONTHS IN ADVANCE

Tournament (Event) Director (page 226)

☐ Recruit a Planning Team. Brainstorm ideas, and adapt this weekend event to fit your particular ministry goals and objectives.

☐ Make sure each team member understands his or her assigned tasks and responsibilities.

☐ Determine if this timeline will work for your area. For example, your geographic location may require making golf course reservations earlier than five or six months in advance. If so, adjust the timeline accordingly.

☐ Decide if this is to be a fund-raising event or just a fun outreach/golf day. Much of what you need to do from this point on will be determined by this decision.

Date: _____   ## 5 MONTHS IN ADVANCE

Tournament Director

☐ Make arrangements with a golf course. The cooperation of a local golf course is key to the success of this event. Ask the golf course to provide golf carts, club rentals (if necessary), and dinner to all participants for a low one-price-per-person greens fee. In exchange, offer to

hold the event in off-peak hours (usually afternoon or evening) and to provide the golf course with publicity. If possible, have the club house provide the awards "banquet" meal (a low-cost hamburger cookout is ideal), including all food, condiments, dessert, silverware, etc. In addition, arrange to sell "dinner-only" tickets to non-golfers who wish to participate. (If the golf course is unable to provide the dinner, work with a caterer.)

☐ Set the date for the event.

Budget Coordinator (page 229)

☐ Set registration fee based on estimated cost of green fees, printing, some prizes, insurance premium for hole-in-one car prize, food and service items for the banquet, and advertising. Remember, the registration fee can be reduced by an aggressive sponsorship goal (see Sponsor Coordinator on page 70).

☐ If this event is to serve as a fund-raiser, work with the other members of the Planning Team to establish a financial goal. A good rule-of-thumb is to have the golfers cover all expenses, and then allow all the donations and sponsorships to go toward the fund-raising goal.

> ❖ *For more ideas and help, refer to job descriptions beginning on page 225.*

Registration Coordinator (page 241)

☐ Develop a registration form. Include a registration deadline and an opportunity for people to indicate whether they are golfers or dinner-only participants, whether or not they are professional or former pro golfers, and who they might like to have in their foursome.

Speaker Coordinator (Optional)
(page 250)

☐ If the decision is made to have a Christian athlete share his or her brief testimony during the dinner, contact potential speakers now.

Date:	**3 MONTHS IN ADVANCE**

Tournament Director

☐ Meet with the planning team to make sure all plans are on track.

Hole-in-One Coordinator

☐ In conjunction with staff members at the golf course, decide which hole should be designated for a hole-in-one prize.

☐ Find an insurer who will give a free car or a certain amount of money to the first player to sink a hole-in-one on a given hole. You will be asked to provide information about the number of players, distance to the designated hole, and other factors. Clarify all conditions that might cause the insurer to refuse payoff. For example: Will the insurer pay if a professional golfer or former pro makes the hole-in-one?

☐ Apply for an insurance policy and pay the premium. Should there be a payout, the money will be used to pay for a car provided by the participating local car dealership.

☐ Make arrangements with a car dealership to have a car (as agreed to by the insurance company) delivered to the golf course on the day of the event and displayed at the tee box of the designated hole.

☐ Clarify who is responsible for any taxes due if someone qualifies for the free car.

Prize Coordinator

☐ Contact local retailers to solicit gift or cash prizes to be awarded for the "Best Of . . ." events. (Possible prize donations could include vacation packages, golf clubs, golfing apparel and accessories, green fees, membership at a fitness center, and restaurant coupons.)

☐ In addition, you will need less expensive prizes for the golfer's grab bag prizes, perhaps enough for approximately half of the people in attendance.

Sponsor Coordinator

☐ It is best if the Prize Coordinator and the Sponsorship Coordinator work together so they are not contacting the same people in the community. For example, the Prize Coordinator might concentrate on retail businesses who might donate products as prizes. The Sponsorship Coordinator might concentrate more on services or corporations (such as banks, insurance companies, and radio or TV stations) who are more likely to donate money than products. Together, determine what strategy will work best in your community.

☐ Contact local businesses to sponsor holes for donations of $50-$100 (or more) per hole. Depending on the number of businesses involved and how aggressive you are, as much as $1,000 or more per hole can be raised. (This could contribute $18,000 or more toward the fund-raising cause.)

Speaker Coordinator (Optional)

☐ Confirm speaker in writing.

Publicity Coordinator

☐ Once the course, date, registration fees, and deadlines are set, begin preparing brochures and flyers to promote the event. (In your advertising, and especially at the event, recognize sponsors who contributed prizes or cash.)

Date: ____	**2 MONTHS IN ADVANCE**

Tournament Director

☐ Check with the contact person at the golf course and banquet facility. Send a deposit if needed.
☐ Keep regular contact with each member of the Planning Team.

Publicity Coordinator

☐ Continue promoting the event. Remember to display posters and flyers at area pro shops and golf courses.

Registration Coordinator

☐ Begin registration.
☐ Collect fees.
☐ Order name tags.

Prize Coordinator

☐ Continue soliciting prizes for the event.
☐ Make arrangements to pick up prizes from the sponsors or provide an address where prizes can be sent or delivered.

Sponsor Coordinator

☐ Finalize sponsors for each of the eighteen holes. Find at least one sponsor for each hole.

Hole-in-One Coordinator

☐ Finalize arrangements with the car dealership and with the insurer for the hole-in-one payout.

Date: ____	**1 MONTH IN ADVANCE**

Tournament Director

☐ Meet with the Planning Team to discuss final plans and to be sure all arrangements are on schedule.

☐ Be sure a signed contract is on file at the church regarding the golf course and meal arrangements.

Publicity Coordinator

☐ Continue promoting the event.
☐ Prepare to mail final press releases to newspapers and local radio and TV stations.

Hole-in-One Coordinator

☐ Mail premium check to insurer.
☐ Confirm all arrangements in writing.
☐ Make sure a signed contract is on file at the church.

Sponsor Coordinator

☐ Have sponsorship signs or banners (naming sponsors) made for display at the registration booth and tee boxes.
☐ Arrange for someone to place the signs at the appropriate locations before the event.
☐ Coordinate with the Photographer to have pictures taken of each sponsor's sign to send with thank-you notes after the event.

Equipment/Supplies Coordinator (page 233)

☐ Make any advance planning necessary for coordinating the setup of all tables, signs, roped-off areas, display of prizes, etc., on the day of the event.

Photographer

☐ Work with the Sponsor Coordinator, Prize Coordinator, Publicity Coordinator, and Tournament Director concerning photos to be taken during the event, including the signs or banners at each hole to send to the sponsors, the prize winners, and general shots of the day's events.

"Best of . . ." Judge

☐ Establish a game plan for determining recipients of the "Best of . . ." prizes in as fair and unbiased a manner as is possible.
☐ Coordinate judging with the Tournament Director and the Prize Coordinator.

Date:	2 WEEKS IN ADVANCE

Tournament Director

☐ Finalize contracts with the caterer and the golf course. Both signed agreements should be on file at the church.
☐ Report the number of participants registered to the golf course and to all the members of the Planning Team.

Publicity Coordinator

☐ Send final pre-event press releases to local radio, TV, and newspapers.

Registration Coordinator

☐ Begin processing registrations and assigning foursomes. Some registrants may indicate the other three in the foursome, while others will be randomly assigned to a group. Try to arrange foursomes so talent is evenly distributed throughout all teams. Foursomes should include both men and women where possible.
☐ Close registration on the deadline.
☐ Make arrangements for two or three others to help run the registration table during the morning hours and at the scheduled time just prior to the awards dinner.

Date:	1 WEEK IN ADVANCE

Tournament Director

☐ Meet with the Planning Team to cover any last-minute needs.

Registration Coordinator

☐ Send a final letter to registrants. Include information regarding the course, program schedule, meal arrangements, and any other details that may be helpful. (A sample letter is found on page 244. Adapt as needed for your event and group.)
☐ Prepare name tag for each participant.

Prize Coordinator

☐ Assemble the grab bag of prizes.
☐ Arrange to transport all prizes to the course or banquet facility.

Hole-in-One Coordinator

☐ Notify the insurance company of any changes to the original contract (i.e., number of golfers participating). All changes must be called in to the insurance company before the tournament begins. (This is crucial because if anything varies from what was actually agreed to in the original contract, the insurance company is not obligated to honor any hole-in-one prize.) Follow up with a hard copy fax to the insurance company of any changes.

Date:	2 TO 4 WEEKS AFTER EVENT

Sponsor Coordinator

☐ See "Followup Guidelines" on page 254.
☐ Send each sponsor a thank you note and a picture taken of the sign or banner at the sponsored hole.

Prize Coordinator

☐ Send each prize contributor a thank you note and the picture taken of their prize being given during the closing meal.

Publicity Coordinator

☐ Send a final news release, along with appropriate photos, to the media announcing the prize winners.

WHITE-WATER RAFTING ADVENTURE

A Non-Navel-Gazing, Soaked-to-the-Bone, Hanging-On-for-Dear-Life, Camaraderie-Building Experience

Event Summary: An exciting, challenging, memory-making white-water rafting adventure—especially appealing to single men. The focus is not on "us" but on the challenge of conquering the river.

Length of Event: 2–4 days

Suggested Theme Verse: Selected verses from Psalms

Ideal Number of Participants: Determined by rafting outfitter (It can be as small as 8–10 or as many as 100 or more.)

Estimated Cost Per Person: Approximately $40–$100, depending on distance to rafting river. (Double this if using chartered buses.)

Facility Requirements: A nice, fast river, plus a campground, retreat center, or motel

Recommended Planning Team: 4–10 people

Advance Planning Needed: Approximately 8 months or less

INTRODUCTION

by Pamela Harper Dodge
Director of Young Adult Ministries
Ward Church
Livonia, Michigan

This is one trip where you are more than along for the ride—white-water rafting is an exciting, challenging experience—one your single adults will always remember.

Since we only do this every other year, we usually get 60 or more people to go. It has become one of our more popular weekend events, especially with the younger singles. And because this trip especially appeals to men, we always have a good number of women who are interested in going.

Because the focus of this event is not on "us" but on the challenge of conquering the river, many healthy relationships are formed. (I'm convinced that many times the best rela-tionships begin when the people are sharing a common objective rather than navel-gazing—primarily focusing on ourselves. And this trip is definitely not navel-gazing when you are soaked to the bone and hanging onto the raft for dear life!) A real sense of camaraderie is developed as people have to stretch themselves, try something new, and take a risk.

This event gives singles an opportunity to do something many of them have never done (but may have always wanted to), to travel together, and to experience Christian fellowship and the grandeur of God's creation.

> **OBJECTIVE**
>
> ❖ To provide a weekend retreat event in which single adults have fun, work together to conquer the river, develop camaraderie, and enjoy the company and fellowship of others.

THE BIG EVENT

SCHEDULE

The following schedule is based on a three-day weekend. Your plans will vary based on the length of your trip and distance from a suitable river. Adjust the schedule as needed.

❖ *Get as many people as possible involved in the planning of this event.*

Friday
7:30 A.M.—Departure
4:30 P.M.—Arrive at event site
5:00 P.M.—Get settled/prepare dinner (Work team #1)
7:00 P.M.—Dinner
8:00 P.M.—Cleanup (Work team #2)
8:30 P.M.—Devotional
9:00 P.M.—Campfire and sing

Saturday
6:00 A.M.—Rise and shine/prepare breakfast (Work team #3)
6:45 A.M.—Eat breakfast QUICK!! (Everyone helps with cleanup!)
7:10 A.M.—Group prayer
(The day's schedule is usually determined by the rafting company.)
7:15 A.M.—Leave for rafting outfitter
8:00 A.M.—Board the rafting buses
4:00 P.M.—Remaining "survivors" return to buses from rafting trip
4:30 P.M.—Bus returns to rafting outfitter
5:00 P.M.—Everyone arrives back at campsite
5:45 P.M.—Prepare dinner (Work team #4)
6:30 P.M.—Dinner
7:30 P.M.—Cleanup (Work team #5)
8:00 P.M.—Devotional
9:00 P.M.—Bonfire, sharing, and sing-a-long

Sunday
7:15 A.M.—Rise and shine/prepare breakfast (Work team #6)
7:30 A.M.—Breakfast (Everyone cleans up!)
8:30 A.M.—Informal worship service
9:30 A.M.—Break camp (Everyone helps!)
11:00 A.M.—Leave for home

PROGRAM IDEAS AND SUGGESTIONS

CAMPING OR HOTEL

One decision that you will need to make is where you will "set up camp." A hotel will be most comfortable, but it will also be most costly. Camping is less expensive and it fits well with the adventure of the river rafting trip. This event will assume that you will camp.

ADVANCE TEAM

It is suggested that a four- to six-person "advance team" take the gear to the site ahead of the group. This allows them to locate a campsite (if none are reserved), set up tents, and prepare the first meal. Depending on the amount of supplies, distance, etc., this team may need to arrive the night before the group (especially true on holiday weekends).

TRANSPORTATION GUIDELINES

To a large extent, the type of transportation needed will be determined by the distance to travel and the anticipated size of group.

Car/Van Transportation—This will be the least expensive means of travel. It also automatically forms small groups for discussion and for getting acquainted. If cars are used:
1. Establish car pools ("arkpools") of three cars each. Each pool keeps tabs on the other cars in their pool, buddy-style.
2. Get several fluorescent-colored tennis balls, one color for each pool of three cars. Cut the tennis balls in half and stick them on the cars' antennas. This makes it easy for cars to recognize others in their pool and in the entire caravan.
3. If possible, borrow or rent a CB radio or cellular phone for each car. This adds a special dimension to the trip—stimulating conversation, joke-telling, keeping track of each other, etc. The more cars involved, the more essential this becomes.
Bus Transportation—If your church has a bus, this may be a good choice. If not, it will

be more expensive. Chartered buses can often add $100–$150/person. One advantage to taking a bus is that it can mean greater safety for your group. This event assumes that your group will use cars or vans.

ICEBREAKERS

The activities and events on this trip are natural icebreakers. If you need help to facilitate the getting-acquainted process, try these ideas.

• **Mix and Match.** To determine who rides in what car, mix people by favorite color, birth month, hobbies/interests, computer preference, how they put toilet paper on the dispenser, etc. Be creative to allow an opportunity for people to get acquainted with new people on the ride to the river.

• **Questions, Questions.** Purchase a question book for each car (such as *201 Great Questions* by Jerry Jones, NavPress, Colorado Springs, 1988). These questions can help people connect, plus create very stimulating, illuminating conversation in each car.

❖ *For more icebreakers, see the Table of Contents.*

• **Have Game, Will Travel.** Purchase a travel games book for each car. Games can help people get better acquainted, plus create real interest and fun for travelers, especially on longer trips.

DEVOTIONS/BIBLE STUDY

Rafting and camping under the stars is a wonderful setting for reflecting on the Psalms. (Possible themes could include "Praise and Adoration," "The Grandeur of God and His Creation," "His Majesty," or "The Attributes of God.") There are three times for a devotional or Bible study (see schedule). Since an event like this may draw a number of seekers, ask three or more group leaders (rather than the staff person or pastor) to do the sharing in a low-key, personal way. For example, they could share their personal testimonies along with what a particular psalm means to them.

Some suggested Psalms that would work well in this setting include: 1, 8, 93, 98, 104, and 145–150. You may also want to look at

Isaiah 43:1-3; 55. Sing several familiar praise and worship songs during each devotional.

EQUIPMENT/SUPPLIES (To be furnished by the event leaders)

- ☐ First aid kit
- ☐ Drinking water containers
- ☐ Extra sunscreen/sunburn ointment (Burns occur easily while on the water for hours.)
- ☐ Toilet tissue; paper plates, cups, and towels
- ☐ Tents (men's, women's, extended dining/meeting), stakes, poles, etc.
- ☐ Lanterns and flashlights with batteries
- ☐ Propane cookstoves/grills for open fires
- ☐ Fire starters (lighter/matches) and back-ups. Make sure several people know how to use them; practice.
- ☐ Cooking pans and utensils, plates, cups, eating utensils, soap, dishtowels, etc.
- ☐ Bug repellent
- ☐ Shovel; ax; hammer; saw; screwdrivers; pliers
- ☐ Duct tape
- ☐ Portable tables
- ☐ Tarps
- ☐ Pocket knife

WHAT TO BRING (See reproducible list on page 79.)

PLANNING THE EVENT

PLANNING TEAM

For this event, you need an Event Director (perhaps an Assistant Event Director) and volunteers to take responsibilities for the event site, budget, publicity, food, registration, worship, transportation, recreation, and equipment/supplies. In addition, if you charter a bus, you will need a Bus Captain.

❖ *The more people who have ownership and involvement in the planning, the greater success you will have.*

Planning Timeline

Event: *White-Water Rafting Adventure*   **Date of event:** _____

Event Director: _____   **Phone:** _____

Thanks for agreeing to serve on our Planning Team. Please check over this timeline for your assigned task(s). Adapt as needed and supplement with information from the generic job descriptions. Highlight your tasks (and due dates) and mark your calendar accordingly.

Date: _____ **8 MONTHS IN ADVANCE**

Most of the planning can be done within eight months. The number of participants and reservation of rafts, campsite, and dates are the most important steps. All other plans hinge on this information.

Event Director (page 226)

☐ Recruit a Planning Team.
☐ Meet with Planning Team to brainstorm ideas and adapt this event to fit your ministry goals and objectives.
☐ Distribute copies of this timeline and related job descriptions. Make sure team members understand their assigned responsibilities. Adapt timeline as needed.

Event Site Coordinator (page 234)

☐ Select the river and rafting outfitter. Local travel agencies or state tourism offices can suggest possible rafting sites. Note: When selecting a river, consider safety. Choose a challenging and fun river run, but not one too hard for the entire group.
☐ Most outfitters have a limited number of people they can take each trip, and long weekends fill up quickly. Determine the minimum/maximum size of your group, based on information from the outfitter.
☐ Put the event date on the church calendar.
☐ Determine lodging accommodations (camping site or motel). Some rafting outfitters provide weekend packages which include meals, lodging, and rafting. While convenient, they usually cost more.

Date: _____ **6 MONTHS IN ADVANCE**

Event Director

☐ Meet with Planning Team to make sure everyone is clear on their areas of responsibility and specific tasks.

❖ *For more ideas and help, refer to job descriptions beginning on page 225.*

Budget Coordinator (page 229)

☐ If the rafting outfitters and campgrounds require advance deposits, get them in.

Date: _____ **5 MONTHS IN ADVANCE**

Event Director

☐ Check the Planning Team's progress.

Registration Coordinator (page 241)

☐ In cooperation with the Planning Team, begin developing a registration form. (See sample form on page 245.) To aid planning, consider including the following:
   Can you provide:
- a car (what is license plate #, year, and seating capacity including the driver)
- a shift at the wheel (help drive)
- a tent (sleeps how many)
- eating area tarp
- coolers for food
- drinking cooler with pour spout, etc.
- guitar
☐ With the Event Director, determine your cancellation/refund policy. Since a final count and payment are usually required in advance by the rafting outfitter and lodging facilities, consider including a "no refund" policy on the registration form.

Transportation Coordinator (page 252)

☐ Decide mode of transportation.

Equipment/Supplies Coordinator (page 233)

This person will also be recruiter and leader of the "advance team."

☐ Estimate rental cost of equipment and supplies (camping and cooking gear, etc.)

Food Coordinator (page 236)

☐ Estimate cost of food. Determine if the Saturday noon meal is included in the rafting outfitter cost.

Recreation Coordinator (page 240)

☐ If schedule and travel distance allow, arrange for other activities or sight-seeing enroute. Determine these activities prior to finalizing transportation arrangements.

Budget Coordinator

☐ Complete cost analysis. Include the following costs: one day rafting, campsite/accommodations, food, transportation, promotion, tent and supplies rental, etc.
☐ Get budget approved by Planning Team.

Publicity Coordinator

☐ Develop a promotion strategy, based on the budget established.
☐ Begin promoting the event as soon as the date, location, and estimated costs are set.

Date:_____	**3 MONTHS IN ADVANCE**

Event Director

☐ Meet with Planning Team to answer questions and resolve problems, if any.

Publicity Coordinator

☐ Continue promoting the event through flyers, posters, verbal announcements, newsletter, and other available means.

Equipment/Supplies Coordinator

☐ Confirm places where you can borrow (or rent) tents and other camping equipment, such as stoves, lanterns, coolers, etc.
☐ Select your "advance team" who will go early to set up camp.

Event Site Coordinator

☐ Reconfirm rafting and lodging details.

Registration Coordinator

☐ Make sure all registrants complete a "Liability Release" form (see sample on page 253.) Completed forms are to be given to the Event Director.
☐ Communicate information gathered on registration forms (expressed interest in helping, driving, bringing items, etc.) to appropriate Planning Team members.

Date:_____	**2 MONTHS IN ADVANCE**

Event Director

☐ If needed, hold a Planning Team meeting to check progress, help answer questions, and resolve any problems.

Transportation Coordinator

☐ Determine how to match cars and riders.
☐ Locate CB radios/cell phones for each car.
☐ Determine possible enroute activities.

Bus Captains Coordinator (page 231)

☐ If traveling by bus, select bus captains.

Worship Coordinator (page 251)

☐ Select at least three people to prepare devotionals and/or personal testimonies.
☐ Together, determine the study and sharing theme for the three devotional times.

- [ ] Find one or more persons to play guitar and lead worship or campfire music.

Food Coordinator

- [ ] Recruit team to help with buying food and organizing meal times.

Publicity Coordinator

- [ ] Recruit one or two people to be official event photographer/videographers. Share that your hope is to give a presentation at a newcomers' brunch or to the entire singles group. Consider a group photo of those on the trip.

| Date: _____ | **1 MONTH IN ADVANCE** |

Event Director

- [ ] Hold a Planning Team meeting to finalize details, check progress, answer questions, and resolve problems, if any.

Food Coordinator

- [ ] Delegate responsibilities to your team for menu planning and purchasing food (ahead of time and on site). Assign your six work teams.
- [ ] If the rafting outfitter does not include a lunch while on the river, make plans for a brown-bag lunch for each participant.

| Date: _____ | **2 WEEKS IN ADVANCE** |

Event Director

- [ ] Check all last-minute details with Planning Team.
- [ ] Provide the church staff with the emergency address and phone number.

Registration Coordinator

- [ ] Close registration.
- [ ] Begin making tent/rooming assignments based on the number of participants.
- [ ] Collect any balances due.

- [ ] Send confirmation letter to all participants with trip details. (See sample confirmation letter on page 244.)

Food Coordinator

- [ ] Finalize last-minute tasks with your team.
- [ ] Designate a captain for each work team.

Transportation Coordinator

- [ ] Prepare a map to the destination for each car navigator. Distribute on departure day.

| Date: _____ | **1 WEEK IN ADVANCE** |

Event Director

- [ ] Final Planning Team meeting to make sure all final arrangements are on track.
- [ ] Make sure you have all "Liability Release" forms. (These are to be kept with you throughout the trip.)

Equipment/Supplies Coordinator

- [ ] Help your "advance team" pick up all tents and other camping equipment.
- [ ] Confirm "advance team" departure time. Note: This team goes early to set up camp, but everyone is responsible for breaking camp before departure.

Budget Coordinator

- [ ] Give money (as approved in budget) to those responsible for purchasing food, supplies, etc.
- [ ] Prepare final payment to rafting outfitter.

Event Site Coordinator

- [ ] Finalize last-minute details (including your estimated arrival time and total number of participants) with campsite and rafting outfitter.

| Date: _____ | **2 TO 4 WEEKS AFTER EVENT** |

- [ ] See "Followup Guidelines" on page 254.

What to Bring

(To be provided by participants)

Space is limited. Only one suitcase or bag and one carry-on case per person is allowed.

- ☐ A mix of warm and cool clothing
- ☐ Swimsuit
- ☐ Towels and washcloth
- ☐ Insect repellent
- ☐ Extra shoes for hiking
- ☐ Sport strap for glasses while rafting
- ☐ Snacks and games for travel time
- ☐ Sunglasses
- ☐ Flashlight with extra batteries
- ☐ Sport drink water bottle
- ☐ Toiletries
- ☐ Soap
- ☐ Toothpaste, toothbrush
- ☐ Small plastic bag for dirty clothes
- ☐ Extra socks
- ☐ Extra cash (for expenses and for meals while traveling)
- ☐ Personal ID and health insurance card
- ☐ Prescription medication
- ☐ A smiling, adventurous attitude
- ☐ Bible, pen and notebook

- ☐ Sleeping bag
- ☐ Pillow
- ☐ Air mattress
- ☐ Rain gear
- ☐ Old tennis shoes (a must for rafting)
- ☐ Sunscreen/suntan lotion

Optional items
- ☐ Christian music cassettes
- ☐ Ball and glove
- ☐ Frisbee, hacky-sack, or Nerf ball
- ☐ Fishing equipment
- ☐ Cap
- ☐ Small folding chair
- ☐ Disposable water camera with film
- ☐ Guitar
- ☐ Thong sandals
- ☐ Tent (if volunteered)
- ☐ Lantern (if volunteered)
- ☐ Large cooler (if volunteered)
- ☐ Portable CB radio (if volunteered)

10 GIVE ME THAT MOUNTAIN!

Character Building through Physical and Spiritual Challenges

Event Summary: A one-day mountain climb (with two days of preparation) in a secluded, peaceful setting that helps single adults break out of comfort zones plus develop commitment and integrity in their relationships. (This event is designed for both experienced and inexperienced climbers including single parents and their children (age 10 and over).

Length of Event: 3 days

Suggested Theme Verse: ". . . Come, let us go up to the mountain of the Lord, . . . He will teach us his ways, so that we may walk in his paths." Micah 4:2

Ideal Number of Participants: 10+

Estimated Cost Per Person: $30–$50, plus travel expenses (airfare, if necessary)

Facility Requirements: Mountain site campground (plus one optional night in a hotel/lodge)

Recommended Planning Team: 5–7 people

Advance Planning Needed: Approximately 4–6 months

Special Instructions: Safety instructions

INTRODUCTION

by Chuck Helvoigt
Director, Single Adult Ministry
Master Plan Ministries
Durango, Colorado

Imagine that you have just topped a crevasse. The view is awesome. And the climb has been exhilarating. You proved that you could go the distance.

Outdoor trips provide a unique setting to help people try new challenges and build lasting relationships. Few events will have the impact on your singles as much as this one can. It helps your singles overcome negative thinking, mental failures, and fears. And in return, it helps them gain a new sense of accomplishment and confidence: "If I climbed this mountain, I know I can tackle other tough challenges in my life."

An event such as this can also be a terrific way to discover new leaders, people who are willing to go beyond the convenient, who hang in when the going is rough, and who seldom quit half-way through. Those who finish such an experience develop a strong sense of camaraderie.

Climbing in a secluded environment and concentrating on personal issues, as well as our relationships, adds a new "mountaintop" perspective to life. This event will certainly be a memory-maker for all involved.

> ### OBJECTIVES
>
> ❖ To stretch your group spiritually and physically.
> ❖ To help participants learn to overcome obstacles in life.
> ❖ To illustrate the value of "stick-to-it-ness" and commitment.
> ❖ To build a team through a common mountaintop experience.

THE BIG EVENT

SCHEDULE

Though your schedule may vary depending on your proximity to the mountains and your starting altitude, plan a three-day trip that looks something like this:

❖ *Get as many people as possible involved in the planning of this event.*

Day One

Spend the first day reaching and establishing a base camp.
1:00 P.M.—Leave for the mountains from the departure point.
5:00 P.M.—Arrive at the base camp location.
6:00 P.M.—Dinner
7:00 P.M.—Meet in small groups prior to a campfire setting.

Day Two

Spend the second day adjusting to a higher altitude, as necessary.
8:00 A.M.—Breakfast
9:30 A.M.—Morning devotions
11:00 A.M.—Activities to get used to the altitude
12:30 P.M.—Lunch
6:00 P.M.—Dinner at the campsite.
7:00 P.M.—Evening devotions/sharing/campfire
9:00 P.M.—Early to bed for an early departure in the morning.

Day Three

Climb the mountain, come back down, break camp, and head for home.
5:30 A.M.—Breakfast
6:15 A.M.—Morning devotions
7:30 A.M.—Begin the climb.
11:30 A.M.—Celebrate on the mountaintop.
12:00 P.M.—Be on the way down.
4:00 P.M.—All people are accounted for back at base camp.
4:30 P.M.—Break camp before dark. Head home.

SCHEDULE COMMENTS

Departure on Day One

If traveling by ground, provide maps, stopping points, and driving times for drivers. If flying, meet at airport two hours prior to flight time.

Arrival at Campsite

The campsite should be no more than three hours from the mountaintop. Set up camp. Keep drinks and frozen or refrigerated items shaded. If coolers are not available, place items in a stream, making certain they won't float away. Prepare the meal.

Activities on Day Two

These could include short, leisurely hikes, rafting, resting, reading, or—if a mountain town or scenic attraction is nearby—sight-seeing or shopping. Participants should begin drinking a lot of water. Either prepare boxed lunches for everyone or, if they are going to be in a town, have them be on their own for lunch.

Climbing

Check and heed weather reports before climbing. Arrive at mountaintop before noon. Afternoon weather patterns can change suddenly and become dangerous to climbers. It is always best to be heading down the mountain by noon and to also make sure everyone is down safely before dark.

Stop often for breaks and snacks. The goal is reaching the top, not speed. Reaching the top is a victory. Record the event on paper, film, and/or video.

Descending

People can stop briefly as needed to eat a pre-packed lunch.

Trip Home

If circumstances allow, plan to stop for dinner on the way home. During dinner, have a time of sharing and evaluating the experience while it is fresh.

IDEAS AND SUGGESTIONS ABOUT THIS TRIP

FOR NON-CLIMBERS

Encourage even the non-climbers in your group to attend. They can still enjoy the wonderful scenery and all other aspects of the trip. In addition, it can be very helpful to have people remain at base camp to keep an eye on supplies, to help prepare meals, and to be tearing down camp on Day Three as the climbers are coming back down the mountain. If there are single parents who have children too young to climb, those at base camp can watch them. (This is a wonderful gift to single parents who might not be able to attend otherwise.) Those who choose not to climb can also take short hikes near base camp.

CHILDREN ARE WELCOME

This can be a wonderful outing for single-parent families, so encourage them to attend. Depending on experience and strength, children as young as eight can participate in the climb. Use wisdom—and always make sure children have an adult nearby. For children too young to climb, arrange for some adults at base camp or back home to watch them.

SAFETY IS ESSENTIAL

Know your people and their limitations. Be especially sensitive to possible altitude sickness with smaller children. And remember that the mountain always wins. (Refer to "Mountain Climbing: Policies and Cautions" on page 92.)

AN OPTIONAL HOT SHOWER

Some groups will want to stay in a hotel or lodge for at least one night. If this is something your group desires, plan to stay in a place where a hot shower is available one night. Adjust your trip expenses accordingly.

❖
For a list of icebreakers, see the Table of Contents.

AN ALTERNATIVE TO MOUNTAIN CLIMBING

If getting to a mountain range is not feasible for your group, consider rock climbing and rappelling. Find an experienced rock climbing guide to work with.

Another option is to use an indoor rock climbing practice course, becoming increasingly popular in many sports facilities across the country. Consider renting such a facility where you actually stay overnight in the facility. An advantage to this setting is its safety and training environment.

DEVOTIONALS

This trip provides an excellent opportunity to study and reflect on God's Word and His promises in a majestic setting. However, the actual time available for formal group study will vary, depending on logistics, base camp facilities, etc.

Get into groups of four to six people each. Stay in the same small groups throughout the event if possible. (Since all climbers need to be in "buddy teams" later, now might be a good time to assign buddies. This allows each buddy team to be in the same small group with one or two other buddy teams. See "Buddy Teams" on Resource 1, page 87.)

Resources 1 and 2 provide a four-part devotional to use on this event (pages 87 and 88). The pages are reproducible and include discussion questions to be used in small groups.

SESSION ONE

Day One, 7:00 P.M.
Length: 90 minutes
Welcome everyone and introduce the study/devotional theme for the event. Divide into designated small groups and use the first set of questions on Resource 1 (page 87).

SESSION TWO/MORNING DEVOTIONS

Day Two, 9:30 A.M.
Length: 90 minutes
Meet in the same small groups. Use the second part of Resource 1 on page 87.

SESSION THREE/EVENING DEVOTIONS

Day Two, 7:00 P.M.
Length: 90 minutes
Meet in the same small groups and use the first part of Resource 2 on page 88.

SESSION FOUR/MORNING DEVOTIONS

Day Three, 6:15 A.M.
Length: 70 minutes
In the same small groups, use the second part of Resource 2 on page 88.

OTHER POSSIBLE STUDIES/THEMES

Depending on the needs and interests of your group, here are some other possible content ideas to consider for this event:

❖ Overcoming spiritual/relational "mountains" in life through Christ (II Corinthians 2:14)

❖ The majesty of God and His creation (Psalm 104)

❖ The power of perseverance and commitment during tough times—running and finishing the race (Hebrews 12:1-12)

❖ Placing our faith in what is solid and lasting (Psalm 121:1-4)

❖ Motivation from the inside out vs. from the outside in (I Thessalonians 2:14)

❖ Being more than conquerors (Romans 8:37)

POSSIBLE SCRIPTURE TOPICS

❖ Caleb in Joshua 14:6-15. Excellent for future battles!

❖ Abraham in Genesis 22:2-14. Good for slaying idols in life.

❖ Moses in Exodus 3. Helps us learn to listen for God's call in our lives.

❖ Elijah in I Kings 18:17-40. Commitment.

❖ Jesus in Mark 9:1-9. See Jesus as He is.

EQUIPMENT/SUPPLIES (To be furnished by the event leaders)

See the reproducible Resource 3 (page 89).

WHAT TO BRING (To be provided by participants)

See the reproducible Resource 4 (page 90).

PLANNING THE EVENT

PLANNING TEAM

For this event, you need an Event Director (possibly an Assistant Event Director) and volunteers to take responsibilities for the event site, budget, publicity, printed materials, registration, small groups, food, transportation, and equipment/supplies. In addition to the above Planning Team, recruit an experienced Fitness Coordinator, Lead Climber, Cook, and First Aid/CPR Specialist.

❖ *The more people who have ownership and involvement in the planning, the greater success you will have.*

Fitness Coordinator: Motivates, challenges, and trains participants in physical fitness in preparation for mountain climbing. Should have good motivational and fitness training skills.

Lead Climber: An experienced climber who knows the route of the climb, is safety minded, able to think on his or her feet, and level-headed in a crisis or emergency situation.

Cook: A cook with strong organizational skills, flexibility, and the ability to cook with a camping stove. Camping experience highly recommended.

First Aid/CPR Specialist: This person needs to be certified or experienced in CPR and first aid.

Planning Timeline

Event: *Give Me That Mountain!*   **Date of event:** _____

Event Director: _____   **Phone:** _____

Thanks for agreeing to serve on our Planning Team. Please check over this timeline for your assigned task(s). Adapt as needed and supplement with information from the generic job descriptions. Highlight your tasks (and due dates) and mark your calendar accordingly.

Date: _____ 6 MONTHS IN ADVANCE

Event Director (page 226)

☐ Recruit a Planning Team.
☐ Meet with Planning Team to brainstorm ideas and adapt this event to fit your ministry goals and objectives.
☐ Distribute copies of this timeline and related job descriptions. Make sure team members understand their assigned responsibilities. Adapt timeline as needed.

Event Site Coordinator (page 234)

☐ Research and select a three- or four-hour climb as "your mountain." Plan to have base camp part way up the mountain.
☐ Buy topographical (TOPO) maps. Contact: U.S. Geological Survey, Box 25286, Denver Federal Center, Bldg, 1810, Denver, CO 80225. Cost: about $4 each plus shipping and handling.
☐ Put the event on the church calendar.

❖ *For more ideas and help, refer to job descriptions beginning on page 225.*

Budget Coordinator (page 229)

☐ Prepare estimated budget.

Publicity Coordinator (page 238)

☐ Prepare a promotional strategy.

Date: _____ 5 MONTHS IN ADVANCE

Budget Coordinator

☐ In cooperation with other Planning Team members, finalize the budget.
☐ Outline payment dates and deadlines.

Publicity Coordinator

☐ Once the date, costs, location, and other details are confirmed, develop and print flyers and brochures.
☐ Begin promoting the event. Use pictures and videos from any previous trips.

Registration Coordinator (page 241)

☐ Have interested individuals sign a preregistration list and reserve the dates.
☐ If needed, help raise scholarship funds and prepare scholarship application forms (sample on page 246).

Date: _____ 4 MONTHS IN ADVANCE

Publicity Coordinator

☐ Continue Promotion.

Registration Coordinator

☐ Begin registration, requiring a deposit. Due to the physical conditioning and training required for most participants, people need to get registered early.

Fitness Coordinator

☐ Develop group and individual fitness programs, including ways to motivate and train participants through talks, demonstrations, practice, videos, and phone calls.

<table>
<tr><td>Date: _____</td><td>

3 MONTHS IN ADVANCE
</td></tr>
</table>

Event Director

☐ With the Planning Team, review progress and make needed mid-course corrections.

Publicity Coordinator

☐ Continue Promotion.

Equipment/Supplies Coordinator (page 233)

☐ With input from Planning Team members, begin reserving/collecting equipment and supplies. Borrowing saves money.
☐ Have tents on hand this month for the Fitness Coordinator to use in training.
☐ Have cooking gear on hand for training sessions next month.
☐ With the Transportation Coordinator, determine the best way to transport equipment/supplies to the mountain.

Fitness Coordinator

☐ Begin training. Divide participants into competing teams to see which group can set up a tent the fastest.
☐ Practice pitching tents at night with only one flashlight.
☐ Focus on lung capacity and leg conditioning. Encourage daily individual training.
☐ Over the next three months, show videos/films on wilderness camping, survival, climbing, etc. Check public libraries and outdoor supply stores for videos. Practice.

Transportation Coordinator (page 252)

☐ Begin planning all ground and air travel.
☐ Begin a search for vehicles (4x4 preferred).

<table>
<tr><td>Date: _____</td><td>

2 MONTHS IN ADVANCE
</td></tr>
</table>

Fitness Coordinator

☐ Continue to encourage, support, and lead the group in fitness training.

☐ Practice using cooking gear with others.

Registration Coordinator

☐ Distribute "Liability Release" forms to all those who have preregistered.
☐ Get final commitments.
☐ With the Planning Team, hold an informational meeting with registrants. Discuss location of the climb, dates, what to bring (see page 90), costs, and payment deadlines. Discuss special medical or diet needs.

Small-Group Coordinator (page 247)

☐ Select small-group discussion facilitators.
☐ Prepare for small-group discussion times.

CPR/First Aid Coordinator

☐ Prepare a comprehensive first aid kit to take along on the trip (see Resource 3 on page 89). Pack contents in plastic bags to waterproof. On the trip, make sure you and others know where it is at all times. To make it highly visible, use a bright colored container/bag.
☐ Be prepared to monitor participants each morning on altitude sickness, dehydration, and hypothermia (see page 92).

Food Coordinator (page 236)

☐ Work with the Cook in preparing menus and all items needed for meals.

<table>
<tr><td>Date: _____</td><td>

1 MONTH IN ADVANCE
</td></tr>
</table>

Event Director

☐ Meet with the Planning Team and the Lead Climber to review progress and what needs to be acquired or done.
☐ Compile a master list of names and phone numbers.

Lead Climber

☐ Familiarize yourself with the trail. Review emergency procedures and contacts.

☐ Review supplies and other details with Planning Team to ensure all is in order.

Fitness Coordinator

☐ Continue providing fitness training.
☐ Keep motivating participants to exercise daily—individually or in groups.

Food Coordinator

☐ Purchase any dehydrated or other specialty foods needed for the trip. (For a list of suggested items, see Resource 5, page 91.)
☐ Recruit helpers as needed.
☐ Continue coordinating plans with Cook.

Transportation Coordinator

☐ Finalize all transportation details.
☐ Provide maps to drivers as needed.

Date: _____	**2 WEEKS IN ADVANCE**

Event Director

☐ Meet with participants. Discuss packing list and tips, finances, equipment preparation (break in boots, etc.), travel information, and journaling. Hiking and camping may be new for some, so clearly communicate policies regarding a buddy system, safety, accountability, and wilderness care. (Pack it in; pack it out. Leave only footprints.)

Food Coordinator

☐ Finalize the menu with the Cook.
☐ Help organize cooking and cleanup teams.
☐ Purchase food in bulk (in biodegradable containers, where possible).
☐ Organize food supplies in packs labeled breakfast, lunch, dinner.
☐ Prepare for any sack lunches to be taken on the climb.

Registration Coordinator

☐ Finalize registration and collect "Liability Release" forms (everyone must complete the form).

Budget Coordinator

☐ Prepare checks as needed for payments and purchases.

Date: _____	**1 WEEK IN ADVANCE**

Event Director

☐ Meet with all participants in a final preparatory meeting. Gather and copy all medical information, liability forms, and emergency information. Take one set of copies on the trip; leave the other on file at the church office. For emergencies, the location of this file should be well known.
☐ If using a payment plan, collect final payment.
☐ Confirm travel details.
☐ Check that everyone has all needed equipment.

Fitness Coordinator

☐ KEEP TRAINING!

Equipment/Supplies Coordinator

☐ Buy supplies you have not been able to borrow. Include extra supplies of all items.

Date: _____	**FOLLOW-UP AFTER EVENT**

Event Director

☐ Plan a meeting with participants in the next one or two weeks to have a final study/devotional and to discuss how the experience affected each participant.
☐ Host a party for your entire single adult group where slides, videos, and pictures of the event will be seen. Have two or three people share their climbing stories.
☐ See "Followup Guidelines" on page 254.

Session One —— Session Two

Get-Acquainted Discussion Questions:

1. What did you usually climb as a child? Were you a good climber?
2. As a child, did you ever get in trouble for climbing something?
3. Where were the closest mountains to where you grew up? When was the first time you saw mountains? How often did you visit them?
4. What was the significance of mountains to you as a child?
5. Describe some obstacle that you had to overcome as a child (such as a bully who beat you up, a difficult subject in school, a health problem, etc.). How did you overcome it? What helped you overcome it?
6. Describe some obstacle that you've had to overcome as an adult. How did you overcome it? What helped you overcome it?
7. Up until now, what has the been the hardest, most challenging thing you've done in life? What was the outcome?
8. What are two real-life mountains (or obstacles) facing you in life right now? (relational, spiritual, physical, etc.)

Close in prayer. Pray for the others in your small group and the obstacles they are facing.

Topic: Attitude (yours, not someone else's)
Objective: To learn how to respond to every situation in life with a positive attitude.
Definition: A mental position with regard to a fact or state.
Scripture Verse: Isaiah 40:27-31.
When you are distressed or discouraged, place your faith and hope in God.

Life, like this mountain climbing experience, provides the test—only *you* have the ability to change your attitude and focus.

Discussion Questions:

1. What was your attitude like when you got out of bed this morning?
2. Think back to when you were a kid. Describe someone you remember who always seemed to have a bad attitude. Why do you think he or she did?
3. Now describe someone who always seemed to have a good attitude. Why do you think he or she did? Other than attitude, what were the main differences between the first and second persons?
4. When do you have a tendency to have a bad attitude? What brings it on?
5. What helps you change a bad attitude into a good attitude?
6. Do you believe that each of us is always and completely responsible for our own attitude? Explain.
7. What determines our attitude? Where does it come from?
8. Attitude has been described as "a mental position with regard to a fact or state." How would you define attitude?
9. In your opinion, is it possible for you to always have a good attitude? Even when the mountain gets steep? Explain.
10. Read Isaiah 40:27-31. What does it have to say about attitude? Do any other verses come to mind?

Close in prayer. Pray for positive attitudes.

Session Three — Session Four

Session Three

Topic: Commitment
Objective: To become a person of your word—to fulfill even difficult promises and commitments.
Definition: An agreement or pledge to some future action; the state of being obligated or emotionally impelled.
Scripture Verses: Nehemiah 5:9-13; 9:7, 8; Hebrews 12:1-3; II Timothy 4:7.

Questions for Reflection:

Briefly reflect on the following:
❖ If you say, "I will come . . . " or "I will do such and such . . . ," do you?
❖ Do people gain or suffer when they count on you?
❖ What promises will you never break?
❖ To whom would you never break a promise?
❖ What makes you break or keep promises?
❖ Could anyone risk their life, reputation, and expectations based on your word only?

Discussion Questions:

1. Describe a time (past or current) when someone let you down by breaking a promise. How did you feel?
2. Describe a time when someone kept their word even though it was a personal hardship. Why did this person do so?
3. Who do you have absolute trust and confidence in, that you could take their word as the gospel? How has this person earned your trust and confidence?
4. "A handshake is binding." "A man's word is as good as gold." True? Why or why not?
5. When is it acceptable to break a commitment or a promise? Explain.
6. What is the price we must pay to become people of our word?
7. How is climbing a mountain similar to keeping a commitment or a promise?
8. What do the above Scriptures say about commitment and keeping one's word?
Close in prayer.

Session Four

Topic: Overcoming (the undeniable victory)
Objective: To understand that victory never comes without effort, but by overcoming an obstacle or some form of adversity.
Definition: To surmount, to overpower, to gain superiority, to win.
Scripture Verses: II Corinthians 2:14; Romans 8:37; Psalm 60:12; I John 5:1-5; Revelation 21:7; II Timothy 4:7.

Questions for Reflection:

1. Describe someone you know who has been an "overcomer." What did this person overcome and how did he or she do it?
2. Is it possible to overcome any and every adversity in life (relational, spiritual, physical, etc.)? Explain.
3. Refer to the two obstacles facing you in life right now (shared in session one). What are the abilities or character qualities you most need to help you overcome these obstacles? How can you acquire these abilities/character qualities?
4. What part do attitude and commitment play in overcoming adversity and challenges in life?
5. What are the rewards for those who overcome? (See Revelation 2:7; 2:17; 2:26; 3:5; 3:21.)
6. How are climbing a mountain and being an overcomer similar?
7. What do the Scripture verses above say to you about being an overcomer?

Close in prayer. Pray for safety today and for help in living victoriously.

Equipment/Supplies

(To be furnished by event leaders)

- ☐ Tents (men's, women's, extended dining/meeting), stakes, poles, drop cloth.
- ☐ Lanterns, mantels, and flashlights.
- ☐ Propane cookstoves and grills for open fires.
- ☐ Fire starters and backups. Don't limit yourself to only one way to start a fire, and make sure several people know how to use each; practice.
- ☐ Cooking pans and utensils, plates, cups, eating utensils, soap, dishtowels, etc.
- ☐ Bug repellent.
- ☐ Topographical (TOPO) map and compass
- ☐ Shovel
- ☐ Toilet tissue (Depending on where you go, you may be lucky to even have a port-a-john available.)
- ☐ Ax
- ☐ Hammer
- ☐ Saw
- ☐ Duct tape
- ☐ Screwdrivers
- ☐ Pliers
- ☐ Portable tables
- ☐ Tarps
- ☐ Water containers (You'll need to supply one gallon of water per person, per day. This includes washing and cleaning.)

- ☐ First aid kit (Also, make a smaller one for the climb itself. It should include matches, Band-Aids, plus something for blisters and scrapes.)
  - ☐ Cold medications*
  - ☐ Pain/discomfort relievers (many)*
  - ☐ Burn ointments
  - ☐ Hydrogen peroxide
  - ☐ Immodium AD
  - ☐ Thermometer
  - ☐ Alcohol wipes
  - ☐ Bandages, large/small (many)
  - ☐ Moleskin
  - ☐ Ace bandages
  - ☐ Adhesive pads
  - ☐ Sling
  - ☐ Tape
  - ☐ Scissors
  - ☐ Tweezers
  - ☐ Water filter
  - ☐ Space blanket
  - ☐ Wire
  - ☐ Knife
  - ☐ Small saw

*Read Resource 6 on page 92 about high altitude applications.

What to Bring

(To be provided by participants)

Pack everything in a duffel-style bag to make transporting and carrying easier. Adjust the list below as necessary, based on altitude, how difficult a climb, and base camp supplies.

Equipment
- ☐ Sleeping bag and foam pad
- ☐ Day pack for climbers
- ☐ Tent (if not already supplied by the leaders)
- ☐ Camera, film
- ☐ Sunglasses, suntan lotion
- ☐ Pocket knife
- ☐ Lighter/matches
- ☐ Flashlight, batteries*
- ☐ Ice ax (optional)
- ☐ Band-Aids/moleskin
- ☐ Water bottle (You can't drink too much water)*
- ☐ Toiletries bag
- ☐ Length of nylon cord (50-100 ft.)
- ☐ Bible, notebook, and pen
- ☐ Soap
- ☐ Cleanup towel
- ☐ Toothpaste, toothbrush
- ☐ Small plastic bag for dirty clothes

Clothes
- ☐ Knee/ankle wraps for descent
- ☐ Hiking boots—broken in
- ☐ Shoes (in addition to hiking boots, for comfortable camp wear)
- ☐ Warm clothes for layering (Temperatures range from 10–85 degrees and conditions can change very fast.)
- ☐ Rain gear/poncho (a must)
- ☐ Hat
- ☐ Wool shirt (year round)
- ☐ T-shirts (long and short sleeves)
- ☐ Jacket (down recommended)
- ☐ Jeans (ones you can get dirty, not just look good in)
- ☐ Shorts (but remember bugs, scrapes, and the cold)
- ☐ Several pairs of socks (wool dries faster, will insulate even when wet)
- ☐ Underwear as needed
- ☐ Warm sleepwear (sweats work great)

*essential safety items

REMEMBER IF YOU BRING IT IN, YOU CARRY IT OUT!

Food Checklist and Cooking Tips

Food Checklist: The following foods are ideal for camping trips. Keep meals simple. Plan to improvise when necessary due to weather conditions. (Note: where possible, take food items in plastic containers that can be rinsed when emptied and reused as water or ice containers.)

Breakfast Food

Biscuit, pancake mix
Syrup
Breakfast or granola bars
Cereal, instant oatmeal (flavored)
Canned fruits
Fruit juices or juice boxes
Bacon, sausage
Bagels

Lunch or Dinner

Bread
Crackers
Canned soups
Pork and beans
Macaroni and cheese*
Cup-o-noodles
Stew/soup mixes
Spaghetti
Chips
Freeze-dried food
Dried potatoes, onions
Canned vegetables
Hamburger/buns
Hot dogs/buns*
Ham
Fresh fruit

Snacks for Climb (or anytime)

Dried fruit
Granola bars
Gorp (trail mix)
Beef jerky
Snack nuts
Fresh fruit
Candy bars
Hard candy (not too sweet)

General Supplies

Coffee/creamer
Canned milk
Sugar/salt/pepper
Butter or margarine
Presweetened Kool-Aid and iced tea
Pickles
Jams/jellies
Canned pop
Cooking oil
Hot chocolate packets
Mustard/ketchup
Cheese (already shredded, in bags)
Cream cheese
Water
Coolers
Can opener

* especially important when children are involved

Cooking Tips:

1. Purchase foods with high altitude instructions to assist in preparation.
2. Once menus are determined and food is purchased, organize food supplies in boxes labeled "breakfast," "lunch," or "dinner."
3. Write menus on cards and place them in the appropriate boxes.
4. Protect food from the elements and animals:
   • Box it tightly, placing it in plastic bags or plastic containers.
   • Hang it from trees overnight.
5. At higher altitudes, water boils much slower than at sea level. Allow for longer food preparation.
6. If you need to use stream water in cooking, boil it for at least two minutes, plus one minute for each thousand feet above sea level. For example, at 10,000 feet boil for a total of 12 minutes.
7. Soaping pots and pans on the underside before cooking over open fires makes them easier to clean.

Mountain Climbing:
Policies and Cautions

The following are some helpful tips to remember as you take part in this mountain-climbing experience.

Use the Buddy System. Make sure that every participant has a designated "buddy" as a climbing partner. No one should climb alone. Those who are less experienced should be teamed with someone who has had more experience. Make sure that each person understands the importance of staying with their buddy, as well as what to do if there is an emergency.

Drink more water/fluids than usual. This is critical. Water direct from a stream should not be consumed. Boil any water taken from local streams for 2 minutes plus 1 minute for each 1,000 feet above sea level..

Be aware of three potential health conditions related to this event. Monitor one another each morning and report any symptoms to our first aid expert. Symptoms take from one to three days to appear, depending on the individual.

ALTITUDE SICKNESS: An illness occurring in persons on high mountains, due to the reduced quantity of oxygen in the air. At 10,000 feet the pressure of oxygen drops to 69%. (At 10,000 it will take two breaths to equal one breath at sea level.) In altitudes over 10,000 feet the breathing rate has to increase to permit the body to absorb the needed oxygen. Altitude sickness is likely to develop in people who do not take time to acclimate themselves.
- **Symptoms:** Headache, shortness of breath, coughing.
- **Key treatment:** Descent to a lower altitude.

DEHYDRATION: The state produced by abnormal loss of body water, the deprivation or loss of water from the tissues. In high altitudes, sweat evaporates as soon as it hits the skin. To avoid dehydration, drink water often, even when you are not thirsty.
- Symptoms: Headaches/dizziness, dry mouth, thirsty, brightly-colored and strong-smelling urine.
- Key treatment: Drink plenty of fluids (especially water), especially before going to bed.

HYPOTHERMIA: Abnormally low body temperature, most likely due to excessive loss of body heat. Hypothermia is a threat to hikers, climbers, and others who spend long periods outdoors during cold, damp weather.
- **Symptoms:** Drowsiness, mental confusion, and pallor. Hands and feet, but especially abdomen, feel cold to the touch. Best way to determine if body temperature is dangerously low is to use a thermometer.
- **Key treatment:** Take individual to a warmer environment. Wrap in space blanket.

11 FOR MEN ONLY

**Building Strong Male Leadership
to Attract Strong Men**

Event Summary: A retreat that challenges single men to live an intentional, focused, purposeful life—and provides an opportunity for them to become a part of an ongoing accountability and growth group.

Length of Event: Friday afternoon–Sunday evening

Suggested Theme Verse: "As iron sharpens iron, so one man sharpens another." Proverbs 27:17

Ideal Number of Participants: 20+

Estimated Cost Per Person: $30–$50

Facility Requirements: Secluded campsite or campground within a 2- or 3-hour drive

Recommended Planning Team: 6–8 people

Advance Planning Needed: Approximately 6 months

INTRODUCTION

by Mark Thrash

Minister of Single Adults and Evangelism

Shandon Baptist Church

Columbia, South Carolina

"For Men Only" is a natural outgrowth of our Single Adult Ministry—a time when men can focus on man-to-man friendships and fellowship. Wonderful camaraderie is established as they work together on various projects. Through these combined ministry projects and efforts, men discover a greater enjoyment of, interest in, and desire to support each other. In the words of Scripture, "As iron shaprens iron, so one man sharpens another" (Proverbs 27:17).

A "male" retreat has several advantages over a coed function. First, a men's retreat typically appeals to the male ego and macho image—spending a weekend roughing it in the woods, cooking over a campfire, sleeping on the ground . . . back to nature!

Second, the absence of women eliminates the need for men to play one-upmanship. Men are more likely to drop the macho facade and to allow you to see them as they really are.

Third, "For Men Only" gives you the opportunity and possibility of developing and building strong, godly men.

Finally, it lays the groundwork for helping men develop accountability relationships in every area of their lives: financial, spiritual, sexual, vocational, and relational.

OBJECTIVES

❖ To provide single men a purposeful and concentrated opportunity to deepen fellowship, to be open and vulnerable, and to lower their guard.

❖ To renew and deepen friendships among men,

❖ To encourage and challenge men in their walk with Christ.

❖ To write a personal "purpose statement" for their life.

THE BIG EVENT

SCHEDULE

Friday

❖
Get as many people as possible involved in the planning of this event.

4:00 P.M.—Leave from designated place.
6:30 P.M.—Set up camp.
7:30 P.M.—Supper
8:15 P.M.—Icebreakers
9:00 P.M.—Introduce retreat theme and speaker. Review weekend schedule.
9:30 P.M.—Determine small groups for weekend.
10:00 P.M.—Free time

Saturday

7:30 A.M.—Breakfast
8:15 A.M.—Quiet-time devotions
9:00 A.M.—Speaker, Session I
9:30 A.M.—Small-group discussion
10:15 A.M.—Break
10:30 A.M.—3-mile nature hike
12:00 P.M.—Lunch
1:00–6:00 P.M.—Free time, volleyball, relay races, etc.
6:30 P.M.—Supper
7:30 P.M.—Testimony
7:45 P.M.—Speaker, Session II
8:30 P.M.—Small-group discussion
9:15 P.M.—Campfire, songs, sharing
10:00 P.M.—Quiet-time devotions

Sunday

8:00 A.M.—Breakfast
9:00 A.M.—Quiet-time devotions
10:00 A.M.—Write a personal purpose statement
11:00 A.M.—Speaker and a time of sharing as a group (Session III)
12:00 P.M.—Lunch (Distribute evaluations, to be completed before departure.)
1:00 P.M.—Break camp and head for home.

PROGRAM IDEAS AND SUGGESTIONS

ICEBREAKERS

You will probably not have the time or interest to do all the icebreakers during this retreat. Choose those that seem to work best for your group, or develop some of your own.

❖
For more icebreakers, see the Table of Contents.

• Get Acquainted

Have each participant pair with a person he does not know well. In five minutes both men should learn all they can so they can introduce each other.

- job
- place of birth
- favorite food and place to eat
- favorite TV show and movie
- biggest mystery about women
- favorite book
- best advice his dad or mom ever gave
- hobbies and special interests
- nickname in high school
- sports played in high school or college
- favorite sport today
- the last time he was with only men
- most admired man in his life
- most admired man in the Bible (other than Jesus)

• Tool Time

In one large group or several small groups, ask the men to respond to the following:

- Name a power tool that best describes your personality.
- Name a power tool that begins with the first letter of your last name.
- Name a power tool that best describes your church at the present time.
- Name a power tool that best describes your home or apartment at the present time.
- Name a power tool that describes your relationships with women.
- What is the worst experience you've ever had with a power tool?

• Car Time

In one large group or several small groups, ask everyone to respond to the following:

- Name a car that best describes your personality.

- Name a car that begins with the first letter of your last name.

- Name a car that best describes your church at the present time.

- Name a car that best describes your home or apartment at the present time.

- Name a car that describes your relationships with women.

- What is the worst experience you've ever had with a car?

NATURE HIKE (SATURDAY, 10:30 A.M.)

The specifics of this hike will be determined by the location and natural surrounding of your retreat site. Find out what opportunities for hiking exist in the area. Can someone from the retreat site lead the hike? Or do you have a real nature lover in your group who might enjoy leading this hike? The ideal walk will be approximately two or three miles long.

ACTIVITIES (SATURDAY, 1:00–6:00 P.M.)

One of the best ways to help the men relax, get comfortable with each other, and build camaraderie is to provide several fun, challenging ways to compete and build team spirit. Divide the men into teams of five to ten. Here are several ideas for team competition.

• Inner Tube Relay

Each team is given one large inner tube. Two men on each team stand back to back with the tube around their waists. They race the other teams from start to finish line. This can be played with only two people from each team competing, or with everyone on each team in a relay race. Rather than having a baton, each pair, upon reaching the designated relay point, must take the inner tube off and get it on the next pair of runners. This continues until all team members have competed.

• Stilt Bowling

Each team is given a pair of stilts. (Stilts can be made out of one-foot sections of PVC pipe, then tied to a person's feet with string or strips of heavy-duty rubber.) The object is to push bowling balls from point A to point B while on the stilts. As with the inner tube relay, this game could also be played as a relay race.

• Obstacle Course

Create a simple obstacle course that could include climbing over a wall, running over a section of tires or logs, climbing a rope ladder, and crawling through a series of upright tires. Use your imagination and creativity. Find out what materials and ideas the retreat site might have for you to consider. Use a stopwatch to see what team can get through the obstacle course the fastest.

• Crazy Volleyball

Set up a regular volleyball net. Consider one or all of the following game ideas:

- Use an egg rather than a volleyball. See which team can play the longest without breaking the egg.

- Try the same game, only with team members' hands tied together.

- Have the receiving team use frying pans.

- Use a water balloon instead of an egg.

- Have each team member wear a construction hat with nails or screws sticking up out of the top of the hat. Each side is given thirty water balloons. See which side can break the most balloons by "butting" the balloons with their hats. (A busted balloon counts only if it is broken in the air by someone's hat. It does not count if it's broken by someone's hands or by falling to the ground.)

- Another way to play this game is to see which side can end up with the fewest popped balloons after a timed period.

DIVIDING INTO SMALL GROUPS

Divide participants into groups of three to five people on Friday evening. It will work best if participants remain in the same small groups throughout the retreat to facilitate relationship building, sharing, and trust.

Quiet-Time Devotions

On page 101 (Resource 1) you will find three passages of Scripture, each one followed by a few questions. These can be used for personal devotions, one passage for each devotional time. Pass out the entire page at one time, or one passage before each devotional time.

Selecting a Speaker

It is not essential that you have an outside speaker for this event. The singles pastor, a key single-adult leader in your group, a respected lay leader in the church, or the senior pastor could do a fine job. However, as is sometimes the case, having a speaker from at least fifty miles away makes him a much "better" speaker. Use your best judgment. Choose a speaker who fits your particular needs and budget parameters and has special appeal with men in your area.

The speaker is responsible for leading two thirty-minute sessions plus a Sunday morning sharing time. The speaker's material should set the tone for the weekend and should be biblically based, spiritually sound, and challenging. Regardless of who the speaker is, it would be very beneficial for him to read several books (see Recommended Resources on page 97) in preparing for the retreat. If he is unable to, ask him to at least read the following chapters:

FOR SESSION ONE
Chapter 3 of *Real Man*, by Edwin Louis Cole
Chapter 1 of *Real Men Have Feelings Too*, by Gary J. Oliver

FOR SESSION TWO
Chapter 1 of *Real Man*, by Edwin Louis Cole
Chapter 1 of *Real Men Have Feelings Too*, by Gary J. Oliver

Two suggested outlines for the speaker, which are reproducible, are found on pages 102 and 103 (Resources 2 and 3). The speaker is encouraged to adapt these as needed for your group, or select other material that may be more suited to your particular needs.

It would also be helpful if the speaker

EQUIPMENT/SUPPLIES (To be furnished by the event leaders)

- ☐ Tents
- ☐ Dishes
- ☐ Washing soap
- ☐ Propane cooking stove(s) (one for every 4-5 men)
- ☐ Rope
- ☐ Pots, pans, kitchen utensils
- ☐ Softball, bat
- ☐ Shovel
- ☐ Ax
- ☐ Deflated tire tube (1 for each team)
- ☐ Fresh drinking water
- ☐ Toilet paper
- ☐ Plastic bags
- ☐ Volleyball and net
- ☐ Balloons for games
- ☐ Eggs and frying pan for crazy volleyball (if played)
- ☐ Construction hats with nails/screws for crazy volleyball (if played)
- ☐ Bowling balls
- ☐ PVC pipe for stilts
- ☐ String or rubber strips
- ☐ Stopwatch (to time relay events)

WHAT TO BRING (To be provided by participants)

- ☐ Tent (if you have one)
- ☐ Bible, paper, pen
- ☐ Comfortable hiking shoes, sneakers
- ☐ Camera
- ☐ Fishing rod (if desired)
- ☐ Personal toiletries
- ☐ Change of clothes (2)
- ☐ Sleeping bag/pillow
- ☐ Guitar (optional)

would write his personal purpose statement prior to the retreat, as an example for the participants as they begin to write their own statements.

"WHAT IS AN ACCOUNTABILITY GROUP?" (SUNDAY, 11:00 A.M.)

Session III is an opportunity to discuss the benefits of being in an accountability group and how to start one. For those who are interested, now is an excellent time to get commitments and determine accountability partners. However, it is important that no one feel pressured or coerced into participating. It needs to be something that is chosen freely.

This can also be an excellent time for singing and worship, and for men to share a testimony and/or the things they learned and benefited from at this retreat.

Accountability Questions

To encourage the men to form accountability relationships, give each participant a "My Accountability Questions" card. (For convenience, make the card about the size of a credit card, or smaller, and have it laminated so each participant can keep it in his billfold or daily planner.)

RECOMMENDED RESOURCES

Real Man, Edwin Louis Cole.(Nashville: Thomas Nelson Publishers, 1993.)

Real Men Have Feelings Too: Regaining a Male Passion for Life, Gary Oliver. (Chicago: Moody Press, 1993.)

The Friendship Factor, Alan Loy McGinnis. (Minneapolis: Augsburg, 1979.)

Man to Man, 201 Focus Group Series. (Littleton, CO: Serendipity House, Inc. 1994.)

Disciplines of a Godly Man, Kent Hughes. (Wheaton, IL: Crossway Books, 1994.)

What Makes a Man, Bill McCartney. (Colorado Springs, CO: NavPress, 1993.)

What God Does When Men Pray, William Carr Peel. (Colorado Springs, CO: NavPress, 1993.)

PLANNING THE EVENT

PLANNING TEAM

For this event, you need an Event Director (possibly an Assistant Event Director) and volunteers to take responsibilities for the event site, budget, publicity, food, printed materials, registration, speaker, small groups, transportation, and equipment/supplies. Unique to this event is the fact that all the Planning Team members and participants are men.

❖ *The more people who have ownership and involvement in the planning, the greater success you will have.*

My Accountability Questions

*As iron sharpens iron,
So one man sharpens another.*

Proverbs 27:17

During the past week/month . . .

1. Have I been with a woman in a way that could be viewed as compromising?

2. Have my financial dealings been filled with integrity?

3. Have I viewed sexually explicit material?

4. Have I spent adequate time in Bible study and prayer?

5. Have I spent quality time and given priority to my family, close friends, and significant people in my life?

6. Have I fulfilled the mandates of what I feel God has called me to do and be?

7. Have I just lied to you?

Planning Timeline

Event: *For Men Only*   **Date of event:** _____

Event Director: _____   **Phone:** _____

Thanks for agreeing to serve on our retreat Planning Team. Please check over this timeline for the task(s) assigned to you. Adapt as needed. Supplement this timeline with information on the reproducible, generic job descriptions found on pages 225-252. Highlight your tasks (and due dates) each time they appear. Mark your calendar accordingly.

Date: _____	**6 MONTHS IN ADVANCE**

Event Director (page 226)

☐ Recruit a Planning Team. Brainstorm ideas and adapt this event to fit your particular ministry goals and objectives.

☐ Make sure each team member understands his assigned tasks and responsibilities.

☐ Determine if this timeline will work and make adjustments accordingly.

☐ Discuss and decide on a theme.

Event Site Coordinator (page 234)

☐ Secure a secluded campsite that is of special interest to men. The site should be within two or three hours of the church.

☐ Put the event date on the church calendar.

❖ *For more ideas and help, refer to job descriptions beginning on page 225.*

Speaker/Workshop Leaders Coordinator (page 250)

☐ The speaker for this event plays a key role and should be someone of particular interest to men, possibly a coach, athlete, musician, or business executive. Enlisting the speaker now provides a better chance of securing the person of your choice.

Budget Coordinator (page 229)

☐ Begin costing the event.

Date: _____	**4 TO 5 MONTHS IN ADVANCE**

Event Director

☐ Meet with the Planning Team for a progress report. Finalize the weekend agenda. With the help of your team, make a list of all the single men in your church or ministry, including those on the fringes. Each person on the list should be individually contacted and invited to the event.

Speaker/Workshop Leaders Coordinator

☐ Finalize the speaker and make sure his theme fits with the weekend plans.

☐ Inquire about any audio/visual needs he may have for the event.

☐ Be sure a signed contract outlining dates, times, and fees is on file.

☐ Pay a deposit, if required.

☐ Get the speaker's photograph and biographical information to the Publicity Coordinator.

Budget Coordinator

☐ Along with the Planning Team, finalize retreat budget and per person costs.

Transportation Coordinator (page 252)

☐ Determine the type of transportation needed. Begin making arrangements.

Publicity Coordinator (page 238)

☐ As soon as the speaker, location, and costs are finalized, have flyers printed. Begin publicity.

Registration Coordinator (page 241)

☐ Begin registration. Have scholarship forms available.

Recreation Coordinator (page 240)

☐ Prepare to provide icebreakers, activities, a nature hike, and games such as tug of war, volleyball, kickball, softball, and relay races.
☐ Secure all the items necessary to carry out these responsibilities.

Food Coordinator (page 236)

☐ Determine the menus. Keep them simple.

Date:	3 MONTHS
_____	IN ADVANCE

Event Director

☐ Meet with Planning Team to make sure they are on track and have everything they need to accomplish their tasks.
☐ Go to strong male leaders to personally ask them to attend the retreat.

Publicity Coordinator

☐ Continue promoting the event.

Registration Coordinator

☐ Encourage men to register for the event.
☐ If early payment is required, collect funds.

Date:	2 MONTHS
_____	IN ADVANCE

Event Director

☐ Meet with the Planning Team to make sure they are on track and have everything they need to accomplish their tasks.
☐ Review the registrations.
☐ Continue going to strong leaders to personally ask them to attend.

Publicity Coordinator

☐ Continue publicity.

Worship Coordinator (page 251)

☐ Recruit someone to serve as the guitar player for singing and worship times.
☐ Begin preparing for leading worship during the retreat.

Speaker/Workshop Leaders Coordinator

☐ If you are planning to provide handouts of the speaker sessions, obtain them now.

Small-Group Coordinator (page 247)

☐ Develop a plan for the most effective, creative method to divide participants into small groups during the retreat.

Equipment/Supplies Coordinator (page 233)

☐ Begin collecting needed camping equipment and supplies. Borrowing supplies greatly reduces costs.

Recreation Coordinator (page 240)

☐ Arrangements for games and activities should be in place.
☐ Communicate any equipment needs to the Equipment/Supplies Coordinator.

Food Coordinator

☐ Purchase non-perishable items.
☐ Ask volunteers to bring snacks.

Registration Coordinator

☐ Scholarship forms should be completed and submitted for approval.

Date:	1 MONTH
_____	IN ADVANCE

Event Director

☐ Meet with the Planning Team to make sure they are on track and have everything they need to accomplish their tasks.
☐ Make personal phone calls to single men that you would like to attend this event.

Publicity Coordinator

- ☐ Continue publicity.
- ☐ Work with the Event Director to make personal phone calls to single men that you would like to attend this event.

Food Coordinator

- ☐ Enlist a cleanup crew to ensure the campsite is left clean.

Small-Group Coordinator

- ☐ If you want small-group facilitators for each group, select and train those people.

Date: _____ 3 WEEKS IN ADVANCE

Event Director

- ☐ Continue making personal phone calls to single men that you would like to attend.

Event Site Coordinator

- ☐ Confirm all arrangements with the campground or facility.
- ☐ Confirm that a deposit has been made.

Transportation Coordinator

- ☐ Confirm travel plans to the event site.

Publicity Coordinator

- ☐ Continue publicity. Make this a priority announcement at your meetings.
- ☐ Continue working with the Event Director to make phone calls to single men.

Date: _____ 2 WEEKS IN ADVANCE

Event Director

- ☐ Meet with the Planning Team to make sure they are on track and have everything they need to accomplish their tasks.
- ☐ Make a last-minute phone call blitz to anyone not yet signed up for the retreat.

Registration Coordinator

- ☐ Close registration.
- ☐ Make room or tent assignments.
- ☐ Collect final payments.
- ☐ Mail a letter to all registrants. (See the sample letter on page 244.)

Date: _____ 1 WEEK IN ADVANCE

Event Director

- ☐ Meet with the Planning Team to make sure the final details are being completed.

Equipment/Supplies Coordinator

- ☐ All necessary items should be collected and ready for the event.

Food Coordinator

- ☐ All supplies, except the perishables, should be ready to take to the event site.

Small-Group Coordinator

- ☐ Confirm participation with all small-group facilitators.

Date: _____ 2 TO 4 WEEKS AFTER EVENT

Event Director

- ☐ Have a meal for all the men who formed accountability groups during the retreat (and for any men who have an interest in doing so). Use this time to encourage one another, answer any questions they might have, and allow the men an opportunity to share how their group is doing.
- ☐ See "Followup Guidelines" on page 254.

For Personal Devotions

Read the Scripture passage. Then write your answers in your notebook.

1. MATTHEW 3:1-17 (SATURDAY, 8:15 A.M.)

How would you have handled the situation if you found yourself in John the Baptist's place?

What was significant about the baptism of Jesus?

Before Jesus did one miracle, what was God saying about Him?

What does this indicate about how God looks at you?

2. MATTHEW 4:1-11 (SATURDAY, 10:00 P.M.)

Note the occurrence of Jesus' baptism, followed by the wilderness temptations. What does that tell you about spiritual highs and lows?

What were Satan's first words to Jesus?

What did Satan's words call into question?

How did Jesus respond to Satan's temptations?

3. LUKE 19:9-10 (SUNDAY, 9:00 A.M.)

Most corporations and successful individuals have a statement of purpose that indicates major goals. What was Jesus' statement of purpose?

Do you have a personal purpose statement? What would you include in such a statement?

Session 1 Outline
Who Am I?

Matthew 4:1-11 (Saturday, 9:00 A.M.)

At its very heart, the temptation of Jesus determined the focus and course of His life on earth. In Satan's words to Christ, "If you are the Son of God," (Matthew 4:3) lies a question of "identity." If Satan can confuse us about our identity, then we lose our focus, purpose, and intention.

I. What has shaped our perceptions about what it means to be a man?
   a. Society, media, advertising, etc.
   b. Our home environment as a child
   c. Role models, heroes, significant others
   d. The church
   e. Women
   f. Other
II. What is the predominant thinking in society about what it means to be a man?
   a. Be macho (Rambo, Charles Bronson, Clint Eastwood, Steven Segal).
   b. Be a successful CEO or company founder (Bill Gates).
   c. Be feelings-oriented (Alan Alda, Kevin Kostner, Robert Redford).
   d. Be strong, stubborn, non-vulnerable (Archie Bunker).
III. Why is there confusion about what it means to be a man?
   a. What is the source of this confusion?
   b. What are the results of this confusion?
      1. Confusion results in a loss of focus and loss of potential. (If we don't know who we are, we don't know where we are going.)
      2. We are blown about, swept under, shifting with the wind (James 1).
      3. We are diluted (an inch deep and half a mile wide, rather than cutting a deep, narrow, powerful channel).
      4. Ineffective living
         a. We listen to too many voices.
         b. We get bogged down by all the choices.
         c. We struggle with decision making.

IV. How do we find our way out of this confusion?
   a. Where do we go to find the answers?
   b. How can we tell who's telling the truth?

V. What can we learn from Jesus' identity?
   a. Jesus' identity revealed (Matthew 3)
   b. Jesus' identity tested (Matthew 3)
   c. Jesus' life focused and affirmed (Luke 19:10)

DISCUSSION QUESTIONS

1. Which of the following types do you feel society most expects you to be?
   The macho man
   The CEO or company founder
   The feelings-oriented type
   The strong, non-vulnerable type
   Other

2. All of us have people we look up to and hold in high esteem. In the past we used the term *hero*. Who is your hero, and why?

3. As a child or young man, who had the greatest influence on what you thought a man should be? Who has the greatest influence today?

4. We are influenced by a variety of sources when constructing an image of the ideal man. Describe the ideal man. What sources have influenced your perception?
   What do women say is the ideal man?
   What do men say is the ideal man?
   What does Jesus say?

5. When do you feel most confused about your male identity or role?

6. What is the strongest influence determining your personal identity?

7. Did Jesus struggle with His identity? If so, how did He resolve it?

8. What can you learn from Jesus as you face the question, Who am I?

Session 2 Outline
The Intention of Jesus
MATTHEW 4:1-11; LUKE 19:9, 10 (Saturday, 7:45 P.M.)

Having affirmed His identity, Jesus focused upon His life, mission, and purpose. What was Jesus' purpose? Leaving Zacchaeus's house, Jesus turned and said, "Today salvation has come to this house, . . . For the Son of Man came to seek and to save what was lost" (Luke 19:9, 10). How can we know our mission and purpose?

I. How did Jesus know His purpose in life?
   a. Scripture knowledge
      1. He refuted Satan's claims by saying, "It is written."
      2. He knew God's Word (Scripture memorization).
      3. Relationships require time and energy. Jesus spent lots of time with His Father (active devotional life).
   b. Discipline—becoming focused. (This is a big part of what it means to be a Christian.)
      1. Spiritual discipline
      2. Mental discipline
      3. Physical discipline (God's temple)
      4. Accountability (Even Jesus had an accountability circle of twelve men. Our hearts are evil. Accountability helps us stay on track.)

II. How can I get a clear picture of my purpose and identity? (How can I put first things first—set priorities?)
   a. Pray about the question, Why am I here? What does God want me to accomplish? (John 10:10)
   b. Begin writing a purpose statement. Be prayerful. To help you get started, write down the following: "I want to have a focused, intentional life. Therefore, I will . . ." or "God has created me to . . ." (You may not be able to complete this statement during the retreat, but it's a start.)

1. Make it a short, succinct statement
2. Be sure it includes the following:
   God
   Family
   Work
   Finances
   Relationships
   Sex
   Time
   Church/ministry

SMALL-GROUP DISCUSSION QUESTIONS

1. Jesus, who was single, was the most focused and intentional man who has ever walked the face of planet Earth. What was His focus?

2. How did Jesus manage to stay focused and intentional? What was His secret?

3. Take a few minutes to theorize about Jesus' statement of purpose for His life. Summarize it.

4. What is your purpose statement for living?

12 "ONCE-UPON-A-TIME" RETREAT

Seeing God's Love through the Eyes of a Child—Again!

Event Summary: A general retreat (which begins on the bus or in the van) that combines group teaching and small "Devotional Group" teams for study, devotions, discussion, and fun activities.

Length of Event: Friday afternoon through Sunday night

Suggested Theme Verse: "I tell you the truth, unless you change and become like little children, you will never enter the kingdom of heaven." Matthew 18:3

Ideal Number of Participants: 20+

Estimated Cost Per Person: $60–$150, depending on facility

Facility Requirements: Retreat facility, conference center, or resort

Recommended Planning Team: 6–12

Advance Planning Needed: 12 months

INTRODUCTION

by Paul Clough
Singles Pastor
Ward Presbyterian Church
Livonia, Michigan

Each year our singles ministry plans a popular spring retreat. A general retreat such as this provides a great opportunity for a change of pace, for some extended time to get to know others, and for a chance to focus on a particular topic that aids our spiritual growth.

One of the keys to the success of this retreat is having everyone in what we call Devotion Groups, small groups of about ten people each. The Devotion Groups meet daily for devotions and prayer, as well as for some of the fun activities. Small groups such as this play a significant role in helping build relationships and encouraging one another to grow in his or her walk with God.

There is always a theme for the weekend and a special speaker and a musician who work together with the ministry leadership to help participants relax, learn, and grow in a non-threatening environment.

After the "mountaintop" experience of a getaway with friends, returning home can sometimes be hard to do, but it can help build stronger people for facing the weeks and months ahead.

OBJECTIVES

❖ To explore what it means to become as little children and respond positively to the Father's love for us.

❖ To encourage fun, fellowship, and spiritual growth through worship, special music, a special speaker, small-group devotions, and fun activities.

THE BIG EVENT

SCHEDULE

Friday

❖ *Get as many people as possible involved in the planning of this event.*

4:00 P.M.—Check-in for bus loading

5:00 P.M.—Depart. Dinner served on the bus in route.

8:30 P.M.—Arrive. Take luggage to your room and gather in the meeting room for refreshments and icebreakers.

9:00 P.M.—Introduction of weekend events

10:00 P.M.—Group singing

10:15 P.M.—Overview of topics

10:30 P.M.—Refreshments followed by bonfire

Saturday

7:30 A.M.—Devotional leaders meet for prayer and last-minute details.

8:00 A.M.—Breakfast

8:45 A.M.—Group singing

9:00 A.M.—Session I

10:00 A.M.—Devotion Groups meet

11:00 A.M.—Group singing

11:15 A.M.—Session II

12:15 P.M.—Lunch

1:00 P.M.—Free time (softball, tennis, volleyball, canoeing, etc.)

5:30 P.M.—Dinner

6:30 P.M.—Concert

7:15 P.M.—Session III

8:30 P.M.—Fun activity (see pages 106-107 for suggestions)

10:00 P.M.—Refreshments followed by bonfire

Sunday

7:45 A.M.—Devotional leaders meet for prayer and report on earlier small groups.

8:00 A.M.—Breakfast

8:45 A.M.—Devotion Groups meet

9:45 A.M.—Group singing

10:00 A.M.—Session IV

11:15 A.M.—Worship/communion/sharing (Devotion Groups sit together.)

1:00 P.M.—Lunch (Hand out evaluations to be filled out before leaving.)

2:00 P.M.—Free time

4:30 P.M.—Check-in for bus loading

5:00 P.M.—Depart. Stop for dinner (you pay!).

9:30 P.M.—Arrive home.

PROGRAM IDEAS AND SUGGESTIONS

BUS RIDE ACTIVITY (FRIDAY NIGHT)

If participants travel to the retreat site as a group on a bus, the Bus Captain is responsible to meet and greet each person individually. The Captain can tell stories, lead singing, play a group game, or do whatever he or she chooses. Eating a box dinner on the bus is a great icebreaker. As the captain passes out the dinners, he or she can introduce each person to the others on the bus (most buses today do have public address systems).

Here's an activity that will help people get better acquainted: Every fifteen minutes the persons in the aisle seats rotate clockwise one seat. (The people on the right side of the bus move back one row and the people on the left move forward one row.) On a two-hour bus ride, everyone will meet eight people. Provide questions to be answered in the fifteen minutes. Either repeat the same questions, which is easiest, or have forty questions—five questions eight times.

Questions that work well are:
• What is your name?
• Where did you grow up?
• What was your favorite activity when you were in elementary school?
• Have you been on a retreat before? If so, what is your favorite memory of that retreat? If not, what are you looking forward to?
• How did you get involved with this group?
• What was your favorite fairy tale or cartoon character as a child? Why? How about today as an adult?

ICEBREAKERS

Icebreakers are great vehicles to get to know one another. In addition, you could use an ice-breaker to divide the participants into their Devotion Groups. This will work with this first icebreaker if you give secret identities to your retreaters that "bunch" together in groups of eight to ten, such as characters from *The Lion King.*

• Famous Persons (Friday night option)

On the back of each person, pin one name of a favorite fairy tale or cartoon pair—Mickey or Minnie Mouse, Cinderella or the Fairy Godmother, Beauty or the Beast, for example. Each person must "discover" his or her identity by asking other people in the room questions about the name that can be answered only with yes or no. Only three questions may be asked of any one person in the room.

Once a person has guessed the name, that person should transfer the card to the front of his or her shirt and continue serving as an "answer person" for others until everyone (or almost everyone) has discovered his or her identity.

Next, everyone should find his or her partner. Allow two minutes for partners to get to know each other's name, favorite fairy tale or cartoon character as a child, and an early childhood memory. Then have each person introduce his or her partner to the whole group (if small enough) or to the Devotion Team (if a very large group).

• Little-Known Secrets (Friday night option)

Duplicate a sheet of paper with twenty-five to thirty squares drawn on it. Each square has a statement in it such as:

> Birthday is in March.
> Has two brothers.
> Likes liver.
> Is left-handed.
> Has lived outside the U.S.
> Is attending first singles retreat.

> Likes jazz music.
> Is a golfer.
> Flies an airplane.

This activity may also be adapted for the event theme. For example, for this "Once-Upon-a-Time" theme, some boxes might read: Had a grade school nickname; Had a crush on a grade school teacher; Hated recess; Wore glasses by age eight; Cried on the first day of school; Carried lunch to school. There are many other possibilities to write in the squares. (If you know of some unusual, but not embarrassing, characteristics about some of your retreaters, be sure to include them!)

❖

For more icebreakers, see the Table of Contents.

Each person must fill in his or her sheet with the signatures of other retreaters. A person's signature must appear only once on the sheet. (If this is a very small group, modify this rule.) The first person to turn in a completed sheet to the Recreation Coordinator wins a prize! Prizes should be inexpensive and humorous (without being insulting), the type you can get at a gag shop. Wrap the prize and have the winner open it in front of everyone. Examples of prizes include pet rocks, candy, and cheap jewelry. Use your imagination!

SKITS (SATURDAY NIGHT)

Skits of all kinds can be fun. Have each Devotion Group develop a five-minute skit. Consider using one of these ideas:

- Skits to best reflect the theme of the weekend
- Skits based on a childhood song
- Skits based on a favorite children's TV show
- Skits that tell a children's story (*Goldilocks and the Three Bears, The Pokey Little Puppy, The Velveteen Rabbit, Cinderella,* or a Dr. Seuss book). Have copies or summaries of these stories available for groups to review.

Either have the groups devise a skit completely on their own or draw a selection from a bowl and then create their own interpretation of the song or story.

CHARACTER COSTUMES

Give each group a paper sack of newspapers and a roll of scotch tape. Their task is to create a costume for one of their members based on a familiar character from a childhood story, movie, cartoon, or book. Each costume should include some kind of description. After a set time limit (fifteen to twenty minutes), stage a fashion show displaying the creations of each team. Encourage creativity.

SCAVENGER HUNT

This old favorite is always fun. Be sure to clearly identify the boundaries of distance, time, and creativity in acquiring the items on the list. Adapt your boundaries and list based on the location of your retreat, the season of the year, and the area of the country in which you live. Here are ideas to get you started:

Rural setting

caterpillar or butterfly
helicopter seed
lightning bug
bird feather, nest, or egg
tin can
gum or candy wrapper
birch or other bark to write on
flat stone or rock for skipping
bandanna
acorn or pine cone
animal cracker
small bag of hay or straw
dandelion (flower or seed) or wild flower

City or neighborhood setting

pacifier
diaper pin
coupon for Kix cereal (or some other kids' favorite)
a school picture
newspaper article about a child's achievement
old valentine
night light
birthday candle
gum wrapper
sucker
children's vitamin
children's Band-Aid (colored or with some cartoon character)
jump rope
sidewalk chalk
matchbox car

DEVOTION GROUPS

Ask that the speaker develop four sessions based on the Scripture and topics provided in the Devotion Group material on pages 112 and 113 (Resources 1 and 2). In other words, the speaker will expand on what the Devotion Groups discuss.

Worship Service

The following schedule is suggested:
Singing (30 minutes)
Opening prayer, call to worship
Scripture reading (portions of Psalm 139)
Singing (one song)
Scripture reading
Message
Singing (one song)
Communion
Sharing (what the retreat has meant, what God has been doing)
Closing song

EQUIPMENT/SUPPLIES (To be furnished by the event leaders)

- [ ] A/V equipment (if not available on site)
- [ ] Items for the icebreakers.
- [ ] Items for recreation as needed
- [ ] Items for the Saturday night fun time
- [ ] Snacks and drinks
- [ ] Prizes
- [ ] Church bulletins and other handouts that those at church would be receiving today
- [ ] Marshmallows, graham crackers, Hershey bars for s'mores at campfire(s).
- [ ] Summaries of children's stories for skits
- [ ] Supplies for Communion

WHAT TO BRING (To be provided by participants)

Include the following items in the letter to registrants (see page 244).

- [ ] Bible and pen
- [ ] Notebook and journal
- [ ] Casual clothing (warm clothes for evening)
- [ ] Toiletries
- [ ] Money for Sunday dinner
- [ ] Flashlight (for bonfires each evening)
- [ ] Equipment for sports they plan to participate in.
- [ ] A great attitude; a desire to grow and be blessed.

PLANNING THE EVENT

PLANNING TEAM

For this retreat, you will need an Event Director and, if your group is large, an Assistant Event Director, and volunteers to take responsibility for the event site, registration, budget, worship, transportation, bus captains, speaker, food, music, small groups, publicity, recreation, and audio/visual needs.

In addition to the above planning team, Devotion Group Leaders are needed. (See Small-Group Coordinator, page 247, for training and tips on leading small groups.) Assign Devotion Group Leaders (one for each eight to ten people) to lead discussions of the speaker's talks.

❖ *The more people who have ownership and involvement in the planning, the greater success you will have.*

Planning Timeline

Event: *"Once-Upon-a-Time" Retreat*   **Date of event:** _____

Event Director: _____   **Phone:** _____

Thanks for agreeing to serve on our retreat Planning Team. Please check over this timeline for the task(s) assigned to you. Adapt as needed. Supplement this timeline with information on the reproducible, generic job descriptions found on pages 225-252. Highlight your tasks (and due dates) and mark your calendar accordingly.

Date: _____ 9 TO 12 MONTHS IN ADVANCE

Event Director (page 226)

☐ Recruit a Planning Team. Brainstorm ideas and adapt this weekend event to fit your ministry goals and objectives.
☐ Make sure each team member understands his or her assigned responsibilities.
☐ Determine if this timeline will work and make adjustments accordingly.

Event Site Coordinator (page 234)

☐ Select and reserve a retreat site. In addition to lodging rooms, you will need one large room for the main sessions and several small rooms (one for each Devotion Group).
☐ Get all details in writing and arrange for a deposit to be paid.

Speaker/Workshop Leader Coordinator (page 250)

☐ Contact and secure the retreat speaker.

Music Coordinator (page 237)

☐ Contact and sign up the special musician.
☐ Ask the musician to provide a mini-concert one evening and to lead worship choruses before each main session and upbeat songs around an evening bonfire.

Budget Coordinator (page 229)

☐ Determine the per-person price.
☐ Prepare budget proposal.

Date: _____ 5 MONTHS IN ADVANCE

Event Director

☐ Hold a Planning Team meeting. Check on progress in each area of responsibility.

Transportation Coordinator (page 252)

☐ Arrange for transportation. If you choose chartered buses, encourage everyone to ride the bus. The retreat begins on the bus!
☐ Send deposit.

Budget Coordinator

☐ Finalize the budget.

❖ *For more ideas and help, refer to job descriptions beginning on page 225.*

Publicity Coordinator (page 238)

☐ Prepare a promotional strategy.

Event Site Coordinator

☐ Confirm arrangements with the facility.
☐ Is a contract on file at the church?
☐ Has a deposit been paid?

Date: _____ 4 MONTHS IN ADVANCE

Registration Coordinator (page 241)

☐ Have scholarship applications available.

Publicity Coordinator

☐ Begin your publicity campaign.

3 MONTHS IN ADVANCE

Date: _____

Event Director
☐ Hold a Planning Team meeting. Check on progress in each area of responsibility.

Bus Captains Coordinator (page 231)
☐ If you use buses or vans for transportation, recruit a Captain for each one.

Small-Group Coordinator (page 247)
☐ Obtain an overview or outline of the speaker's four talks. Rewrite as needed the Devotion Group material based on the speaker's content. (See pages 112 and 113.)

Registration Coordinator
☐ Have scholarship application forms available.
☐ Begin registration.

Food Coordinator (page 236)
☐ Coordinate with the retreat facility all menus and meal preparation.

2 MONTHS IN ADVANCE

Date: _____

Recreation Coordinator (page 240)
☐ Organize small teams (three to five people each) to help plan the special activities.

Small-Group Coordinator
☐ Recruit Devotion Group Leaders and set training dates. Devotion Group Leaders are responsible for the following: meeting for prayer each morning and leading two discussion groups Saturday and Sunday mornings; helping group members get acquainted; using the Devotion Group Material (Resources 1 and 2 on pages 112 and 113) or material provided by the speaker.

Registration Coordinator
☐ Continue registration.

Worship Coordinator (page 251)
☐ Prepare for the worship times.

Event Materials Coordinator (page 233)
☐ Make a list of all materials that will be needed. Plan to produce or photocopy materials as needed.

1 MONTH IN ADVANCE

Date: _____

Event Director
☐ Check on progress in each area.

Registration Coordinator
☐ Collect final payment of all registrants.
☐ Recruit someone to prepare name tags. They should also include room and Devotion Group assignments. Be creative.

Food Coordinator
☐ Arrange for snack foods for Friday and Saturday evenings.
☐ Also plan for the bonfire drinks and s'mores.

3 WEEKS IN ADVANCE

Date: _____

Event Site Coordinator
☐ Call the contact person and give the number of people who will be attending.
☐ Confirm all other arrangements.

Transportation Coordinator
☐ Confirm all transportation details.
☐ Provide maps to all drivers.

| Date: _____ | **2 WEEKS IN ADVANCE** |

Event Director
☐ Hold a Planning Team meeting. Check on progress in each area of responsibility.

Registration Coordinator
☐ Send a letter to all registrants with final information about the retreat. (See the sample on page 244.)
☐ Begin a roommate list.

Speaker and Music Coordinators
☐ Confirm retreat details and make final arrangements.

Small-Group Coordinator
☐ Divide participants into groups of five to eight people.
☐ Assign a small-group leader and meeting room to each group.

| Date: _____ | **1 WEEK IN ADVANCE** |

Small-Group Coordinator
☐ Hold one Devotion Group Leaders training session with all the group leaders.
☐ Also, arrange to meet with the leaders each morning before breakfast to address any concerns, to review the day's activities, and to pray together.

Food Coordinator
☐ Arrange to pick up food that is perishable.

Worship Coordinator
☐ Borrow or buy Communion supplies: bread, grape juice, communion cups, and trays.
☐ Plan the communion service.
☐ Plan to be available all weekend as a counselor.

Publicity Coordinator
☐ Put the last notice in the church bulletin.

Registration Coordinator
☐ Finalize the list of attendees, showing any balance due.
☐ Finalize the roommate list.

Budget Coordinator
☐ Write checks for the speaker, musician, event site, and bus company.

Event Materials Coordinator
☐ With assistance from the Registration Coordinator, assemble a materials folder for each participant. Make up extra folders to allow for last-minute registrants.
☐ Organize all other materials as needed.

Bus Captains Coordinator
☐ Assemble envelopes for the Bus Captains. Include bus driver tips, map, five trash bags, first-timer stickers (any fun sticker will do), and other instructions if needed.

| Date: _____ | **2 TO 4 WEEKS AFTER EVENT** |

☐ See the "Followup Guidelines" on page 254.

Devotion Group Material

SATURDAY MORNING

1. Open with prayer.

2. Introductions. Find out a little bit about each person's family and work. Then ask questions such as:
• Who has never been on a singles retreat before? (Welcome them to the retreat experience.)
• How did you hear about this retreat?

3. Icebreaker. Complete the following sentence with a favorite memory: "Once upon a time I . . ."

4. Read the Scripture passage on which this retreat theme is based: Matthew 18:1-5.

5. Get-acquainted activity. Ask each person in your group to respond to the following get-acquainted questions:
• Share something about your childhood. How does it relate to you today as an adult?
• What do you miss most about childhood?
• What does it mean to humble yourself like a child?
• In what ways are you still childlike? No longer childlike? Why?

6. Response to Scripture. Read Romans 12:1, 2 and ask volunteers to respond to these discussion questions:
• In what ways do you tend to conform to the world?
• What are some of the world's major influences on you? How have you tried to break away from them?
• How do you "renew" your mind?
• How does this help in "testing and approving" what is God's will?

7. Prayer. Share prayer requests and close in prayer for each other.

Devotion Group Material

SUNDAY MORNING

1. **Open with prayer.**

2. **Response to Scripture.** Read I John 1 and/or 4. Then ask people to respond to the following questions:

I John 1
• What childhood memory is as clear today as the day it happened?
• Are you afraid of the dark?
• What do you do when a movie gets scary?
• What does it mean to walk in the light? Walk in the darkness?
• How is this test useful in determining the choices you make in your life?
• As you get older, do you find it easier or harder to forgive your close friends and family? Why?

I John 4
• What characteristics or strengths did you get from your father? Your mother?
• What family event or experience stands out as an example of the closeness of your family?
• What kind of love is John talking about in this chapter?
> Warm feeling
> Brotherly love
> Sacrificial love
> Material giving
> Absence of malice
> Forgiveness of sins
> All of these
• How is God's love expressed through Jesus? Through people?
• How is such love suppressed through fear?
• How is such love made complete or perfect?
• What experiences have you had where love cast out fear? Where fear cast out love?

3. **Summary.** How does the message that God is love (I John 4:8, 16) relate to the message that God is light (I John 1:5)?

4. **Prayer.** Share prayer requests and close in prayer for each other.

13 A GATHERING OF CHRISTIAN SINGLES

An Interdenominational, Area-Wide Holiday Event

Event Summary: An interdenominational holiday weekend retreat providing an opportunity for those from smaller churches to be involved in a large retreat for Christian singles.

Length of Event: Friday evening–Monday noon

Suggested Theme Verse: ". . . being confident of this, that he who began a good work in you will carry it on to completion until the day of Christ Jesus." Philippians 1:6

Ideal Number of Participants: 75+

Estimated Cost Per Person: $60–$150, depending on cost of facility

Facility Requirements: Retreat facility, conference center, or resort

Recommended Planning Team: 10–15 people

Advance Planning Needed: Approximately 9–12 months

INTRODUCTION

by Linda Hardin
General Coordinator of Single Adult Ministries
and Women's Ministries for the
Church of the Nazarene
Kansas City, Missouri

OBJECTIVES

❖ To provide an annual retreat for single adults throughout your area/region to encourage all single adults toward acceptance and wholeness in Christ
❖ To encourage singles to seek a more vibrant faith and to serve and minister to others.
❖ To equip them for practical living.
❖ To provide opportunities for building a broader network of single Christian friends.

Many churches are too small to do a singles retreat or conference on their own. As a result, single adults from these churches often feel left out and isolated. Here is an idea that can be adapted for any denominational group, for a community-wide retreat, or for a cluster of churches who might want to combine resources for this event. It provides an opportunity for single adults from a state or region to gather together for growth, fellowship, and inspiration.

A retreat like this helps those from smaller churches plug in to something larger, make friends, and be reminded that they are not the only Christian singles (or single parents) around. This becomes a place to find encouragement, to connect, to network, and to grow—a bridge on the journey to developing new friendships.

Another important aspect of this retreat is that we always try to have some special "outward focus." This may involve raising funds during the retreat for a special missions project or cause.

Either the Memorial Day or Labor Day weekend is chosen to allow more time at the retreat, while requiring as little time off work as possible.

THE BIG EVENT

SCHEDULE

Friday

4:00–6:00 P.M.—Registration
6:00–7:00 P.M.—Dinner
7:00–8:00 P.M.—Informal wind-down time. (Show a video?)
  8:00–9:00 P.M.—What's Happening (introduce workshop leaders, promote activities, explain Talk-It-Overs, announcements, etc.)
  9:00–10:00 P.M.—Devotions led by the main speaker
  10:00–11:00 P.M.—Concert or more informal "mixer" activities, icebreakers, table games, volley-ball, etc.
  Talk-It-Overs (optional)

❖ *Get as many people as possible involved in the planning of this event.*

Saturday

7:00–7:30 A.M.—Devotions
7:30–8:30 A.M.—Breakfast
8:45–9:30 A.M.—Icebreakers, announcements
9:30–10:30 A.M.—Workshop Session 1
10:30–10:45 A.M.—Break
10:45–11:45 A.M.—Workshop Session 2
12:00–1:00 P.M.—Lunch
1:15–6:00 P.M.—Free time, tours, and various activities (canoe trip, craft time, scavenger hunt, swimming, organized sports, etc.)
  Talk-It-Overs (optional)
6:00–7:00 P.M.—Dinner
7:30–9:00 P.M.—General Session
9:00–9:30 P.M.—Break
9:30–10:30 or 11:00 P.M.—Talent Night

Sunday

7:00–7:30 A.M.—Devotions
7:30–8:30 A.M.—Breakfast
8:30–9:30 A.M.—Workshop Session 3
9:45–10:30 A.M.—Special emphasis (if you have selected one, for example, share how to sponsor a child through a relief agency)
10:45–12:00 A.M.—General Session
12:00–1:00 P.M.—Lunch
1:00–1:15 P.M.—Group picture

1:30–5:30 P.M.—Wacky Olympics, free time, softball game, fishing derby, etc.
  Talk-It-Overs (optional)
6:00–7:00 P.M.—Dinner
7:30–9:00 P.M.—General Session
9:00–9:30 P.M.—Bonfire, singing, testimonies
9:45–10:30 P.M.—Talk-It-Overs (optional)

Monday

7:00–7:30 A.M.—Devotions
7:30–8:30 A.M.—Breakfast
8:30–9:30 A.M.—Workshop Session 4
9:45–11:00 A.M.—Closing General Session/Communion
11:15 A.M.—Farewells/departures (Note: You might consider serving Communion at the Sunday evening General Session rather than Monday morning.)

PROGRAM IDEAS AND SUGGESTIONS

ICEBREAKERS

When using icebreakers with a large group, breaking into groups of 8–12 usually works the best. This allows people to mix, laugh together, and get to know each other by name.

❖ *For more icebreakers, see the Table of Contents.*

• **Stay between the Lines**

In teams of 8–12 people, have each team count off (1, 2, 3, etc.) and stand between two lines (drawn or marked with tape on floor) placed 18 inches apart. Each team member keeps the same number throughout the game.

As a leader calls two or more numbers, the people having the numbers are to trade places without falling or stepping on or outside the lines. If numbers "3" and "10" are called, then the people with those numbers (within each team) trade places. As the game progresses, three or four numbers are called at a time. The team with the most people still standing inside the lines after a designated amount of time is declared the winner.

- **Human Knots**

Have each team of 8-12 stand in a tight circle. Everyone then joins hands with two other team members, *but not with the persons standing next to them.* (Each team is soon a tangled mess of arms and hands.) With a stopwatch running, everyone tries to untangle and form a complete circle—without ever letting go of the hands they started with. The fastest team wins.

- **Pass the Piece of Purple Paper**

Each team forms a line. The person at one end passes objects to the other end. (Suggestions: paper plate, bright blue balloon, tiny toy truck, piece of purple paper, or anything else that could easily become a tongue twister.) While passing this object, each person states his or her name, the name of the preceding person, and the object's name. For example, "My name is Chris, this is Anjali, and this is a piece of purple paper." As soon as an object reaches the other end, the first person passes another one. The first team to complete passing all the items down the entire line wins.

- **Well, I've Never . . .**

This can be an entertaining way for adults to get to know more about each other. Give each person as many beans as there are team members. For example, if there are 12, each person would have 12 beans. One at a time, each person states one thing he or she has *never* done (traveled outside the country, flown a plane, met a President, etc.). Others who have done it give the individual one bean. Whoever runs out of beans first (or has the least beans) wins as the most adventurous.

- **Let's Build**

Give each team one sheet of paper (81/2" x 11") and an equal stack of 3" x 3" paper squares. The object is to see which team can build the highest, self-supported item within a three minute limit. (Optional: Give each team a pair of scissors and a roll of scotch tape.)

WORKSHOP SESSIONS

Workshops need to reflect the wide range of ages and interests of those attending. As topics and speakers are decided, take time to analyze the choices. Would I find something appealing in each time slot if I were a man? a woman? never married? a single parent? divorced? widowed? Because new people attend each year, it may be helpful to include divorce and grief recovery, single parenting, self-esteem, and sexuality workshops each year.

Suggested workshop topics to consider:

Finding God's Will	Cooking for One
Friendship Factor	Stress Management
Single Parenting	Divorce Recovery
Grief Recovery	Dating As Adults
Financial Planning	Car/Home Maintenance
Personality Types	Interpersonal Relationships
Great Devotions	Sex and the Single Adult
Great Prayer Times	Spiritual Formation
Journaling	Self-Esteem
Time Management	Marketplace Christianity

GENERAL SESSIONS

Content of the general sessions and morning devotions will be determined by the conference theme. A special speaker does the general sessions and Planning Team members lead the morning devotions. Select a conference theme based on the needs of your area singles. Here are a few suggestions:

Surviving and Thriving in a Post-Christian Society
God: A Present Help
A Love Affair with God
Running the Race
Successfully Single

SPECIAL FEATURES

Afternoon activities need to be light. Most people struggle to stay awake in meetings or workshops scheduled right after lunch.

- **Wacky Olympics**

These non-athletic, fun activities allow most people to participate. "Olympics" include three-legged races, water balloon toss, "plunger ball" (use a plunger as the bat with a rubber ball), and other creative relays.

Teams compete for prizes. Prizes might include different colored ribbons with self-adhesive strips, bookmarks, wrapped candies, certificates, first place in next meal line, etc. Try to acknowledge all participants in some way. Use your creative genius!!

• Talk-It-Overs

Talk-It-Overs (TIOs) are optional discussion/support groups, offered during free times or late evenings. Their purpose is to provide a setting where individuals receive support, encouragement, and help as they discuss a particular topic or need. Discussion leaders need to be knowledgeable about the topic and selected in advance. (Area pastors or counselors may make very good TIO leaders.) Design the TIOs to meet your group's needs and interests. Consider TIOs based on situations (never-married, divorced, widowed, single parent, etc.) and interests (personal outreach, specific hobby, etc.) Scheduling TIOs early in the retreat can be a good way for people to connect with others of like interests.

• Talent Hour

Most people like an opportunity to share their talents and abilities. During the registration process, have people indicate their interest in participating in the Talent Hour. To control content and better plan the evening, consider screening what people intend to do or provide appropriate material (skits, etc.) for them to choose from. Talent may include drama, magic, instrumental or vocal music, clean comedy, etc.

Once you've held several annual retreats, consider having a spoof "funeral" for those who have "departed from the wonderful world of singleness." This is meant to be fun, even ridiculous. Begin with "wailers" entering the room with lit candles and their heads covered with sheets, blankets, etc. Their conversations and comments about the "departed" can cause many good laughs. ("Poor Joe. Now he can't drink orange juice straight from the carton!")

Be creative as this "service" is planned. Keep the tone of this act on the light side and sensitive to any who may have recently lost a loved one through death.

• Comic Facial Make-over

This activity involves four people—two make-up artists and two models. The make-up artists stand behind the models and, without looking at them, apply the models' make-up. Be sure to cover the models with capes and have make-up remover available. Select participants prior to the retreat and make sure they do NOT practice! For additional laughs, include both men and women.

Here's a variation. Place a sheet around the models and seat them in front of a large sheet or curtain. The people applying the makeup stand immediately behind the models and put their hands through slits in the curtain so it appears as though their arms are those of the models. This adds to the slapstick humor as it looks like the model is applying the makeup in a very messy fashion.

NEW FRIENDSHIPS

An important aspect of any singles event is to meet new friends. Here are some ideas to get people connected.

• Table Captains

Round tables at meals encourage more interaction. At each table, have a preselected Table Captain to help facilitate introductions, guide discussion, and make people feel welcome and cared for. Table Captains remain at the same table and everyone else shifts at each meal. To ensure this mixing, assign persons to tables by birth date (or month), birth order, favorite color, color of paper drawn as they enter the room, or some other creative method.

To aid discussion, distribute copies of Resource 1, "Table-Talk Questions" (page 123), to all Table Captains. An excellent source for questions is *201 Great Questions* by Jerry D. Jones (NavPress, Colorado Springs, 1988).

• Birthday Club

If you use this idea, make sure it is announced early in the weekend. Distribute copies of Resource 2 (top half of page 124). Have interested people complete the form and place it in a box. Before the retreat ends, each person who submits a form draws one from the box. He or she stays in contact with the person on the form throughout the year with prayer, encouragement, and birthday greetings.

• Mug Exchange

To make the Mug Exchange work, this information must be included in the confirmation letter concerning "what to bring."

Interested participants bring a mug from home. Distribute copies of Resource 3 (bottom of page 124) and have each person complete it and place it inside the mug. The mug is put into a brown lunch sack and placed in a barrel (box). Following one meal (perhaps Sunday dinner), each person who placed a mug in the barrel takes a mug and then finds the person whose mug they have selected. This helps insure that partners meet face to face.

The mug is kept by the one who selects it as a reminder to pray for and to send occasional greetings to the person who brought the mug.

EQUIPMENT/SUPPLIES (To be furnished by the event leaders)

- [ ] Items needed for icebreakers (refer to descriptions on pages 115 and 116)
- [ ] Items needed for Wacky Olympics events (refer to page 116)
- [ ] Items needed for registration (pens, tape, paper clips, envelopes, stapler, etc.)
- [ ] Blank "Birthday Club" forms (page 124)
- [ ] Box for "Birthday Club" forms
- [ ] Blank "Mug Exchange" forms (page 124)
- [ ] Brown lunch sacks for "Mug Exchange"
- [ ] Barrel or large box for "Mug Exchange"
- [ ] Copy of Resource 1 for each Table Captain
- [ ] Prizes for icebreakers, games, and Wacky Olympics

WHAT TO BRING (To be provided by participants)

- [ ] Bible
- [ ] Notebook/journal
- [ ] Bedding (depending on the facility being used)
- [ ] Informal clothes and swimsuits
- [ ] Alarm clock
- [ ] Favorite table game (optional)
- [ ] Toiletries
- [ ] Gym shoes
- [ ] Mug for exchange (optional)

PLANNING THE EVENT

PLANNING TEAM

For this event, you need an Event Director (possibly an Assistant Event Director) and volunteers to take responsibilities for the event site, budget, publicity, printed materials, registration, speaker, music, food, recreation, transportation, and equipment/supplies. In addition to the above Planning Team, recruit a Table Captain Coordinator and a Talent Night Coordinator.

Table Captain Coordinator (Refer to Small-Group Coordinator, page 247): Understands the value of interaction, getting people acquainted and hospitality in a retreat setting. Can recruit and organize all Table Captains for this event.

Talent Night Coordinator: Motivates and challenges people to show off their talent. Has a sense for what makes a good program. Organizes the retreat Talent Night.

Because this event is designed to be done by more than one church, make sure that the planning team consists of participants from some or all of the churches involved. This allows the various participating churches to have a greater sense of ownership and responsibility for the event.

❖
The more people who have ownership and involvement in the planning, the greater success you will have.

Planning Timeline

Event: *A Gathering of Christian Singles*   **Date of event:** _____

Event Director: _____   **Phone:** _____

Thanks for agreeing to serve on our retreat Planning Team. Please check over this timeline for your assigned task(s). Adapt as needed and supplement with information in the generic job descriptions. Highlight your tasks (and due dates) and mark your calendar accordingly.

Date: _____ 1 YEAR IN ADVANCE

Event Director (page 226)

☐ Recruit a Planning Team.
☐ Meet with the Planning Team to brainstorm ideas and adapt this event to fit your ministry goals and objectives.
☐ Distribute copies of this timeline and related job descriptions. Make sure team members understand their assigned responsibilities. Adapt timeline as needed.
☐ Discuss possible locations, workshops, speakers, musicians, etc. Select a theme.

Event Site Coordinator (page 234)

☐ Select and reserve a retreat site.
☐ Secure meeting rooms for the general sessions and workshops as well as the game events such as icebreakers and Wacky Olympics. (Sometimes, one open, flexible room will work for both.)
☐ Once the site is confirmed, place the dates and location on the church calendar (plus give this information to all Planning Team members/churches).

Date: _____ 9 TO 10 MONTHS IN ADVANCE

Speaker/Workship Leaders Coordinator (page 250)

☐ Start searching for a general session speaker and workshop leaders. Discuss expectations, retreat theme, fees, dates, etc.

☐ Once confirmed, send an agreement to each for his or her signature.
☐ Work with the general session speaker to finalize topics to be addressed. Suggest several possible specific issues—but allow the speaker some flexibility.
☐ Determine the number of workshop topics based on the expected number of participants and the number of meeting rooms available. For groups of 75 or less, provide two or three options for each time slot. For retreats with more people, offer four or five options per session. For suggested topics see page 116. Plan to repeat popular workshops in two or three time slots.

Music Coordinator (page 237)

☐ Determine what kind of music is needed and select the Worship Leader. If possible, find one person who can lead worship, congregational singing, and also provide "special music."
☐ Begin contacting potential musicians.

Date: _____ 7 TO 8 MONTHS IN ADVANCE

Event Director

☐ Meet with the Planning Team to ensure that established objectives (see page 114) are being incorporated into this event.

Budget Coordinator (page 229)

☐ With the Planning Team, begin estimating costs for the event.

Food Coordinator (page 236)

☐ Determine the number of meals, snacks, and other refreshments needed. Inform the Event Site Coordinator, who will communicate with the retreat site facility.

❖ *For more ideas and help, refer to job descriptions beginning on page 225.*

Publicity Coordinator (page 238)

- [ ] Once the event theme, location, general session speaker, and at least some of the workshop leaders have been determined, begin preparing flyers, brochures, and other printed promotional material.
- [ ] If the Mug Exchange is planned, communicate this information in the promotion and/or in the confirmation letter.
- [ ] Work with the Registration Coordinator.

Date:	5-6 MONTHS
	IN ADVANCE

Publicity Coordinator

- [ ] Begin promoting the event. Mail or deliver brochures to all known singles groups in the area, inviting them to attend.
- [ ] Have a representative at all major area singles functions to promote the event.
- [ ] Recruit assistants from sponsoring churches/areas to help with promotion.

Registration Coordinator (page 241)

- [ ] Establish registration procedures and deadline. Begin registration.
- [ ] If scholarship funds are available, supply the application forms now (see sample form on page 246).
- [ ] Since a talent night production is part of this event, include this information on the registration form. Have participants indicate their interest and proposed act.

Speaker/Workshop Leaders Coordinator

- [ ] Make sure a signed agreement from the speaker and each workshop leader is on file and any deposits have been paid.

Music Coordinator

- [ ] Obtain signed agreement(s) from musicians and check payment of deposits.
- [ ] Determine the type of sound equipment that is needed.

Table Captain Coordinator (pages 118 and 248)

- [ ] Begin gathering a team of individuals who will facilitate discussion at meal times.

Date:	3 MONTHS
	IN ADVANCE

Event Director

- [ ] Meet with the Planning Team to discuss progress.
- [ ] Establish schedule for the weekend.
- [ ] Select three Planning Team members to provide morning devotions at the retreat.

Publicity Coordinator

- [ ] Use funny skits to help promote the event at area Sunday school classes.
- [ ] Have publicity assistants do the same in their churches/area.
- [ ] Promote through area church bulletins.

Registration Coordinator

- [ ] Continue registration. Remind people of registration and scholarship deadlines.

Table Captain Coordinator

- [ ] Continue selecting table captains who will facilitate discussion at meal times.
- [ ] Become familiar with the suggested list of discussion starters (Resource 1 on page 123). Add to or adapt these as desired.

Transportation Coordinator (page 252)

- [ ] Determine the best modes of transportation for this event.
- [ ] Begin making plans.

Recreation Coordinator (page 240)

- [ ] Plan various activities for the weekend based on those available at the event site or in the host city. Plan to include both physical and non-physical activities.

- [ ] Select individuals to be responsible for special activities throughout the weekend, such as 5K run/walk, Wacky Olympics, fishing derby, softball game, late-night volleyball, etc.
- [ ] Check on availablity of all equipment.

Talent Night Coordinator

- [ ] Develop the initial arrangements for Talent Night. Talent will be presented by those in attendance.
- [ ] Determine who will emcee this event. The musician often does a good job. But determine this based on the abilities represented by those involved.

Event Site Coordinator

- [ ] With the facility, select a location for the Sunday night bonfire. (If this is not possible to do outdoors, consider a fireplace or some other indoor "bonfire" option.)

Speaker Coordinator

- [ ] Recruit people to serve as Talk-It-Over leaders. Consider workshop leaders, area pastors, counselors, or some of the more spiritually mature retreat registrants.
- [ ] Develop an initial list of possible Talk-It-Overs (see page 123).

Date: _____ **2 MONTHS IN ADVANCE**

Equipment/Supplies Coordinator (page 233)

- [ ] Work with the Planning Team to make sure all necessary equipment/supply items arrive at the retreat site as needed.

Audio/Visual Equipment Coordinator (page 228)

- [ ] Work with the Event Site Coordinator regarding audio/video needs for the workshops, program, and general sessions.

Music Coordinator

- [ ] Confirm travel and lodging arrangements for the musician(s).
- [ ] Plan a worship service for Sunday morning. Finalize worship leaders.
- [ ] Coordinate with the Event Coordinator, who will be responsible for serving Communion and related details.

Talent Night Coordinator

- [ ] Finalize Talent Night details.
- [ ] Make sure each performer will bring own equipment and props.

Speaker Coordinator

- [ ] Review plans with the speaker and workshop leaders. Assist as needed.
- [ ] Confirm travel and lodging arrangements.

Registration Coordinator

- [ ] Scholarship applications are now due (or will be soon). Send them to the proper authority for approval.
- [ ] Inform applicants of awarded funds.
- [ ] Order name tags and name tag jackets.

Date: _____ **1 MONTH IN ADVANCE**

Publicity Coordinator

- [ ] Make final promotional efforts.
- [ ] Contact publicity assistants to see what they can do to help in their area/church for a final promotional push.

Registration Coordinator

- [ ] Close preregistration at the deadline. All pre-registration payments/deposits should now be due.
- [ ] As the weekend approaches, contact the Event Site Coordinator to adjust attendance figures as needed.
- [ ] Begin preparing the final letter to registrants. (A sample letter is found on page 244. Adapt as needed for your event.)

Event Materials Coordinator

☐ Have event schedule, table captain materials, maps, final letter to registrants, and any other copied material ready for assembly and/or mailing.

Table Captain Coordinator

☐ Finalize plans with Table Captains. Ask them to attend a brief training time two hours ahead of the retreat start time.
☐ Determine and prepare icebreakers as needed for the retreat.
☐ Recruit other Table Captains to help lead and organize the icebreakers.
☐ Gather needed materials for each icebreaker.

Speaker Coordinator

☐ Finalize and confirm Talk-It-Over leaders and sessions.

Date: _____	**2 WEEKS IN ADVANCE**

Registration Coordinator

☐ Contact the Event Site Coordinator again to adjust attendance figures as needed.
☐ Mail informational packets to those going on the retreat. Work on this with Event Materials Coordinator.

Budget Coordinator

☐ Prepare checks to pay speaker, workshop leaders, musician(s), and other expenses pertaining to the retreat. Have checks ready to disburse during the retreat.

Date: _____	**1 WEEK IN ADVANCE**

Event Director

☐ Make certain that each participating church office (and key staff members) have the event emergency telephone numbers where participants can be reached.

☐ Meet with the Planning Team to cover any last-minute details and make final checks on all other arrangements.

Registration Coordinator

☐ Start preparing name tags. Make room assignments.

Event Site Coordinator

☐ Confirm all arrangements with the event facility.

Food Coordinator

☐ Send the final number of registrants to the food preparation person at the event site.

Transportation Coordinator

☐ Confirm all drivers and provide them with maps to the event location. (If helpful, also provide a list of passengers and points of departure.)

Date: _____	**2 HOURS IN ADVANCE**

Event Director

☐ Meet briefly with the Planning Team for final details and prayer.

Table Captain Coordinator

☐ Meet with all the Table Captains for a 30-45 minute training session. Go over "Small-Group Facilitor Guidelines" (page 248) and "Table-Talk Questions" (Resource 1, page 123).

Date: _____	**2 TO 4 WEEKS AFTER EVENT**

☐ See the "Followup Guidelines" on page 254.

Table-Talk Questions

What is your number one goal for the next year? For the next five years?

What has been the most enjoyable vacation you've ever taken? Why?

If you could vacation (or travel) anyplace in the world, where would you go?

What are your hobbies?

What is your concept of the ideal mate? Do you know someone who has a mate like this? Or is it just an unrealistic fantasy?

What do you feel is the greatest challenge in forming and maintaining relationships?

Is it possible to establish and maintain a "best friend" relationship with a person of the opposite sex? If so, how?

What is the biggest advantage of being single?

What is the biggest disadvantage of being single?

On a scale of 1-10, (1=Let's not talk about it; 10=I love it!) where are you in accepting your singleness?

If you could be with either the most attractive person in the world, or the most intelligent, which one would you choose and why?

If you could change one thing in your life, what would it be?

When do you feel most loved?

What is the funniest thing that has happened to you this past year?

Describe a recent time when you felt God's presence in a special way.

What is it about you today that your high school classmates would have least expected?

What is one thing you are doing with your life that you probably could not do if you were married?

Do you think there is really anything to birth order theories? Explain.

What was your favorite animal/pet as a child? What is your favorite as an adult?

What aspect of your potential do you think you have least realized/accomplished?

If you were going to totally change your career, what would you do?

Which of your grade school memories is the strongest? Why?

What made you decide to come to this retreat?

Birthday Club

It's a proven fact that we each have one birthday a year!

Everyone needs encouragement from time to time, and hearing from a friend is always a welcome blessing.

Since we all like receiving friendly mail, do the friendly thing by filling out the following information and dropping it in the nearest (and only) birthday box, located in the dining hall.

NAME: _____ BIRTHDAY: _____

(Year optional)

ADDRESS: _____

CITY: _____ STATE: _____ ZIP: _____

List any other special times when a word of encouragement would help:

Before the end of the retreat, each person who completes one of these forms will draw a "Birthday Club" form from the "Birthday Box." Then it is up to you to encourage the person whose name you draw over the next year—especially at birthday time!!

Mug Exchange
Information Form

NAME: _____ BIRTHDAY: _____

(Year optional)

ADDRESS: _____ PHONE: _____

CITY: _____ STATE: _____ ZIP: _____

Tell a little about yourself (work, where you grew up, favorite color, etc.)

Please share some needs that your prayer partner can help you pray about this year.

Please complete this form, place it inside your mug, then wrap and place the mug in the "Mug Barrel."

14 A COMMUNITY OF CARING

A Mini-Vacation Getaway with Friends

Event Summary: A weekend getaway that provides an opportunity for singles to vacation with other Christian singles, focusing more on fun, rest, and play and less on teaching and study. A great way for singles to build relationships in a relaxed environment.

Length of Event: Friday–Monday

Suggested Theme Verse: "Carry each other's burdens." Galatians 6:2

Ideal Number of Participants: 50+

Estimated Cost Per Person: $80–$140

Facility Requirements: Vacation-setting conference center, resort, or mountain lodge

Recommended Planning Team: 12–15 people

Advance Planning Needed: Approximately 6–12 months

INTRODUCTION

by Charles Roberts
Minister of Singles
Peachtree Presbyterian Church
Atlanta, Georgia

Over the years this has been one of our most popular single-adult outings and is fast becoming a tradition in our ministry. We always select a holiday weekend (usually Memorial day), which allows us a little extra time to travel, spend more time together, and enjoy a wider variety of destinations and activities. For simplicity and comfort, we usually select a lake or ocean resort setting. This provides an exciting, relaxing, fun getaway.

This weekend can be a wonderful time to discover new leadership as people show initiative, helpful attitudes, kindness, and character.

There are few things we do each year that are more effective in being a memory-maker and in creating a sense of community.

THE BIG EVENT

SCHEDULE

Friday

7:00–8:00 P.M.—Arrival
8:00–9:30 P.M.—Welcome, overview of weekend, ice-breakers, and refreshments
9:30–11:30 P.M.—Informal, late-night conversations

Saturday

8:15 A.M.—Breakfast
9:00–10:00 A.M.—Program (see below)
10:00–10:30 A.M.—Refreshment break
10:30 A.M.–12:00 P.M.—Program (continued)
1:00–5:00 P.M.—Lunch and unstructured activities
6:00 P.M.—Dinner
7:30 P.M.—Free time

> ❖ **Get as many people as possible involved in the planning of this event.**

OBJECTIVES

❖ To enable single adults to build a sense of community during an inexpensive weekend vacation with other singles.

❖ To challenge single adults spiritually and to give them an opportunity to rest and play.

Sunday

8:30 A.M.—Worship (If possible, do this in an outdoor setting such as on the beach.)
9:30 A.M.—Breakfast
10:00–5:00 P.M.—Beach or sports (lunch on your own)
6:00-9:00 P.M.—Dinner and entertainment

Monday

9:30 A.M.—Breakfast
11:00 A.M.—Checkout

PROGRAM IDEAS AND SUGGESTIONS

BANDANNAS

Have a bandanna for everyone. The bandannas will be used during the Trust Walk on Saturday morning. If possible, have your weekend logo, theme, and dates printed on the bandannas. These become a nice keepsake to remember the weekend.

ICEBREAKERS (FRIDAY)

• Quaker Questions

Have each person answer these questions:
1. Where did you live when you where age 12?
2. What was winter like there?
3. How was your home heated?
4. What was the emotional center of warmth in your home then?
5. How old were you when God first became more than just a word to you?

• Test Your Intuition

Have people in each small group pair up, look into the eyes of their partner, and try to guess—without any help—answers to the following questions. (Think of more questions.)
1. In what state was this person born?
2. What kind of car does he drive?
3. Has she received a speeding ticket in the past five years?
4. Does he sing in the shower?

5. When she is driving, what type of music does she listen to?

After both partners have guessed their answers, see who had the best intuition.

SATURDAY, 9:00–10:00 A.M.

• **Trust Walk.** Have everyone pair off, then take turns being blindfolded and guided by their partner as they walk around—to illustrate what it means to TRUST another person.

• **Bamboo Barrier.** Divide into groups of eight to ten people and face the challenge of getting over a barrier. Place a piece of bamboo (or a 2 x 4, a long stick, or a piece of rope) between two supports (for example, chairs stacked on top of each other) about five or six feet off the ground. Have each group figure out a way to get everyone over the barrier without touching it, moving it, or going under it! Learn a lot about teamwork!

> ❖ **For more icebreakers, see the Table of Contents.**

Possible discussion questions:
1. What did it feel like to have a difficult barrier facing you?
2. How did it feel to need someone's help to get over it?
3. How did it feel to help others get over the barrier?

• **Talk: Becoming the Body of Christ.** Next, offer a talk about the need for Christian community, based on Galatians 6:2 and Romans 12:15. Keep it simple, asking people to respond with what they learned about themselves based on their experiences that day. Point out that the purpose of the entire group is to become the Body of Christ!

10–10:30 A.M., REFRESHMENT BREAK

10:30 A.M.–12:00 P.M.

• **Roleplay the Good Samaritan.** Read the story of the good Samaritan (Luke 10:25-37) and give people the opportunity to act it out.

Identify three distinct roles:

1. The one who was hurt: If you have ever felt a specific hurt in your life that has not yet healed, go to the center of the room and lie down.

2. The Samaritan: If you feel helpful, full of love and compassion, go to one side of the room.

3. The innkeeper: If you feel full of kind words, faith, and prayers, go to the other side of the room.

Before asking people to move to one part of the room, give them three to five minutes to think about which role best fits them. After everyone has made a choice and moved, instruct the Samaritans to go to the wounded, help them up, and take them to an innkeeper, who offers a prayer for them. If the majority are in the center of the room, read II Corinthians 1 together. Talk about the compassion that we have received and the importance of caring for one another. Once everyone has been helped, close by singing "Amazing Grace."

SATURDAY NIGHT

Organized Games and Activities

Plan a large group activity for Saturday night. Ideas include skits written and "auditioned" by those at the event. Plan a scavenger hunt, and provide prizes. Activities may include a golf tournament, tennis tournament, snorkeling, fishing, cruising, bike riding, or jogging.

Another idea for Saturday night would be to have a large puzzle for the entire group to put together. In advance of the event, have an artistically inclined person do a large, colorful painting of something that represents your group or church. It could be the theme of your weekend, a benediction that your church uses every Sunday, the logo of your singles ministry, or a Scripture passage. The larger this painting is, the better.

Once the painting is done, cut it into as many pieces as you expect people to attend. Then have everyone help put this puzzle together again. Once the puzzle is complete, have everyone take a piece of it as a reminder of the weekend together.

EQUIPMENT/SUPPLIES (To be furnished by the event leaders)

- ☐ Games, recreational gear
- ☐ Refreshments (if not provided by the facility)
- ☐ Prizes to be awarded
- ☐ Bandannas for everyone

WHAT TO BRING (To be provided by participants)

- ☐ Sleeping bag or bedding (if needed)
- ☐ Toiletries
- ☐ Bible, pen, notebook
- ☐ Spending money for free time
- ☐ (Optional) Guitar
- ☐ Swimsuit
- ☐ Suntan lotion
- ☐ Beach blanket
- ☐ (Optional) Gear for snorkeling, golf, tennis, etc.
- ☐ Tennis shoes

PLANNING THE EVENT

PLANNING TEAM

For this event, you need an Event Director (possibly an Assistant Event Director) and volunteers to take responsibilities for the event site, budget, food, publicity, event materials, registration, small groups, music, worship, recreation, transportation, audio/visual equipment, and equipment/supplies. In addition, you may want to consider including a bus captain and an artist (for the large puzzle) on your Planning Team.

❖ *The more people who have ownership and involvement in the planning, the greater success you will have.*

Planning Timeline

Event: *A Community of Caring*   **Date of event:** _____

Event Director: _____   **Phone:** _____

Thanks for agreeing to serve on our Planning Team. Please check over this timeline for the task(s) assigned to you. Adapt as needed. Highlight your tasks (and due dates) each time they appear. Mark your calendar accordingly.

Date: _____ **6 TO 9 MONTHS IN ADVANCE**

Event Director (page 226)

☐ Recruit a Planning Team and brainstorm ideas. Adapt this weekend event to fit your particular ministry goals and objectives.
☐ Make sure each team member understands his or her responsibilities.
☐ Determine if this timeline will work and make adjustments accordingly.

Event Site Coordinator (page 234)

☐ Select and reserve a retreat site.
☐ Put the date on the church calendar.

Date: _____ **5 MONTHS IN ADVANCE**

Food Coordinator (page 236)

☐ Plan meals and snacks for the weekend. Negotiate the cost.

Transportation Coordinator (page 252)

☐ Determine the best mode of transportation. Make any rental arrangements now.

Budget Coordinator (page 229)

☐ Along with the Planning Team, develop a working budget for the event.

Publicity Coordinator (page 238)

☐ Begin collecting the information needed for a brochure.

Date: _____ **4 MONTHS IN ADVANCE**

Publicity Coordinator

☐ Have your promotional piece printed and distributed in your church.
☐ Begin promoting the event through the church bulletin.

Event Site Coordinator

☐ Confirm your arrangements with the event site.

Date: _____ **3 MONTHS IN ADVANCE**

Event Director

☐ Meet with the Planning Team to discuss progress.
☐ Establish a schedule for the weekend.
☐ Recruit someone to lead the program on Saturday morning.

Music Coordinator (page 237)

☐ Recruit musicians for the event.

Publicity Coordinator

☐ Take the publicity packet to each singles Sunday school class to promote the event. Be creative.

Registration Coordinator (page 241)

☐ Begin the registration process.

Recreation Coordinator (page 240)

☐ Begin organizing icebreakers, games, and activities.
☐ Determine if prizes will be awarded, and the criteria for each.
☐ Recruit an artist to do the large puzzle.

❖ *For more ideas and help, refer to job descriptions beginning on page 225.*

Equipment/Supplies Coordinator (page 233)

☐ Check with the Planning Team for any equipment/supplies that are needed.
☐ Make arrangements to buy, borrow, or rent items as needed.

Event Materials Coordinator (page 233)

☐ Check with the Planning Team for any printed materials needed for event.
☐ Make arrangements to have any such materials printed.
☐ Determine the art work for the bandannas. Order enough bandannas for everyone expected to attend.

Bus Captains Coordinator (page 231)

☐ If buses or vans are to be used, arrange for Bus Captains.

| Date: _____ | **2 MONTHS IN ADVANCE** |

Event Director

☐ Meet with the Planning Team to check on progress.

Audio/Visual Equipment Coordinator (page 228)

☐ Communicate with the facility regarding needs for the event.

Music Coordinator

☐ Work with musicians to prepare all music for the event.

Worship Coordinator (page 251)

☐ Recruit people to plan a worship service for Sunday morning.
☐ If desired, arrange to serve communion.

Small-Group Coordinator (page 247)

☐ Recruit small-group facilitators as needed.

| Date: _____ | **1 MONTH IN ADVANCE** |

Registration Coordinator

☐ Make last-minute appeals for registration.
☐ Provide an estimated attendance figure to the Planning Team and to the facility.
☐ Set up a roommate list.

Recreation Coordinator

☐ Have any prizes selected and ready.

Food Coordinator

☐ Begin purchasing food as necessary, and recruit helpers as needed.
☐ Coordinate transportation of food with the Equipment/Supplies Coordinator.

Transportation Coordinator

☐ Finalize all transportation plans.

Equipment/Supplies Coordinator

☐ Arrange for transportation of all equipment and supplies.

Event Materials Coordinator

☐ Prepare informational packets and deliver them to the Registration Coordinator.
☐ Have other needed materials printed for the event (including bandannas).

| Date: _____ | **1 WEEK IN ADVANCE** |

Registration Coordinator

☐ Distribute informational packets to those going on the retreat.

| Date: _____ | **2 TO 4 WEEKS AFTER EVENT** |

☐ See the "Followup Guidelines" on page 254.

HOW EFFECTIVE IS OUR SINGLES MINISTRY?

A Time to Evaluate and Look Ahead

Event Summary: A 24-hour leadership retreat that challenges participants to evaluate the singles ministry and to set goals for the year ahead. It is designed to help your leadership team gain new insight and ideas for how to build a sense of "family" in your group as well as to have a more effective ministry with single adults in your church and community.

Length of Event: Friday evening–Saturday evening

Suggested Theme Verse: "Let them give thanks to the Lord for his unfailing love and his wonderful deeds for men. Let them sacrifice thank offerings and tell of his works with songs of joy." Psalm 107:21, 22

Ideal Number of Participants: All of the leadership team

Estimated Cost Per Person: $15–$50, depending on facility chosen

Facility Requirements: Retreat center or church

Recommended Planning Team: 3–6 people

Advance Planning Needed: Approximately 6 months

INTRODUCTION

by Dr. Paul M. Petersen
Senior Pastor
Westminster Presbyterian Church
Aurora, Illinois

In her book, *Fashion Me a People*, Maria Harris begins with the task of *koinonia* (community), rather than with teaching or worship, because she feels community-building is the initial educational ministry of the church.

If the task of building fellowship or community in the local church is critically important, it is an even higher priority in Single Adult Ministry, because one of the differentiating factors of a single adult versus married ministry is the need to create a non-matrimonial, non-nuclear, non-biological family. This is a need that the church is uniquely designed to meet, but often does not.

This 24-hour leadership retreat—using Harris's book as a springboard—is designed to provide both community and an evaluation process for your leadership team. In a Single Adult Ministry, evaluation of past ministry is critical for two reasons. The first is the same as any successful church ministry: the need to learn from and improve on past experience, to build a more effective ministry, to correct mistakes, as well as celebrate successes. Secondly, since Single Adult Ministry is relatively new in many churches, there is a limited history to compare or contrast against.

This retreat can help your leadership team gain new insight and ideas for how to build a sense of "family" in your group—to have a more effective ministry with single adults in your church and community.

OBJECTIVES

❖ To encourage single adult leaders to:
  1) build a sense of community;
  2) help singles feel more welcomed and included in your church;
  3) evaluate their past programs and ministries; and,
  4) set objectives and goals for the future.

THE BIG EVENT

SCHEDULE

Friday

8:00 P.M.—Gather at retreat site
8:30 P.M.—Community-Building Exercise:
  Resource 1

❖
Get as many people as possible involved in the planning of this event.

Saturday

8:00 A.M.—Breakfast
8:45 A.M.—Personal prayer and devotions
9:15 A.M.—Presentation of "Six Tasks for Community"
10:00 A.M.—Evaluation Exercise: Resource 2
11:45 A.M.—Lunch break, free time
2:00 P.M.—Individual Goal Setting: Resource 3
5:00 P.M.—Dinner break
6:30 P.M.—Group Goal Setting: Resource 4
7:30 P.M.—Worship
8:00 P.M.—Dismiss

PROGRAM IDEAS AND SUGGESTIONS

If your leadership team numbers eight or larger, divide into groups of four or five. It is best to remain in the same small groups throughout the retreat.

SESSION 1

Friday Night, 8:30 P.M.–10:00 P.M.

Goals: That new, deeper friendships among the leadership team would begin.

That the leaders are challenged to step back and look at the ministry with new eyes, new perspectives.

Use Resource 1, "Inclusion Questionnaire," (pages 135 and 136) as a tool to get discussions started about group members' involvement in your church. After each person has completed the questionnaire, discuss the

results and the responses to the Resource 1 questions in each small group.

SESSION 2

Saturday Morning, 9:15 A.M.–11:45 A.M.

Goals: Help each leader establish their personal ministry goals.

Help the group build a strong sense of community.

It is required that the leader of this 24-hour retreat read Maria Harris's book, *Fashion Me a People: Curriculum in the Church*—in particular those sections referred to in the footnotes of this event. The material on her six tasks for a healthy community need to be understood, developed, and presented Saturday morning from 9:15–10:00.

Use Resource 2, "Evaluation Questions," (page 137) as your guide. Continue meeting in the same small groups.

SESSION 3

Saturday Afternoon, 2:00 P.M.–4:30 P.M.

Goal: Set goals for 6–12 months to improve individual ministry areas.

This is "free time" for individuals to pray, ponder, and write down goals for their own ministry and life, using Resources 3 and 4 (pages 138 and 139).

SESSION 4

Saturday Evening, 6:30 P.M.–7:30 P.M.

Goal: Set some key goals for 6–12 months for the entire Single Adult Ministry.

Based on the work done in sessions two and three, and using Resources 3 and 4, establish goals for the ministry as a whole. Come back together so each small group can report to the large group. If the various

❖
For a list of icebreakers, see the Table of Contents.

small group goals are compatible, move forward with your goals for the year! If they are too diverse, agree on a way to prioritize, deciding which goal should be tackled first, second, third, etc.

WORSHIP SERVICE

Saturday Evening, 7:30 P.M.–8:00 P.M.

Use this time as a celebration of your ministry together, and as a time to commit to prayer the goals you have agreed on.

Suggested Order of Service

❖ Sing two or three familiar songs.
❖ Read a Psalm about God's presence, such as Psalm 106 or 107.
❖ Pray in small groups, asking for God's presence with your ministry.
❖ Read a New Testament passage dealing with community, such as Ephesians 4.
❖ Pray a benediction, asking for God's blessing upon your ministry "family" and your goals.

EQUIPMENT/SUPPLIES (To be furnished by the event leaders)

☐ Book: *Fashion Me a People: Curriculum in the Church* by Maria Harris (Louisville, Kentucky: Westminster/John Knox Press, 1989)
☐ Photocopies of Resources 1-4 (pages 135-139)
☐ Newsprint and markers (optional)
☐ Snacks

WHAT TO BRING (To be provided by participants)

☐ Bible, notebook, pen/pencil
☐ Casual dress
☐ Overnight toiletries (if staying overnight somewhere other than home, which is recommended for community building)

PLANNING THE EVENT

PLANNING TEAM

For this retreat, you will need an Event Director (and possibly an Assistant Event Director) and volunteers to take responsibility for the event site, registration, budget, transportation, and food.

❖ *The more people who have ownership and involvement in the planning, the greater success you will have.*

Planning Timeline

Event: *How Effective Is Our Singles Ministry?* **Date of event:** _____

Event Director: _____ **Phone:** _____

Thanks for agreeing to serve on our retreat Planning Team. Please check over this timeline for the task(s) assigned to you. Adapt as needed. Supplement this timeline with information on the reproducible, generic job descriptions found on pages 225-252. Highlight your tasks (and due dates) each time they appear. Mark your calendar accordingly.

Date: _____ | **6 MONTHS IN ADVANCE**

Event Director (page 226)

☐ Recruit a Planning Team. Brainstorm ideas, and adapt this weekend event to fit your particular ministry goals and objectives.

☐ Make sure each team member understands his or her assigned tasks and responsibilities.

☐ Determine if this timeline will work for your area and make adjustments accordingly.

☐ Decide who will present the materials and facilitate the discussion times. (It is recommended that one of the pastors or the singles ministry director, who knows the ministry well, do the facilitating.) Whoever is chosen, it is important that that person read the book, *Fashion Me a People: Curriculum in the Church*, by Maria Harris (Louisville, Kentucky: Westminster/John Knox Press, 1989).

Event Site Coordinator (page 234)

☐ With the Planning Team's input, carefully choose a facility for the weekend (your church possibly may be the best place for this event). The facility will set the tone for the event.

☐ Put the dates on the church calendar.

Budget Coordinator (page 229)

☐ Begin estimating costs for the event.

Registration Coordinator (page 241)

☐ Communicate to all your leaders the dates of the event and make sure they know that they are requested or expected to attend.

☐ Prepare scholarship application forms if applicable.

Date: _____ | **5 MONTHS IN ADVANCE**

Budget Coordinator

☐ Finalize budget with the Planning Team.

Date: _____ | **3 MONTHS IN ADVANCE**

❖ *For more ideas and help, refer to job descriptions beginning on page 225.*

Event Director

☐ Meet with the Planning Team to discuss the program schedule, progress of plans, etc.

Event Site Coordinator

☐ Check to be sure a signed contract is on file at the event site and at the church.

☐ Make sure all details are correct.

☐ Verify that a deposit has been paid and received.

Food Coordinator (page 236)

☐ Begin making plans for simple and inexpensive snacks for the weekend. Provide coffee, pop, and juice. Cheese, crackers, cut fruit, and baked goods will go a long way for less money.

☐ Determine what meal arrangements you need to make.

<table>
<tr><td>Date: _____</td><td>

2 Months
in Advance

</td></tr>
</table>

Registration Coordinator

☐ Continue registration. Encourage people to preregister as much as possible.

<table>
<tr><td>Date: _____</td><td>

1 Month
in Advance

</td></tr>
</table>

Event Director

☐ Meet with the Planning Team to discuss all plans for the event. Make sure everything is on schedule.
☐ See to it that whoever is presenting the material has read Harris's book by now.

Registration Coordinator

☐ Sign up those who are planning to attend.
☐ If your ministry team is large so that not everyone knows each other, order name tags and name tag holders.
☐ Secure someone to prepare the name tags one week in advance of the event.
☐ Begin preparing a confirmation letter to registrants. (Adapt the sample letter on page 244 for your group and event.)

Event Site Coordinator

☐ Confirm all plans for the event site.
☐ Send a program schedule to the contact person.
☐ Check details of the payment plan.

Food Coordinator

☐ Finalize plans for meals and refreshments.
☐ Purchase the non-perishables.

Event Materials Coordinator (page 233)

☐ Gather all needed supplies.
☐ Make copies of resources as needed.
☐ Assist Registration Coordinator in preparing the confirmation letter.

<table>
<tr><td>Date: _____</td><td>

1 Week
in Advance

</td></tr>
</table>

Event Director

☐ Meet with the entire Planning Team to discuss all plans and cover any last-minute details.

Registration Coordinator

☐ Give the number of those preregistered to the Event Site, Food, and Event Materials Coordinators.
☐ Mail confirmation letters to the registrants.

Event Site Coordinator

☐ Send out an update on the number of participants expected. Confirm all reservations.
☐ With input from the Planning Team, create and maintain a list of all items and services needed while at the facility. Coordinate these needs with the retreat facility.

Food Coordinator

☐ Confirm all meal and refreshments plans.

<table>
<tr><td>Date: _____</td><td>

2 to 4 Weeks
after Event

</td></tr>
</table>

Event Director

☐ Receive from each ministry team or group a list of the five-month objectives for each ministry area. For the next five months, followup each month to check on progress and accomplishments. Provide help and encouragement as needed.
☐ See the "Followup Guidelines" on page 254.

Inclusion Questionnaire

Fill in this sheet by yourself (it should take only a few minutes). Then share your responses and discuss the questions on the next sheet in your small group.

The following characteristics have been found to be the primary reasons people are attracted to a particular church. Which of these characteristics are the reason you attend your church? Which of these characteristics would be the primary reason you would select a church if you were to move to another city in the next year? Within each column, rank the reasons in order from 1 to 15, with 1 as the most important to you and 15 as the least important.

Reasons I Started Attending My Church	What I'd Look For in Selecting a New Church If I Moved	
_____	_____	The opportunities to participate in community service
_____	_____	Living near the church
_____	_____	The social/fellowship activities of the church
_____	_____	Friends and/or relatives belong to or attend the church
_____	_____	The quality of friendliness and/or concern among members
_____	_____	The quality of the preaching and teaching
_____	_____	The variety of program options
_____	_____	The prestige or status of the church in the local community
_____	_____	A specific program that was available: _____
_____	_____	The opportunities for leadership by members of the church
_____	_____	The quality of pastoral care and concern provided by the church staff
_____	_____	The style of worship in the church
_____	_____	The attention given to children by the church
_____	_____	Other: _____
_____	_____	Other: _____

1. Are there any differences in why you selected your current church and why you would select a new church if you were to move? Please explain.

(Continued)

From FASHION ME A PEOPLE by Maria Harris. © 1989 Maria Harris. Used by permission of Westminster John Knox Press. In addition to Harris's material, the writer has added characteristics particular to Singles Ministry.

2. Think back to when you first began attending this church. What was it that helped you feel included? Please explain.

3. In your opinion, what is the most appealing characteristic about your church to newcomers or visitors? Why?

4. What is the most appealing characteristic about your singles group? Why?

5. What are three things your singles group could do to help it become more appealing to newcomers?

6. What would it take to make those three things happen?

7. What could your group be doing now to help people feel more included?

8. What is one thing you plan to do personally to help enhance the attractiveness of your church's singles ministry in the next six months?

From FASHION ME A PEOPLE by Maria Harris. © 1989 Maria Harris. Used by permission of Westminster John Knox Press. In addition to Harris's material, the writer has added characteristics particular to Singles Ministry.

Evaluation Questions

Continue meeting in the same groups. Write out your answers to questions 1-4. When completed, discuss them in your small group. After each person answers, allow time for your group members to respond and give further input if they desire. They may see things you do not! Then, as a group, brainstorm responses to question 5. Have a "secretary" (chosen by your group) take notes for record keeping and future reference.

1. Specifically, what do you want to accomplish in your particular area of ministry responsibility in the next six months (or year)?

2. Why is this your objective?

3. What are you doing now to help accomplish this objective?

4. What would help you to be better equipped to accomplish this objective?

5. According to author Maria Harris, there are six requirements to developing healthy community. How does your ministry objective (as described above) help fulfill any or all of these six requirements?

AS A PARISH: (a community of believers):
1) **Inclusion** (making people of diverse backgrounds and perspectives feel welcomed and included):

2) **Leadership** (making many leadership opportunities available to a wide variety of people within the congregation):

3) **Outreach** (promoting the Gospel, faith, and social justice beyond the four walls of the church building):

AS A FAMILY: (an intimate community of sojourners):
4) **Presence** (being genuinely and lovingly involved in each other's lives):

5) **Receptivity** (being ready and willing to really listen to one another):

6) **Responsibility** (taking action; responding to one another after you have listened):

Evaluation Questions

Below are the three qualities Maria Harris names as central to a church's life-giving power[2]. As a group, brainstorm five things under each heading you can do to improve your singles ministry. Then choose which one you will implement this month, and which for each of the following four months. (Remember to also include how you plan to implement each one.)

INCLUSION (making people of diverse backgrounds and perspectives
feel welcomed and included):   month

1. _____   _____
2. _____   _____
3. _____   _____
4. _____   _____
5. _____   _____

LEADERSHIP (making many leadership opportunities available to
a wide variety of people within the congregation):   month

1. _____   _____
2. _____   _____
3. _____   _____
4. _____   _____
5. _____   _____

OUTREACH (promoting the Gospel, faith, and social justice beyond
the four walls of the church building):   month

1. _____   _____
2. _____   _____
3. _____   _____
4. _____   _____
5. _____   _____

From FASHION ME A PEOPLE by Maria Harris. © 1989 Maria Harris. Used by permission of Westminster John Knox Press. In addition to Harris's material, the writer has added characteristics particular to Singles Ministry.

Evaluation Questions

Below are three things indicated by Harris that are required for "family."[3] If single adults are to be family for each other, we need to examine how we fulfill these roles both individually and corporately. As a group, brainstorm five things under each heading you can do to improve your singles ministry. Then choose which one you will implement this month, and which for each of the following four months. (Remember to also include how you plan to implement each one.)

PRESENCE (being genuinely and lovingly involved in each other's lives):   month

1. _____   _____
2. _____   _____
3. _____   _____
4. _____   _____
5. _____   _____

RECEPTIVITY (being ready and willing to really listen to one another):   month

1. _____   _____
2. _____   _____
3. _____   _____
4. _____   _____
5. _____   _____

RESPONSIBILITY (taking action; responding to one another after you have listened):
                                                                        month

1. _____   _____
2. _____   _____
3. _____   _____
4. _____   _____
5. _____   _____

From FASHION ME A PEOPLE by Maria Harris. © 1989 Maria Harris. Used by permission of Westminster John Knox Press. In addition to Harris's material, the writer has added characteristics particular to Singles Ministry.

16 BECOMING A WINNING TEAM

A Development Retreat for New Leaders

Event Summary: A team-building retreat for a new leadership team which includes a short work project and opportunities to learn how to work most effectively together.

Length of Event: Friday evening–Saturday afternoon

Suggested Theme Verse: "From him the whole body, joined and held together by every supporting ligament, grows and builds itself up in love, as each part does its work." Ephesians 4:16

Ideal Number of Participants: Entire leadership team

Estimated Cost Per Person: $10–$35

Facility Requirements: Campground, private cabin, condo, or vacation home (near a potential work project)

Recommended Planning Team: 8–10 people

Advance Planning Needed: 6 months or less

Special Instructions: Participants should receive and complete an abbreviated Myers-Briggs temperament test (contained in the book Please Understand Me) and a Houts Inventory of Spiritual Gifts two weeks before the event. (See page 142 for information about administering the Myers-Briggs Type Indicator® test.)

INTRODUCTION

by Jerry Swanson
Pastor for Single Adults and Men's Ministry
College Avenue Baptist Church
San Diego, California

OBJECTIVES

To help a new singles ministry leadership team
❖ build relationships and friendships
❖ better understand how each member contributes uniquely to the team, approaches tasks, and makes decisions
❖ learn how to contribute to the mission of the singles ministry
❖ discover spiritual gifts of each team member
❖ encourage one another
❖ work together on a service project

Every healthy, growing single adult ministry will have a steady inflow of new leaders. As a result, there will be the need to develop a new leadership team—sometimes as often as once or twice every year.

This overnight retreat is designed to take a new group of leaders and begin to mold them into a team, help them understand the other team members, learn how each can contribute to the mission of your singles ministry, and allow them to observe each other in a multifaceted context. It is also an excellent opportunity to better understand leadership styles and decision-making styles and how to most effectively run your leadership meetings.

This retreat will often become the defining moment when the team establishes their identity and ministry purpose and vision. The bonding and development that occur are exciting, rewarding, and enriching.

THE BIG EVENT

The best time to hold this retreat is after the new team members have been oriented to their positions by the respective outgoing leaders. To maximize the benefits of this retreat, plan to meet during the first month of the new team members' terms or office.

> ❖
> **Get as many people as possible involved in the planning of this event.**

SCHEDULE

Your schedule may vary depending on travel time and service project. Use the following schedule as a guide.

Two weeks in advance

Hand out to each of the leaders the two tests that will be used during this retreat. Ask them to complete the tests, self-score them per the instructions, and bring them to the retreat. (The two tests, described later, are an abbreviated version of the Myers-Briggs Type Indicator® and the Houts Inventory of Spiritual Gifts. If you are qualified to administer the actual Myers-Briggs Type Indicator® [see requirements on page 142], you will need to do so several weeks in advance in order to evaluate the results of the test for each team member.)

Friday

6:00 P.M.—Leave from church
7:00 P.M.—Dinner at a fast-food restaurant on the way
7:30 P.M.—Continue travel to event site
8:00 P.M.—Arrive and settle in at event site
8:30 P.M.—Session I: "The Seven Most Significant Events of My Life"
9:30 P.M.—Singing, devotional, and group fellowship
10:00 P.M.—(Optional) Late night sitcoms and discussions

Saturday

8:00 A.M.—Breakfast
9:00 A.M.—Session II: "Please Understand Me"

10:00 A.M.—Break
10:30 A.M.—Session III: "Understanding My Spiritual Gifts"
11:30 A.M.—Prayer and Devotional
12:00 P.M.—Lunch
1:00 P.M.—Leave for work project
4:30 P.M.—Complete work project and clean up
5:00 P.M.—Leave for home (allowing participants adequate time to get home, rest, and prepare for Sunday)

RETREAT COST

To minimize the burden on your volunteer leaders, keep the costs for this event as low as possible. This is especially important if you make this a required attendance for the new leadership team. This can be accomplished by one or more of the following suggestions:

1. Use a condo, cabin, beach house, or private home owned by someone in the church who would be willing to let you use it for little or no cost. (If appropriate, your team work project could be to fix up or paint at this facility as a way to say thanks for the free weekend rent.)

2. Except for the first evening dinner, prepare meals as a team.

3. When possible, cover the retreat costs out of your singles ministry budget.

The goal is for the leadership team to have little out-of-pocket expense for this retreat.

WORK PROJECT

Due to time limitations, this project will need to be relatively small and close to the retreat site. It could include cleaning, fence-fixing, yard work, maintenance, light repair, or painting at a church, an elderly person's home, or the retreat facility where you are staying. The actual project is not as important as is the act of serving others as a team in some helpful way. It is also an excellent way for team members to get better acquainted and to observe how members of the team approach a task;

how their temperament style influences tasks; and how they work together, use tools, take initiative, lead, organize, and exhibit character.

RESOURCES

There are two primary resources that you need to do this retreat effectively:

1. The book, *Please Understand Me*, by David Keirsey and Marilyn Bates (Del Mar, CA: Prometheus Nemesis Books, 1979) for Session Two. It would be helpful for the retreat leader to be quite familiar with this book as a preparation tool. Indeed, it would be good to provide a copy of this book for each member of the leadership team. Included in the book is an abbreviated Myers-Briggs test, along with directions for participants to complete their own scoring.

In order for you to administer the complete Myers-Briggs Type Indicator®, you must have completed a course in psychological tests and measurements at an accredited university or college. For more information, or to obtain copies of the Myers-Briggs test, contact:

Consulting Psychologists Press, Inc.
3803 E. Bayshore Road
P. O. Box 10096
Palo Alto, CA 94303
415-969-8901

2. The "Houts Inventory of Spiritual Gifts" for Session Three. These inventories may be available through your church or bookstore, or contact:

Charles E. Fuller Institute
P. O. Box 91990
Pasadena, CA 91109-1990
1-800-999-9578

The cost is approximately $3.50 per copy (usually quantity discounts are available), and the tests are self-scoring and contain definitions of all the gifts.

Several other helpful spiritual gifts tests are also available. Contact your pastor or your local Christian bookstore for more information.

(Remember that it is important that each participant receive and complete both the Myers-Briggs test [or an abbreviated version] and the spiritual gifts inventory *in advance* of the retreat. There is not adequate time during the retreat for these tests to be administered.)

GROUP PHOTO

Sometime during the retreat (possibly right before Saturday lunch or at the project worksite) take a group photo. Upon returning, make sure each member of the team receives a nice, framed copy of this photo. Plus, place a copy on the singles ministry bulletin board.

If your budget allows, have the name of the leadership team professionally placed on the frame, such as "(group name) Singles Ministry Leadership Team Retreat, Fall 19__." This group photo helps build camaraderie, a sense of pride and purpose, and reminds the team of the good relationships initiated and nurtured during the retreat.

Also consider having photos (or video) taken throughout the weekend to show the entire group back home, either in a special program or prominently displayed on the bulletin board. This helps create interest for others to be involved in future leadership teams.

PROGRAM IDEAS AND SUGGESTIONS

DEVOTIONAL TIMES

Emphasize Ephesians 4:16 as the theme. The focus of your devotional time is on how the team leaders need each other. If one member does not participate, all are weakened; when each person does his or her part, all are strengthened and blessed.

SESSION I (FRIDAY, 8:30 P.M.)

"The Seven Most Significant Events of My Life"

1. Give everyone some construction paper and colored pens.

2. (15 minutes) Ask them to think through each period of their life.

Ages 1-5	Carefree preschool days
6-8	First years of school (a new world of learning)
9-11	Homework (and braces)
12-14	Jr. High (absolutely clueless)
15-17	Know it all
18-21	The world is yours (freedom if you want it)
22-on	The real world . . .

3. (20 minutes) Draw a picture or symbol that represents the significant events during each age period. You may want to tag each period with a phrase or description that captures that period of your life. (Remind everyone that artistic ability is not a prerequisite!)

4. (25 minutes) Discuss each person's pictures and symbols. (Unless you have a small leadership team, it is usually best to have people share in groups of three or four people. Another possibility, if time allows, is to have everyone change small groups at least once so they can share their story with a second small group. But don't overdo it.)

• **Optional Icebreaker (Baby Pictures)**

Have each participant bring a copy of his or her baby picture (without showing it to any other participant). Upon arrival, all pictures are to be given to the retreat director who will then number them and tape them to a wall.

❖
For more icebreakers, see the Table of Contents.

Time participants and see who can guess which baby pictures belong to whom. The first person to figure out which picture belongs to which person wins.

• **Optional Discussion Starter**

Ask, "If our group was a train, what part would you play and why? Would you just be along for the ride, would you be the engine, or would you be the caboose? In what way does your part help the train get to its destination?" Discuss these questions as a group.

• **Optional Late-Evening Fun**

Bring along some taped segments of some popular TV sitcoms such as "Seinfeld," "Friends," or even some old classics such as "The Andy Griffith Show." Watch one or two, paying special attention to the different temperament types of people on the show and how they do or do not get along.

Then discuss the following:

1. Who in your group is most like some of the temperament types on the show? In what way?

2. Of the people on the show (based on their temperament), what role would they best play on your leadership team? What contributions could they make? Why?

3. What leadership role would be least suitable for them? Why?

4. Of the different temperament types on the TV show, how would they be accepted or treated if they came to your singles group?

SESSION II (SATURDAY, 9:00 A.M.)

❖ "Please Understand Me"
(Myers-Briggs Type Indicator®)
❖ Possible biblical reference: I Corinthians 12
(Different parts of the same body)

The goal of this session is to better understand some of our natural, inborn gifts and temperament styles. This in no way is intended to be a comprehensive, "final word" on the subject. But it is a helpful way to open a window to see some of the things that make us tick, helping us better understand why each of us tends to do things the way we do.

During this session, discuss the results of the Myers-Briggs test, either completed and scored in advance by each participant or administered by you or another qualified tester. Depending on the size of your leadership team, you may choose to talk about these as an entire group or continue discussion in small groups of three or four.

1. Distribute the "Temperament Worksheet/Discussion Starter" handout (Resource 1, page 149).

2. Using the type overview description found either in the book, *Please Understand Me*, or in the Myers-Briggs testing instrument, give a brief overview of each temperament style; the weaknesses, strengths, and importance of each; and why it is helpful for each other to know the different styles as a leadership team.

3. Go around the room and ask each person to tell his or her temperament type. Encourage the other members to write down each person's type on their worksheet so they can refer back to it during the day as needed. (It can also be fun to ask for a show of hands for all the Es, all the Is, and so forth. This typically gives rise to some fun comments about the strengths and weaknesses of different types—plus comments of surprise about how some of the group members' types turned out. It also allows participants to get a feel for the makeup of their leadership team.)

4. Finally, using the "Temperament Worksheet/Discussion Starter" (Resource 1, page 149, lead a discussion about the strengths, weaknesses, and uses of the leadership team's unique set of temperament types.

Session III (Saturday, 10:30 a.m.)

❖ "Understanding My Spiritual Gifts" (Houts Inventory of Spiritual Gifts)
❖ Possible biblical reference: Romans 12 (Building up the body of Christ by making use of differing gifts)

The goal of this session is to identify and gain a better understanding of our God-given spiritual gifts. As with temperament types, this in no way is intended to be a comprehensive, "final word" on the subject. But it is a helpful way of understanding some of the specific gifts God has given us to use toward the building up of the body of Christ.

Discuss the results of the Houts Inventory of Spiritual Gifts, completed and scored in advance by each participant. Depending on the size of your leadership team, you may talk about the results of the Inventory as an entire group or in small groups of three or four.

1. Give a brief overview of spiritual gifts, their importance, and why it is important for the leadership team to know what they are and who possesses which one(s).

2. Ask each participant to complete the "Spiritual Gifts Worksheet/Discussion Starter" handout (Resource 2, page 150), and then, using the handout, lead a discussion about the group members' spiritual gifts.

3. Discuss how understanding teammates' gifts and temperament help one another resolve conflict, plan, and work together more effectively as a team.

4. Have each person affirm and encourage two or three others in their group about their unique gifts and temperament—as well as about how those gifts and temperament benefit the singles ministry.

5. Have each participant write on an index card the following:
   • A new insight I've learned today about me and how I work with others . . .
   • A new insight I've learned about our leadership team . . .
   (When members of the leadership team complete the sentences, ask them to place their card in an envelope and seal it. Then ask them to write their name on the envelope. As you collect the envelopes, announce that these envelopes will be returned to them at a later leadership team meeting [two to four months later] to remind them of what they learned about themselves and others during the weekend.)

6. Close the session in prayer. (Allow people adequate time to pray together in small groups.) Enjoy the sense of God's greatness through the assembling of a multi-gifted, multi-talented team. It is rewarding to know that each person has been called and appointed to serve a specific function on the team.

EQUIPMENT/SUPPLIES (To be furnished by the event leaders)

- [ ] To be distributed to each participant at least two weeks in advance of the retreat:
  • An abbreviated version of the Myers-Briggs Type Indicator®, in the book, *Please Understand Me*
  • Houts Inventory of Spiritual Gifts
- [ ] (Optional) The Myers-Briggs Type Indicator®, to be administered to each participant and evaluated in advance of the retreat
- [ ] 3x5 cards and envelopes (enough for each participant)
- [ ] Copies for each participant of the Temperament and Gifts Worksheet/ Discussion Starter (Resources 1 and 2)
- [ ] Construction paper and colored pens
- [ ] Tools, as needed, for work project
- [ ] (Optional) Videotape of a TV sitcom for a Friday night discussion starter
- [ ] (Optional) Extra copies of the book, *Please Understand Me*

WHAT TO BRING (To be provided by participants)

- [ ] Sleeping bag
- [ ] Toiletries
- [ ] Completed and scored abbreviated Myers-Briggs test and Houts Inventory of Spiritual Gifts test
- [ ] Work clothes, gloves
- [ ] Money for Friday evening dinner
- [ ] Bible, pen, notebook
- [ ] Camera
- [ ] (Optional) Guitar
- [ ] (Optional) Baby picture

PLANNING THE EVENT

PLANNING TEAM

Having each member involved in the planning of this retreat is an excellent way for the new leadership team to begin working together.

For this event, you need an Event Director (possibly an Assistant Event Director) and volunteers to take responsibilities for the event site, budget, event materials, worship, registration, food, transportation, and equipment and supplies. (The person responsible for equipment and supplies may also serve as the Work Project Coordinator for this retreat.) For this event, the speaker or teacher (probably the singles ministry pastor or leader) will most likely be the Event Director.

In addition to the above Planning Team, recruit a Work Project Coordinator. (As mentioned above, it may be possible to have the Equipment/Supplies Coordinator also serve as the Work Project Coordinator.)

❖ *The more people who have ownership and involvement in the planning, the greater success you will have.*

Planning Timeline

Event: *Becoming a Winning Team*   **Date of event:** _____

Event Director: _____   **Phone:** _____

Thanks for agreeing to serve on our leadership retreat Planning Team. Please check over this timeline for the task(s) assigned to you. Adapt as needed. Supplement this timeline with information on the reproducible, generic job descriptions found on pages 225-252. Highlight your tasks (and due dates) each time they appear. Mark your calendar accordingly.

| Date: _____ | **6 MONTHS IN ADVANCE** |

Event Director (page 226)

Since this retreat is designed to be one of the first things a new leadership team does, they will not have the luxury of planning ahead six months. As a result, it will be necessary for you to lay some of the groundwork and determine various options ahead of time.

☐ Find two or three options for a retreat site. If it is possible to wait until the new team meets to confirm your site, allow the new team to help make this decision. If that option does not exist for you, confirm the site.

☐ Begin making arrangements for possible work projects (see "Work Project" on page 141). Remember that the event site will need to be very near the work project.

☐ Mark the dates on the church calendar.

☐ Begin estimating costs for the event.

☐ As you recruit or select your new leadership team, begin letting the new leaders know about the date for this retreat. (It should be required attendance for all new leaders.)

| Date: _____ | **4 MONTHS IN ADVANCE** |

Event Director

☐ Order copies of the Myers-Briggs Type Indicator® test (and/or the book *Please Understand Me*) and the Houts Inventory of Spiritual Gifts test for each participant. (See page 142 for ordering information.)

| Date: _____ | **2 MONTHS IN ADVANCE** |

Event Director

☐ Even though the new leadership team may not have begun their duties, the new team members should be confirmed by now.

☐ Begin preparing the three workshop sessions. Information for these workshops is provided on pages 142-144. Adapt these sessions as needed for your group.

☐ Begin thinking about who will be responsible for the Friday evening and Saturday noon devotionals. Is this something that you will do, or will you delegate this to the Worship Coordinator?

☐ If you or someone you know is qualified to do so, administer and begin evaluating the results of the Myers-Briggs Type Indicator®.

❖ *For more ideas and help, refer to job descriptions beginning on page 225.*

| Date: _____ | **5 WEEKS IN ADVANCE** |

Event Director

☐ Hold a planning meeting with the new leadership team. If it has not already been done, determine who will fulfill specific responsibilities for the retreat.

☐ Remind team members that this retreat is required for all new leaders.

☐ (Optional) If you choose to have the TV sitcom discussion on Friday night, delegate to someone the responsibility for taping and bringing the videos.

Event Site Coordinator (page 234)

☐ If the Event Director has not already done so, finalize all details for the retreat site.
☐ Confirm that a signed contract for the event site is on file in the church office.
☐ Verify that any required deposit has been made.

Equipment/Supplies Coordinator

(page 233) *(For this retreat, also serving as the Work Project Coordinator)*

☐ If the Event Director has not already done so, begin finalizing all details for the work project. For instance, what will the project be? What tools and supplies will be needed?
☐ Working with the Planning Team, determine what other supplies will be needed for the retreat.

Food Coordinator (page 236)

☐ Determine what meals are needed at the event site. If your group will be cooking their own meals, plan a menu. Snacks are needed for Friday evening; breakfast and lunch are needed for Saturday.
☐ Begin coordinating cooking and cleanup teams for each meal.
☐ Ask for volunteers to provide the snacks.

Registration Coordinator (page 241)

☐ Since this retreat is designed for leaders only, the registration duties will be light. Begin registration for the event.
☐ If scholarships will be awarded, supply the application forms now (see page 246).

Budget Coordinator (page 229)

☐ Gather information from the various Planning Team members to determine budget needs.
☐ Work with the Event Director to finalize a budget, determine costs each participant

will need to pay, if any, and determine how costs will be covered.

Worship Coordinator (page 251)

☐ Determine which group members are musically inclined and can assist in leading singing on Friday evening.
☐ Determine (with the Event Director) who will be responsible for the devotional on Friday evening and Saturday noon. If the Event Director has requested that you be responsible, begin planning the devotionals.

Transportation Coordinator (page 252)

☐ Determine what mode of transportation will be used for the event (most likely a car pool or the church van).

Date:	3 WEEKS IN ADVANCE

Event Director

☐ Hold another Planning Team meeting to confirm that everything is on schedule.
☐ Check on the final arrangements for the work project.
☐ Arrange for one of the participants to take photographs or videotape portions of the retreat. Make arrangements for a group photograph.

Equipment/Supplies Coordinator

☐ Finalize any last-minute details for the work project. (Make sure all tools and supplies are arranged for.)

Registration Coordinator

☐ Scholarship application forms should be sent to the proper person for approval.
☐ Inform any individuals receiving a scholarship of the amount awarded.

<table>
<tr><td>Date: _____</td><td>

2 WEEKS IN ADVANCE

</td></tr>
</table>

Event Director

- ☐ Check on the progress made by each Planning Team member.
- ☐ Proof master copies of all the event materials, and then have the Event Materials Coordinator reproduce them.
- ☐ Distribute copies of both the abbreviated Myers-Briggs test (in *Please Understand Me*) and Houts test to each retreat participant. Instruct them to bring the completed and scored tests with them to the retreat.

Event Site Coordinator

- ☐ Send a copy of the event schedule to the contact person at the event site.

Event Materials Coordinator

- ☐ In cooperation with other Planning Team members, copy and prepare all event materials for assembly (schedule, workshop handouts, maps, etc.).

Transportation Coordinator

- ☐ Confirm transportation arrangements.

Food Coordinator

- ☐ Recommend two or three restaurants that are on the way to the event site—places where the team could eat Friday evening.

<table>
<tr><td>Date: _____</td><td>

1 WEEK IN ADVANCE

</td></tr>
</table>

Event Director

- ☐ Meet with the Planning Team to confirm that all final details are in place.

Equipment/Supplies Coordinator

- ☐ Confirm that all work project supplies are ready for transport to the event site.

Registration Coordinator

- ☐ In coordination with the Event Materials Coordinator, send a final letter to all attendees outlining the events, times, schedule, and what to bring. (A sample letter is found on page 244. Adapt the letter to meet the needs of this event.)
- ☐ Finalize a count of the attendees and give that count to the Food Coordinator, Event Site Coordinator, Event Director, Event Materials Coordinator, and Transportation Coordinator.
- ☐ Make final sleeping room assignments.

Food Coordinator

- ☐ Purchase food supplies (non-perishables).
- ☐ Gather any other cooking supplies that are not provided at the event site.
- ☐ Complete a cooking and cleanup schedule that involves all participants.

Transportation Coordinator

- ☐ Give all drivers a map to the event site, along with a list of assigned riders.

Event Site Coordinator

- ☐ Check in with the event site. Provide a final number of those registered to attend.
- ☐ If the site is a private dwelling, be sure to obtain the keys to it.

Budget Coordinator

- ☐ Prepare payments as needed.
- ☐ Provide Food Coordinator with money for purchasing food.

<table>
<tr><td>Date: _____</td><td>

2 TO 4 WEEKS AFTER EVENT

</td></tr>
</table>

Event Director

- ☐ Work with the photographer to purchase copies of the group photo (nicely framed, if possible) for each participant.
- ☐ See the "Followup Guidelines" on page 254.

Temperament Worksheet/Discussion Starter

My Name _____

My Position/Responsibility on the Singles Ministry Leadership Team _____

_____

My Temperament Type _____

1. Please find your type on the test summary (either in the book, *Please Understand Me* or on the Myers-Briggs Type Indicator® testing instrument. Read the overview description of your type. Do you think it accurately describes you?

2. Share with the group the weaknesses and strengths of your type.

3. How does your type tend to make decisions and resolve conflict?

4. What kind of tasks or responsibilities are best suited for your type?

5. Is your current leadership position a good fit for you? Why or why not?

6. As a group, discuss the strengths of your temperament in the context of your current single adult ministry leadership position and responsibilities.

7. Based on your temperament and leadership position and responsibilities, in what areas do you need the most help and encouragement?
   (For example, the activities coordinator may be an introverted person who was given the position because of organizational and detail abilities. Since introverted people tend to do things alone—which may lead to fatigue, burn-out or discouragement, and which does not lend itself well to nurturing and mentoring other leaders who might be able to take their place at some point—surround the introverted person with a group of people who will assist with the assigned tasks.)

8. Based on your temperament type, what members of the leadership team might be the most difficult for you to understand or work well with? In what ways do you (or can you) complement one another? What steps can you take to learn to understand each other and work together more effectively?

Remember, we don't have to think alike to love alike!

Spiritual Gifts Worksheet/Discussion Starter

My Strongest Spiritual Gifts are _____

_____

1. What new thing did this test show about your gifts? What did it confirm that you already felt (or knew) about your spiritual gifts?

2. Share with the group the weaknesses and strengths that may arise from your spiritual gift(s).

3. Based on this inventory, what kind of tasks and responsibilities are best suited for you?

4. Is your current leadership position a good fit for you? Why or why not?

5. As a group, discuss the strengths of your spiritual giftedness in the context of your current single ministry leadership position and responsibilities.

6. Based on your spiritual gifts and current leadership position and responsibilities, in what areas do you need the most help and encouragement?

7. After discussing both temperament type and spiritual gifts, where would you like to see more opportunities for personal growth? What responsibilities or tasks within the church would you like to begin doing more of? Less of?

17 LEADERSHIP BOOT CAMP

Helping Single Adults Lead with the Right Heart

Event Summary: A concentrated leadership training and team-building event designed to equip leaders to be a cohesive unit, plus give them a better vision for what God wants to accomplish through them in your church and community.

Length of Event: Friday evening—Sunday afternoon

Ideal Number of Participants: Preferably no more than 20 hand-picked leaders.

Estimated Cost Per Person: $35–$85, depending on the facilities

Facility Requirements: Retreat or hotel conference center

Recommended Planning Team: 8–12 people

Advance Planning Needed: Approximately 8–12 months

INTRODUCTION

by Norman Yukers
Minister with Singles
Rehoboth Baptist Church
Tucker, Georgia

One of the reasons the military has a boot camp is because the camp forces recruits to learn to rely on their drill instructor. The same is true for ministry leadership. My goal for our volunteer leaders is for them to depend on me as I depend on them—for all of us to blend together as a cohesive unit, a team.

Over the years I've found that the format for this weekend event is an excellent way to build a cohesive unit, to encourage people to work together, to communicate more effectively, to become better prepared to minister to others, and to understand the heart and dreams of one another. It also allows leaders to get to know each other in an informal retreat setting.

This is one event in which I hand-select those who will attend. (I invite people that I have been watching, those who have been showing servanthood and leadership qualities.) My goal is to have a mix of previous leaders (about one-third of the total group), with the remainder being potential leaders. This allows the more experienced leaders to "buddy up" with a new crop of leaders.

This event gives me a chance to observe them in action and find various teachable moments in the process. During this event, I intentionally seek ways to affirm each person's leadership abilities and my own desire for them to be a part of our singles ministry team.

OBJECTIVE

❖ To sharpen the skills necessary to be a lay leader in a growing, active singles ministry.

THE BIG EVENT

SCHEDULE

Friday

7:00–7:30 P.M.—Arrival, check-in, registration

7:30–8:00 P.M.—Introductions and overview of weekend

8:00–8:30 P.M.—Icebreaker

8:30–9:00 P.M.—Snacks/Refreshments

9:00–10:00 P.M.—Session 1

10:00–10:45 P.M.—Small groups (in groups of 3–4, determined by birth month)

10:45 P.M.—Free time

❖
Get as many people as possible involved in the planning of this event.

Saturday

7:30–8:15 A.M.—Breakfast

8:15–8:30 A.M.—Cleanup

8:30–9:00 A.M.—Worship and prayer

9:00–10:00 A.M.—Session 2

10:00–10:45 A.M.—Small groups (in groups of 3–4, divided by favorite ice cream flavor)

10:45–11:15 A.M.—Break

11:15 A.M.–12:00 P.M.—Team-Building exercise #1

12:00–1:30 P.M.—Lunch

1:30–1:45 P.M.—Cleanup

1:45–7:00 P.M.—Recreation/free time

7:00 P.M.—Dinner

8:00–9:00 P.M.—Session 3

9:00–9:30 P.M.—Small groups (in groups of 3–4 each, divided by gender)

9:30–9:45 P.M.—Refreshment break

9:45–10:30 P.M.—Team-Building exercise #2

Sunday

7:30–8:15 A.M.—Breakfast

8:15–8:30 A.M.—Cleanup

8:30–9:30 A.M.—Session 4

9:30–10:15 A.M.—Small groups (in groups of 3–4, divided by favorite pro sport)

10:15–10:30 A.M.—Break

10:30–11:30 A.M.—Worship/Communion

11:30–12:00 P.M.—Pack, check out, etc.

12:00 P.M.—Lunch

1:30 P.M.—Depart

MEAL TIMES

If possible, cook your own meals during this retreat. It can be a valuable part of the team-building process. Divide your group into five teams, one team for each meal. Each team will be responsible for preparing their designated meal as well as doing the cleanup following the meal. Since there is minimal time in the schedule, use disposable items as much as possible to keep cleanup time at a minimum.

SCHOLARSHIPS

Depending on your budget limitations, one thing to consider is paying all or most of the costs of this retreat out of your budget. Since this is your hand-picked leadership group, paying their way can be a worthwhile investment. However, if this is not possible, develop a scholarship fund to help those who might not be able to attend otherwise.

PROGRAM IDEAS AND SUGGESTIONS

ICEBREAKER

Here are some great ways to help your group members get better acquainted.

• **Wagon Wheel**

To play "Wagon Wheel," take on the role of wagon master and divide your group into two circles, one inside the other. Ask those in the outer circle to face those in the inner circle, and vice versa. Then give the following instructions:

1. Rotate in opposite directions until I, the wagon master, shout, "Whoa!"

2. When I ask a question, share your answer with the person you are facing.

3. When I say go, start rotating again.

This is a fun get-acquainted game! Make sure the players introduce themselves to each other if they are not acquainted. For the questions, make use of the list on Resource 1, page

❖
For more icebreakers, see the Table of Contents.

158, or make up your own. At the end of the game, ask volunteers to tell about some of their most unusual answers.

TEAM-BUILDING EXERCISES

One of the goals of this retreat is to help your leaders develop as a team. Here are several ideas that can help them accomplish that goal. (The objective of each of these exercises is to help a group of people learn to work together while listening to instructions from the group leader.) Select one or more of the following to use during your retreat.

• The Puzzle

1. Divide your participants into teams of 4-5 people each. Designate one person to be the group leader.

2. Give each team a puzzle to put together. (Note: Before the retreat, find an appropriate picture for a puzzle and make multiple copies. Cut half of the copies into several pieces and put them into separate plastic bags. Take the remaining half of the copies of the original picture and place one in each bag in such a way that it cannot be viewed.)

3. Give one bag to each group leader, instructing them to remove the uncut picture without letting other team members see it.

4. Direct the leaders to place the puzzle pieces on the floor or table in front of their team members.

5. Next, the leader instructs his or her team members on how to put the puzzle together. (Remember that only each small group leader can see the original picture. It is up to the group leader to give instructions to the other group members on how the puzzle goes together.)

(For added fun, offer a prize to the first team that can finish its puzzle.)

• Blindfold Obstacle Course

1. Select a representative sample of people who will be blindfolded. (Ideally this will be no fewer than four or five people, but it should not be more than half of your total group. Determine the number that works best for you based on the time available.)

2. Select a "guide" for each person who is blindfolded.

3. Have all of the blindfolded persons go into a room where they cannot hear the instructions about the obstacle course.

4. Explain the obstacle course to the guides and to the remainder of the group. (Beforehand, designate one or two people to develop an obstacle course either inside or outside, or both. The obstacles could be a maze of barricades, old tires, chairs, barrels, ropes, water, etc. Make it moderately challenging, but keep safety in mind.)

5. Instruct one guide at a time to go to the room and bring out one blindfolded person. The objective is for the guide to assure the blindfolded person that he or she can be trusted to give instructions to help the blindfolded person through the obstacle course. The guide can only give verbal instructions and cannot touch or hold the person blindfolded in any way. (Example: "Take one step then turn left. Take three steps, then climb over the barrel. Turn right at 2:00 and walk 4 steps.")

6. Continue this process, one guide and blindfolded person at a time, until each has completed the course. (Due to time limitations, everyone may not be able to participate in this activity. However, everyone will be able to learn by observing.)

Observe how well the blindfolded person listens to instructions from his or her guide, as well as how the guide earns trust and effectively communicates instructions. Once this activity is complete, discuss what the participants felt and learned from this process. How well can they rely on one another? How important is clear communication and trust? How well do they follow instructions? What are the implications for a ministry team?

(Keeping safety in mind, if you want to add some excitement to this activity, use a timer and give prizes to the partners who get through the obstacle course in the least time.)

• **Lego Construction**

1. Have an ample supply of colored Lego building blocks.

2. Divide your participants into teams of 4-5 people each. Designate one person in each group to be the team leader.

3. Give each leader a model of something that has been built with Legos prior to the retreat. Only the leader of each team is allowed to see this model.

4. The leader must give verbal instructions to his or her team to build an identical model as the one done beforehand. (Example: "Take two red Legos and place them on top of the row of four blue Legos.")

5. Using a timer, see which team is first able to assemble an identical item based solely on their leader's verbal instructions.

Discuss what was learned in the process about the importance of communication and teamwork.

• **Other Games**

Other team-building exercises could include games such as Charades, Pictionary, or Taboo. If your retreat center has a ropes course available, this would be an excellent team-building activity to consider.

In today's world, communication is a very important leadership skill. Effective leaders have to know how to communicate clearly to those they are leading. And a good leader will understand the value of learning how to communicate to different people in different ways, recognizing that different forms of communication are required to get the task completed.

RECOMMENDED RESOURCES

Terry Hershey has written an excellent four-session outline for a retreat such as this. (See *Young Adult Ministry*, written by Hershey and published by Group, © 1986, pages 100-102.) This outline is provided on Resource 2, pages 159-160.

Another outstanding resource is *The Leading Edge*, by Gerry Peak (The Sampson

Company, © 1994). This is an interactive Sunday school leadership training program that includes a leader's guide, a workbook with discussion questions, four 12-minute video lessons, an overhead transparency kit, a reproducible audiocassette (with four 15-minute lessons of additional teaching), a promotion kit, and a reproducible "Certificate of Achievement." The cost for this program is $129.95 (plus shipping and handling). For more information, call (214) 387-2806 or write Sampson Ministry Resources; 5050 Quorum, Suite 245; Dallas, TX 75240.

The four sessions in *The Leading Edge* are as follows:

SESSION ONE: "Every Single Possibility— Discovering the Potential of Single Adult Ministry." Focus: To lead participants to identify dynamic realities of the growing single adult population and to commit themselves to reaching and evangelizing single adults with the Gospel of Jesus Christ. Theme Verse: Mark 8:23b-25.

SESSION TWO: "Every Single Sunday Morning—Keys for Making Sunday Morning Exciting." Focus: To lead participants to identify at least four elements that will build an effective, exciting Sunday morning Bible study program with single adults. Theme Verse: Mark 6:35-37a.

SESSION THREE: "Every Single Week—The Magnetic Power of an Ongoing Ministry." Focus: To lead participants to identify three approaches for using special events and emphases to meet the spiritual, physical, emotional, and social needs of single adults. Theme Verse: John 21:25.

SESSION FOUR: "Every Single Step of Faith —Establishing and Growing a Single Adult Ministry." Focus: To lead participants to identify three basic concepts for growing a single adult ministry and to commit to reaching single adults for Jesus Christ. Theme Verse: Matthew 5: 14-16.

Another excellent and recommended resource is *Giving the Ministry Away: Empowering Single Adults For Effective Leadership* by Terry Hershey, Karen Butler, and Rich Hurst. Beginning on page 185 of this book, you will find an easy-to-use, step-by-step guide to a leadership training retreat, such as this one.

Other Resources

- George Barna, *Vision*. (Ventura, CA: Regal Books, 1992).
- Stepehen Covey. *Principle-Centered Leadership*. (New York: Summit Books, 1991).
- Oswald Sanders, *Spiritual Leadership*. (Chicago: Moody Press, 1974).

EQUIPMENT/SUPPLIES (To be furnished by the event leaders)

- ☐ Flip charts
- ☐ Overhead transparencies and projector
- ☐ Dry erase boards
- ☐ VCR (The more mediums used, the more effective the teaching will be.)
- ☐ Tape or CD player.
- ☐ Name tags
- ☐ Icebreaker materials
- ☐ Recreational gear for Saturday afternoon free time
- ☐ Team-building materials/props/supplies
- ☐ (Optional) Games that instill teamwork
- ☐ (Optional) Workbook/note sheets for each participant

WHAT TO BRING (To be provided by participants)

- ☐ Casual clothes
- ☐ Sleeping bag/bedding
- ☐ Toiletries
- ☐ Bible, pen, notebook
- ☐ Journal
- ☐ Camera
- ☐ Recreational items (softball, volleyball, Frisbee, etc.)

PLANNING THE EVENT

PLANNING TEAM

For this event, you need an Event Director (possibly an Assistant Event Director) and volunteers to take responsibilities for the event site, budget, printed event materials, registration, small groups, transportation, food, worship, and equipment and supplies. In addition, you may want to consider having a Recreation Coordinator if your scheduled time and interest allow.

The role of speaker will most likely be covered by the Event Director (probably the Singles Minister or leader).

❖ *The more people who have ownership and involvement in the planning, the greater success you will have.*

Planning Timeline

Event: *Leadership Boot Camp*   **Date of event:** _____

Event Director: _____   **Phone:** _____

Thanks for agreeing to serve on our retreat Planning Team. Please check over this timeline for the task(s) assigned·to you. Adapt as needed. Supplement this timeline with information on the reproducible, generic job descriptions. Highlight your tasks (and the due dates) each time they appear. Mark your calendar accordingly.

Date: _____	**5 TO 6 MONTHS IN ADVANCE**

Event Director (page 226)

☐ Recruit a Planning Team. Brainstorm ideas, and adapt this weekend event to fit your particular ministry goals and objectives.
☐ Make sure team members understand their assigned tasks and responsibilities. (Note: Additional planning team members can be added later as hand-selected participants for this retreat are invited.)
☐ Determine if this timeline will work for your area and make adjustments accordingly.

Event Site Coordinator (page 234)

☐ Secure camp or conference site.
☐ See that a deposit is paid, if required.
☐ Mark the date on the church calendar.

Budget Coordinator (page 229)

☐ Begin estimating the per person costs for this event.

Date: _____	**4 MONTHS IN ADVANCE**

Event Director

☐ Determine the study material to be used during the retreat. If materials need to be ordered, do so now.

Transportation Coordinator (page 252)

☐ Determine the best mode of transportation.

Date: _____	**3 MONTHS IN ADVANCE**

Event Director

☐ Contact and personally invite all prospective participants for this retreat. Ask for their commitment. Remember that all potential leaders should be invited, as well as several past key leaders. (If your group elects leaders, attendance at this event should be a mandatory part of the acceptance procedure.)
☐ Recruit the additional members of the Planning Team.
☐ Have a meeting with all Planning Team members.

Registration Coordinator (page 241)

☐ Begin registration.
☐ If scholarship funds are available, prepare and supply application forms.

Event Site Coordinator

☐ Check to be sure a signed contract is on file at the event site and at the church.
☐ Make sure all details are correct.
☐ Verify that a deposit has been paid and received at the event site.

Food Coordinator (page 236)

☐ Begin plans for refreshments and meals at the event site.

❖ *For more ideas and help, refer to job descriptions beginning on page 225.*

Date: _____ | 2 MONTHS IN ADVANCE

Event Director

☐ Hold a Planning Team meeting to troubleshoot where needed and to check on progress.

Equipment/Supplies Coordinator (page 233)

☐ Confirm what equipment (such as audio/visual) is available for use at the event site.

Worship Coordinator (page 251)

☐ From the list of those attending, ask musically talented people to lead the singing for Saturday and Sunday sessions.
☐ Inform the Equipment/Supplies Coordinator of any needed audio/visual equipment.

Recreation Coordinator (Optional) (page 240)

☐ Plan a variety of games and activities. Make all the needed arrangements.

Date: _____ | 1 MONTH IN ADVANCE

Registration Coordinator

☐ Collect all moneys due.
☐ Submit scholarship applications to the Event Director for processing.
☐ Inform recipients of funds granted.

Transportation Coordinator

☐ Confirm all transportation details.

Worship Coordinator

☐ Recruit a qualified person to acquire and transport communion elements to the event site and to serve Communion at the event.

Event Site Coordinator

☐ Send a copy of the event schedule to the contact person at the event site.
☐ Check details of the payment plan.

Equipment/Supplies Coordinator

☐ Check with all Planning Team members concerning equipment and supplies needed at the retreat.
☐ Make arrangements to have those items ready and available at the retreat.

Event Materials Coordinator (page 233)

☐ Have event schedule, small-group materials, maps, final letter to registrants, and any other copied materials ready for assembly or mailing.

Food Coordinator

☐ Finalize all meal preparation and cleanup crew details.

Date: _____ | 1 WEEK IN ADVANCE

Event Director

☐ Meet with the Planning Team to be sure all plans are on track.

Registration Coordinator

☐ Send a letter to all participants confirming the event details. Adapt the sample letter on page 244 for your event.

Date: _____ | 2 TO 4 WEEKS AFTER EVENT

☐ See the "Followup Guidelines" on page 254.

Questions for "Wagon Wheel"

1. In the third grade, where were you living and how many brothers and sisters did you have?

2. As a kid, what was your favorite TV show? Why?

3. Who was the most important influence in shaping your view of God?

4. What gives you a lot of satisfaction?

5. If you could ask God one question, what would you ask Him?

6. Who is your favorite music group?

7. Where is your favorite vacation spot?

8. What makes you really angry?

9. What makes you want to cry?

10. Who or what makes you laugh a lot?

11. What were your favorite and least favorite school subjects?

12. If you could marry a famous person, who might he or she be?

13. What was your youth group like?

14. How much time do you spend on the phone each day?

15. What gets you in hot water with your parents?

16. Who is your favorite movie star?

17. If you could live for one year anywhere in the world, where would it be?

18. Did you ever try chewing tobacco?

19. Did you ever get in trouble with the police?

20. What is your favorite thing to do on a Saturday night?

21. What is your favorite hobby?

22. What is your favorite food?

23. What is your dream car?

24. What was the "in" dance at your high school?

25. What do you save money for?

26. Where did you first hold hands?

27. What was your most embarrassing moment?

28. When was the first time you were kissed by someone outside your family?

29. What was your hairstyle like when you were thirteen years old?

30. What household chore do you hate doing?

31. What's one thing you've tried that you never want to do again?

32. As a child, what did you usually do on July 4th?

33. Who do you admire most?

34. Where do you go when you want to be alone?

35. Where do you go or to whom do you go for advice when you have a problem?

36. What is your greatest fear?

37. Have you been really hurt in your life? When?

38. If you could change one thing about yourself, what would it be?

39. What do you like most about yourself?

40. What is your favorite room in your house?

Our Role As Ministers

Session One:
Our Identity in Christ

(II Corinthians 5:17-21)
Every Christian is a minister. There is not an elite group of "those who minister," and an average group of the rest who are "ministered unto." This is "our church," not "my church" or the "pastor's church." As ministers, God has done the following in each of us.

❖ He has given us His Word (II Timothy 3:16, 17; Ephesians 3:1-5, 7-11).
❖ He has equipped us with His power (Ephesians 1:18-20; 3:14-20).
❖ He has given us His character (Romans 8:29; Ephesians 4:13).
❖ He has equipped us with spiritual gifts (Romans 4:7-13; I Corinthians 12—14).

Questions:
1. Would it make a difference in what we do if we were to say that every believer is a minister?

   How would that affect our group?

2. How do we communicate this truth to others?

3. What does this truth do to our understanding about our identity in Christ?

Session Two:
Our Significance to the Body

(I Corinthians 12:12-26)
We need the body and it needs us. There is no such thing as a hierarchy of "superior giftedness." Simply because someone is "the pastor" doesn't mean that person is more necessary for the body. In fact, the Bible is clear that the weakest, most vulnerable parts are quite necessary.

   Our goal with one another is *building up*. We need to see that the Christian faith is not something one person can do in isolation. We all have a role as builders in each others' lives.

Questions:
1. Why do we see some persons as essential for the body and others as dispensable?

2. How might the message of I Corinthians 12 change the way we view each other?

3. In what ways does this principle apply to leadership?

(Continued)

Adapted from *Young Adult Ministry* by Terry Hershey.

  159

Session Three:
Our Spiritual Giftedness

(I Corinthians 12—13; Ephesians 4; I Peter 4:10)

❖ **Faith.** You must believe you are gifted. God doesn't ask us to do what He hasn't equipped us to do (John 15:16; I Corinthians 12:7).
❖ **Prayer.** God doesn't want us to pray only that we'll satisfy a curiosity. He asks of us a commitment (John 4:2).
❖ **Awareness.** Be aware of the gifts available to believers.
❖ **Responsibility.** In what type of service are you presently involved?
❖ **Common sense.** Consider your desires; consider the needs of others; consider your experience; confirm others.

The purpose of my gift is not to wear an identification badge, but to propel me into service. Read I Peter 4:10. How do we find our niche?

Questions:
1. What does I Peter 4:10 mean practically to you?

2. Are you aware of your niche? Explain.

3. Are any of the five steps listed above helpful? In what ways?

Session Four:
Our Duty As Salt and Light

(Matthew 5:13-16)

God says that we are models (I Thessalonians 1:7) and ambassadors (II Corinthians 5:17). What does that mean? It means we don't just float through life in a vacuum. We are bearers of God's message of peace. We have the message that turns the world upside down (Acts 17). We do not live only for ourselves.

What does it mean to be salt?

❖ Salt brings out taste; it brings out the best in people.
❖ Salt is a preservative—a preservative against moral decay.
❖ Salt adds zest and excitement.

Questions:
1. Does it make a difference that you are God's ambassador? If so, in what ways?

2. How does our call to be salt affect our leadership position?

3. In what specific ways can you be more like salt?

18 LEADERSHIP VISION TRIP

Gaining New Ideas and Perspectives for Your Ministry

Event Summary: Taking your leadership team to another city to visit a singles ministry for a weekend to gain new ideas, perspective, and possibilities for ministry with single adults. An opportunity to spend concentrated, quality time together as a leadership team while expanding your vision for ministry.

Length of Event: 2–3 days

Suggested Theme Verse: "Never be lacking in zeal, but keep your spiritual fervor, serving the Lord." Romans 12:11

Ideal Number of Participants: 5–15

Estimated Cost Per Person: $39–$89 (depending on number of nights, meals, etc.)

Facility Requirements: Host church accommodations (hotel optional)

Recommended Planning Team: 2–4 people

Advance Planning Needed: Approximately 5–9 months

INTRODUCTION

by Douglas Peterson
Associate Minister of Adults
Calvary Church
Grand Rapids, Michigan

There's nothing like a change of perspective to get the creative juices flowing. One of the best benefits of a Vision Trip for your Single Adult leadership team is the change of perspective that it provides—spending a weekend visiting another singles ministry. Instead of being in charge, your team can relax, observe, and recharge. The Vision Trip is an opportunity to experience, explore, and learn from a successful singles ministry in a setting and location other than what you're familiar with.

This networking encounter will generate wonderful new ideas and outlooks for ministry with single adults. Your leadership team will return excited, refreshed, and eager to discuss

new ministry possibilities for your church. The enthusiasm they bring back and share can be contagious—serving as the spark that may just ignite a very special and effective new activity or program.

The Vision Trip is also great fellowship. There is something quite special about being together with your key leaders, sharing ideas, laughing, praying, and just going through the routines of a weekend together. The trip builds unity, grows friendships, and promotes mutual understanding and shared purpose. You'll love it!

OBJECTIVES

❖ To increase the vision for single adult ministry.
❖ To promote creativity in ministry.
❖ To encourage networking.
❖ To provide fun and fellowship.

THE BIG EVENT

SCHEDULE

❖

Get as many people as possible involved in the planning of this event.

Friday

3:00 P.M.—Gather and depart

6:00 P.M.—Check in at hotel, clean up, eat dinner

7:00 or 7:30 P.M.—Activity with host church singles group

Saturday

8:00 A.M.—Breakfast

9:00 A.M.—Meet with leadership of host church Singles Ministry

10:15 A.M.—Break

10:30 A.M.—Reconvene meeting

12:00 P.M.—Lunch with host singles team

1:30 P.M.—Free time (shopping, sightseeing, etc.)

5:00 P.M.—Depart for home

OR

6:00 P.M.—Meet at hotel or restaurant for dinner

7:00 P.M.—Attend Saturday evening services/singles event at host church

10:00 P.M.—Coffee and dessert

Sunday

8:00 A.M.—Breakfast

9:30 A.M.—Attend Sunday morning worship

12:30 P.M.—Lunch

1:30 P.M.—Depart for home

4:30 P.M.—Arrive home

SELECTING THE HOST CHURCH

Your goal of gaining new perspectives and insights must be carefully considered here. It's important to select a host church that has an exciting and growing single adult ministry. Although larger ministries usually offer more activities to observe and be a part of during the weekend, focus on finding the ministry that offers the most to your leadership team.

When contacting potential host churches, inquire about the focus of their ministry. Does it primarily deal with young, never-married singles? Older, single-again individuals? Single parents? Inquire as to what key activities are planned for the coming year and if there is a particular weekend they would recommend for you to visit. You will want to participate in as many new and different events and activities as possible at your host church.

As a leadership team, also discuss the areas you would most like to learn about. What are the specific needs of your ministry? Select a host church that is strong in the areas where your ministry needs to grow.

One of the criteria for selecting a host church is to make sure their leadership team will commit to interacting with your team for a few hours sometime during the weekend. Generally this works best from 9:00 A.M. to noon on Saturday. Following the meeting everyone can go out to lunch together and continue sharing in a more informal setting.

It is also important to consider distance when selecting the host church. Try to choose one that is within a 3–4 hour drive of home. This allows your leadership team to spend more time at the host church than traveling.

TRAVEL ARRANGEMENTS

There are several travel options, depending on your resources and the size of your leadership team. Car pooling can be done. However, it tends to break up the group and limit the "road fellowship." Church vans are a better choice, allowing more people to ride together. Consider chartering a bus and going in real style (although it will increase your costs). This way everyone keeps together and no one has to drive. If train schedules allow, another option would be to combine this event with the "Train Trip Adventure" on page 19.

Whatever method is chosen, all costs are shared by the participants (unless your church budget can help out). Remember that you want to keep the cost at a figure that allows for maximum participation, yet provides a quality, comfortable experience for everyone. If the distance is a bit long, the Planning Team will want to check to see if there are any interesting places along the way that would serve to break up the drive as well as enhance the trip experience.

LODGING ARRANGEMENTS

It may be possible to stay in the homes of the members of the host church. This would need to be coordinated by their leadership team. There are advantages and disadvantages. The good news is that it saves bucks. It also provides additional interaction and fellowship with those of the host church. The bad news is that it breaks up your group, making schedules harder to keep, sharing impressions more difficult, and diminishing the unity-building aspects of the trip.

The better choice may be to stay in a hotel and enjoy the amenities offered by whirlpools, in-house exercise rooms, saunas, and the joy of a private bathroom! Also, when staying together in one hotel, all vehicles are in the same place and schedules are easier to arrange and keep. When making reservations, ask for corporate rates or weekend specials. Some hotels may also offer free breakfast.

As with travel, choose the lodging arrangements that will best meet your team's objectives and needs.

PROGRAM IDEAS AND SUGGESTIONS

FRIDAY EVENING

Leave your home church in time to provide an opportunity to spruce up before the Friday night event. This may mean leaving around 3 or 4 P.M. Most of your team will be able to do this if given ample notice. Typically, a Friday activity will begin around 7 or 7:30 P.M. Since the Planning Team has picked this weekend carefully in advance, there is probably a highlight event for the host church and something your singles will really enjoy. One group has visited everything from large group Bible studies, to square dances, to full-length Christian drama presentations.

As time permits after the Friday night activity, consider stopping at a local restaurant for dessert. Or, if staying at a hotel, some may want to skip the dessert and get back for a swim or a soak in the whirlpool. Or maybe you can do both.

SATURDAY MORNING

As mentioned earlier, Saturday morning may be the best time to meet with the single adult leadership of the host church. Give your singles ample time to have breakfast prior to the meeting. The meeting should last until noon, giving you nearly three hours to interact and learn. Out of this discussion will come new insights, perspectives, and ideas. Have someone take notes during this meeting.

❖ For a list of icebreakers, see the Table of Contents.

Here are some suggested questions to bring to this meeting (You may want to send these questions in advance so the host church can be prepared.):

❖ How is your ministry organized and why?

❖ What is the focus of your ministry?

❖ What is the most difficult aspect of ministry with single adults? Most rewarding?

❖ What types of activities and programs do you do? Which ones seem to be working best and why?

❖ How do you recruit volunteer leaders?

❖ How do you train volunteer leaders?

❖ What seems to work best to help you reach the unchurched?

❖ How do you welcome/followup on newcomers?

❖ Do you have a mission statement? If yes, what is it? And how did you develop it?

❖ What do you want your ministry to look like in 1 year? 2 years? 5 years?

❖ How did you come to be involved in this ministry?

❖ What would be your three most important suggestions/recommendations for others doing single adult ministry?

After the meeting, everyone could eat lunch together and continue the dialogue.

SATURDAY AFTERNOON

This is a very important part of the weekend. Plan for Saturday afternoon to be kick-back time—some good, old fashioned R&R. With careful advance planning, various activities and points of interest in the host city can be identified. It could just be spending time shopping the malls or outlet stores. Or visit major attractions, museums, sporting events, or historical points of interest. Some of the team may just want to return to the hotel to swim, read, relax, or rest. Plan to meet for dinner around 6 P.M. at a nice restaurant.

SATURDAY NIGHT/SUNDAY MORNING

Vision trips can be one or two nights in length. Ideally, your host church singles ministry will also have a Saturday night activity that you can visit. If not, possibly another singles ministry in the area will. Either way, plan to worship at the host church on Sunday morning. This allows you to see the single adult ministry in the Sunday setting. .

THE TRIP HOME

Whether you return home Saturday evening or Sunday afternoon, plan to eat at a special restaurant enroute home.

It is advantageous to have some discussion questions for your leaders to talk about on the trip home. Debriefing immediately after an event is much better than waiting a week or a month—capitalize on this experience while it is fresh and energizing. Discuss such questions as:

❖ What one thing from the host church's ministry stands out to you?

❖ What was the most creative idea you had as a result of something you experienced or observed this weekend?

❖ How could our ministry most benefit from what we observed/learned?

❖ What would you now like to do differently in our ministry, if anything?

❖ How has this trip helped expand your vision? What new dreams are you dreaming?

❖ Is there something in your particular area of ministry responsibility that you feel discouraged about? If so, why?

❖ Is there something in your particular area of ministry responsibility that you feel encouraged about? If so, why?

EQUIPMENT/SUPPLIES (To be furnished by the event leaders)

☐ Discussion Questions to use with host team (see page 163)
☐ Discussion Questions to use with your team on return home (on this page)
☐ Maps and sightseeing information for host city

_____

WHAT TO BRING (To be provided by participants)

☐ Change of comfortable clothes and toiletries based on number of nights
☐ Dress clothes, if needed for Sunday morning worship
☐ Swimsuit and/or workout clothes
☐ Bible, notebook, pen/pencil
☐ An inquisitive, teachable attitude

PLANNING THE EVENT

PLANNING TEAM

For this event, you need an Event Director (possibly an Assistant Event Director) and volunteers to take responsibilities for the event site, budget, registration, and transportation.

❖ *The more people who have ownership and involvement in the planning, the greater success you will have.*

Planning Timeline

Event: *Leadership Vision Trip*   **Date of event:** _____

Event Director: _____   **Phone:** _____

Thanks for agreeing to serve on our Vision Trip Planning Team. Please check over this timeline for your assigned task(s). Adapt as needed and supplement with information in the generic job descriptions. Highlight your tasks (and due dates) and mark your calendar accordingly.

Date: _____ | 4 TO 6 MONTHS IN ADVANCE

Event Director (page 226)

☐ Recruit a Planning Team.
☐ Meet with Planning Team to brainstorm ideas and adapt this event to fit your ministry goals and objectives.
☐ Distribute copies of this timeline and related job descriptions. Make sure team members understand their assigned responsibilities. Adapt timeline as needed.

Budget Coordinator (page 229)

☐ Begin developing a proposed budget.

Event Site Coordinator (page 234)

☐ Research potential host churches and bring this information to the team for a decision on which ministry to visit.
☐ Be the contact person between the Planning Team and the selected host church. In consultation with the Planning Team, make all schedule arrangements for activities with the host church.
☐ Gather information from hotels near the host church, including costs, amenities, check-in and check-out times, etc.

Transportation Coordinator (page 252)

☐ Make all transportation arrangements.
☐ Plan the route, including any enroute stops.

Date: _____ | 4 MONTHS IN ADVANCE

Event Director

☐ Meet with Planning Team for updates on progress.

Event Site Coordinator

☐ Recommend to the Planning Team all accommodation arrangements.

Budget Coordinator

☐ With the Planning Team, finalize the budget and establish the cost per participant.

Registration Coordinator (page 241)

☐ Along with the singles ministry director, identify key leaders who should particpate on this trip. Send them personal invitations.
☐ Prepare the scholarship application form.

Date: _____ | 3 MONTHS IN ADVANCE

Event Director

☐ Conduct meeting of Planning Team for updates on progress.

Registration Coordinator

☐ Follow up invitation letters with phone calls or in-person invitations.
☐ Sign up leaders planning to attend and begin collecting deposits.

Budget Coordinator

☐ Make arrangements to pay any necessary hotel deposits, etc.

❖ *For more ideas and help, refer to job descriptions beginning on page 225.*

Date:	**2 MONTHS** **IN ADVANCE**

Event Director

- ☐ Conduct a Planning Team meeting for updates on progress.
- ☐ Prepare discussion questions to be used during the meeting with the host church (see suggestions on page 163).
- ☐ Send a copy of the questions to the host church for their advance preparation.
- ☐ Schedule a follow-up debriefing meeting for participants to share what they learned and observed. Plan to include key singles who were unable to go on this trip.

Event Site Coordinator

- ☐ Propose Saturday afternoon free-time activities/sightseeing to Planning Team.
- ☐ Confirm schedule with the host church.

Registration Coordinator

- ☐ Scholarship applications are now due.
- ☐ Determine with the singles ministry director who receives scholarship assistance, and in what amount.
- ☐ Notify scholarship recipients.

Date:	**1 MONTH** **IN ADVANCE**

Event Director

- ☐ Conduct a meeting of the Planning Team for updates on progress.

Event Site Coordinator

- ☐ Re-confirm accommodations and schedule with host church.
- ☐ Let the host church know how many people will be coming on this trip.

Transportation Coordinator

- ☐ Confirm final transportation arrangements.

Date:	**2 WEEKS** **IN ADVANCE**

Registration Coordinator

- ☐ Finalize attendance list.
- ☐ Send a written confirmation to participants which includes the schedule and emergency phone numbers which they can leave with family or friends (see sample, page 244).
- ☐ Collect all registration fees.

Date:	**2 TO 4 WEEKS** **AFTER EVENT**

Event Director

- ☐ Following the trip send appropriate thank-you note to the host church.
- ☐ Provide a written summary of things shared during the Saturday morning leadership meeting between the vision trip participants and the leadership of the host church. Distribute a copy to all ministry leadership and to your senior pastor.

All Leaders

- ☐ Following the trip, the Planning Team should make arrangements to have some of those who participated share what they learned and what new perspectives they may have gained with the other single adult leaders in your ministry who didn't attend. This will not only bring everyone in on what has been learned, but will serve to build enthusiasm for the next Vision trip.
- ☐ See the reproducible "Followup Guidelines" on page 254.

19 COMMUNITY IN SOLITUDE

A Break from the Rat Race

Event Summary: A guided, group spiritual formation retreat that includes extensive time in reflection, prayer, Bible reading, and community building, as well as small-group sharing and encouragement time.

Length of Event: Friday evening–Sunday afternoon

Suggested Theme Verse: "But those who hope in the Lord will renew their strength. They will soar on wings like eagles; they will run and not grow weary, they will walk and not be faint." Isaiah 40:31

Ideal Number of Participants: 10+

Estimated Cost Per Person: $50–$150, depending on facility costs

Facility Requirements: Monastic, peaceful setting recommended

Recommended Planning Team: 4–10 people

Advance Planning Needed: 6–9 months

INTRODUCTION

by Dr. Paul M. Petersen
Senior Pastor
Westminster Presbyterian Church
Aurora, Illinois

The world is a busy place that seems to revolve at a faster and faster pace. We need time to collect ourselves. "Community in Solitude" is a reflective weekend providing an opportunity to unwind away from the pressures of our world and to spend extensive time in reflection, prayer, Bible reading, and small group time.

This event is not a "silent retreat," where no interaction among participants is allowed. Rather, it is a guided, group retreat where interaction is essential to the process. The vehicle for group guidance and interaction is the "Spiritual Formation Group." These small groups are designed to provide nurture and encouragement. Through questions and prayer, personal growth is encouraged, and each member becomes committed to the spiritual growth of others in the group.

A topic is presented in an "Interlude with God" (time alone with God), followed by an opportunity to discuss it in the Spiritual Formation Groups (small groups). The third component is worship. Time is set aside to praise and honor God.

The event provides an opportunity for Christian singles to experience an interlude with God, in an uncluttered setting. "Community in Solitude" provides an opportunity for Christian community building through the collective sharing of the individual "Interludes with God."

OBJECTIVES

❖ To provide a time for spiritual reflection and community building, unhindered by the pressures and hectic pace of the world.

THE BIG EVENT

SCHEDULE

❖ *Get as many people as possible involved in the planning of this event.*

Friday

7:30–8:30 P.M.—Registration, settle in

8:30–9:30 P.M.—Snacks, time to get acquainted

9:30–10:00 P.M.—Introduction by the Leader

10:00–10:30 P.M.—Spiritual Formation Groups meet to get acquainted

10:30–11:00 P.M.—Evening Worship (Scripture and prayer)

11:00 P.M.—A Time of Quiet (Reading, praying, journaling, sleeping)

Saturday

6:30–7:30 A.M.—Optional small-group prayer or reflective exploration of facility grounds

7:30–8:00 A.M.—Morning Worship (Scripture and prayer)

8:00–8:30 A.M.—Breakfast

8:30–9:00 A.M.—Leader explains Spiritual Formation Group process and the "Interludes with God." Hand out first Interlude questions (Resource 3).

9:00–10:30 A.M.—Interlude with God #1

10:30–11:30 A.M.—Session 1—Prayer (in Spiritual Formation Groups)

11:30 A.M.–12:00 P.M.—Free Quiet Time with God in prayer and reflective Scripture reading anywhere on the retreat grounds

12:00–1:00 P.M.—Lunch (In groups of two or three, discuss what God has been saying to you)

1:00–2:30 P.M.—Interlude with God #2

2:30–4:00 P.M.—Session 2—Holiness (in Spiritual Formation Groups)

4:00–5:30 P.M.—Free Quiet Time

5:30–6:30 P.M.—Dinner (Sit and share with people who are not in your Spiritual Formation Group.)

6:30–6:45 P.M.—Free Quiet Time

6:45–7:30 P.M.—Evening Worship (Scripture and prayer)

7:30–8:00 P.M.—Free Quiet Time

8:00–9:00 P.M.—Interlude with God #3

9:00–10:00 P.M.—Session 3—The Holy Spirit (in Spiritual Formation Groups)

Sunday

7:30–8:00 A.M.—Breakfast

8:00–9:00 A.M.—Morning Worship and Communion

9:00–9:30 A.M.—Free Quiet Time

9:30–10:30 A.M.—Interlude with God #4

10:30–11:30 A.M.—Session 4—The Word (Spiritual Formation Groups)

11:30 A.M.–1:00 P.M.—Brunch

1:00–2:00 P.M.—Interlude with God #5 (Prepare yourself to reenter the world)

2:00–3:00 P.M.—Session 5—Compassion (Spiritual Formation Groups)

3:00–3:30 P.M.—Debriefing: "Some Thoughts on Reentry" (Leader)

3:30 P.M.—Check-out/Depart for home

PRE-EVENT READING

The following suggested Scripture passages and books will help participants prepare for and follow up the retreat.

SCRIPTURE

Psalm 25	Psalm 27	Psalm 31
Psalm 33	Psalm 37	Psalm 40
Psalm 39	Psalm 95	Psalm 104
Psalm 106	Psalm 145	Psalm 130
Lamentations 3	Isaiah 8	Isaiah 25
Isaiah 40	Isaiah 49	Isaiah 64
Habakkuk 3	Hosea 12:6	Micah 7:7
Luke 12	Acts 1	
I Corinthians 10	Ephesians 2:11-22	

BOOKS

A Kempis, Thomas, *The Imitation of Christ* (Greensburg, PA: Barbour and Co., Inc., 1984).

Bridges, Jerry, *The Practice of Godliness* (Colorado Springs, CO: NavPress, 1991).

____, *The Practice of Holiness,* (Colorado

Springs, CO: NavPress, 1991)

Hurnard, Hannah, *Hind's Feet on High Places*, (Wheaton: Tyndale House Publishers, 1977)

Foster, Richard, *Celebration of Discipline*, (HarperSanFrancisco, 1978).

Larson, Bruce, *The Presence: The God Who Delivers and Guides*, (HarperSanFrancisco, 1984).

Nouwen, Henri, *The Way of the Heart* (New York: Ballantine/Epiphany Books, 1983).

Packer, J.I., *Knowing God*, (Downers Grove, IL,: InterVarsity Press, 1973.)

Phillips, J.B., *Your God Is Too Small* (New York: Macmillan Publishing Co., 1961).

Tozer, A.W., *The Pursuit of God* (Harrisburg, PA: Christian Publications, Inc., 1982).

PRE-EVENT TRAINING

One of the most important aspects of this event takes place in small groups called Spiritual Formation Groups. It is the purpose of the groups, and thus of the group facilitators, to encourage and challenge each individual to get the most out of the experience.

The time spent in the Spiritual Formation Groups should be a time of growth, the birth of something new in each person's life—individually and collectively. Group facilitators need to help people realize and feel God's love for them. Growth is a process. Anguish and frustrations are a normal part of the process.

Use the material in this section, Resource 1, "Community in Solitude Overview" (page 175) and Resource 2, "Training Bible Study" (page 176) in training the Spiritual Formation Group Facilitators.

To train facilitators, schedule two training sessions. For example:

SESSION 1 (TWO WEEKS BEFORE RETREAT)

Show an event schedule. Discuss the benefits of this type of retreat as shown on page 167. Explain the "Community in Solitude" process, using Resource 1. Conduct a Bible study using Resource 2. The Bible study will help facilita-

tors explore what reflective time with God really means. Review the process—worship and personal time with God, followed by group interaction on the same topic. Give an "Interlude with God" assignment for facilitators to complete before Session 2. Use one of the assignments on Resource 3, page 177, designed for the retreat, or develop three or four questions of your own.

SESSION 2 (ONE WEEK BEFORE RETREAT)

Begin with a practice Spiritual Formation Group in which facilitators share their "Interlude with God" experiences. Review the process. Remind facilitators that the purpose of the Spiritual Formation Groups is sharing and encouragement, not teaching or seeing how much head knowledge exists in the group. Encourage the facilitators to do the following within their groups.

- Pray for each member.
- Tolerate differences with patience.
- Treat all members of the group as family, for each one is a brother or sister in Christ.
- Allow each member the right to express frustrations with the process. For some, this retreat will not be easy, as most people are uncomfortable with silence and unstructured time.
- Be careful not to provide rote answers or a quick fix. Remember, God is at work in each one of us, sometimes in a very painful way. Sometimes our real motive in providing a rote answer or quick fix is that we have a need to hide our own pain.
- Be honest with your feelings and share them with your group.
- With an attitude of prayer, silently reflect on what is being said, individually and collectively.

Hand out questions to be used in the Spiritual Formation Groups during the event (Resource 4, page 178). Pray together for those who will be attending the event.

PROGRAM IDEAS AND SUGGESTIONS

ICEBREAKERS

At 8:30 on Friday evening there is an opportunity to enjoy snacks and to get to know the others on the retreat. Since this is a reflective retreat, a quiet icebreaker giving your participants a chance to get to know one another is helpful.

• Signature Boxes

One of the more popular icebreakers—and so variations are found in other chapters as well—is the autograph sheet with 25-30 boxes on a sheet of paper, each with a descriptive phrase, that needs a signature. Suggested descriptive phrases include: never been on a singles retreat before; has read the entire Bible through in one year; has been parachuting; attends church at least fifty times a year; etc.

❖ *For more icebreakers, see the Table of Contents.*

The object is to be the first one to fill your sheet with the signatures of people who fit the descriptions. Depending on your numbers you may want to limit how many boxes one person can sign on a given sheet.

• Four Quaker Questions

Consider using these questions during the opening Spiritual Formation Groups on Friday evening (10:00–10:30 P.M.).

1. Where did you live when you were ten years old?
2. How was your home heated when you were ten years old?
3. What was your favorite room in your home when you were ten years old?
4. When did God become more than just a name to you?

WORSHIP AND COMMUNION

Bringing in an outside speaker as the retreat leader who facilitates the process of the weekend is not necessary. Someone who is accustomed to small groups and the spiritual formation process within your own church or ministry can provide that leadership.

For the worship/communion services it is recommended that the Retreat Leader develop devotional talks (5-10 minute) based on the five session topics. Use the materials below and Resources 2, 3, and 4 (pages 176-178) as a guide. The topics and Scriptures are:

Session 1: Prayer—Psalms 51; 57:7-9; 92:1-5; 93:1-5; 97:1-12; 139:23, 24; I Corinthians 2:9-12; Ephesians 1:16-18

Session 2: Holiness—I Chronicles 16:8-36; I Corinthians 1:1-3; Ephesians 1:1-10; Colossians 3:1-17; I Peter 1:13-16

Session 3: Holy Spirit—John 17:5-15; Acts 10:34-48; Galatians 5:16-26

Session 4: The Word—John 1:1; I Corinthians 15:1-11; Colossians 3:15-17; II Timothy 3:14-17; I Peter 2:1-3

Session 5: Compassion—Psalm 85; Isaiah 58:6-11; Amos 5:21-24; Matthew 5:23, 24

Worship services are to be kept simple: some meditative Scripture reading, a short devotional thought from the Leader, and some prayer, both corporate and personal. Singing is not planned, but can easily be placed in the worship services if desired, using an available piano, a guitar, or simply your voices giving praise to God.

The communion service should also be simple. The easiest is for the participants to come forward one by one and to take of the bread and the cup. Then they return to their seats in quiet meditation. This fashion of Communion keeps with both the community and the solitude aspects of the weekend. (However, another meaningful option would be to serve Communion within each small group.)

QUESTIONS FOR SPIRITUAL FORMATION GROUPS AND INTERLUDES WITH GOD

Adapt the questions in Resources 1 and 2 (pages 175-176) for your particular group. Every question does not need to be discussed or used as written. The assignment for Interlude with God #1 is handed out on Saturday at the 8:30 A.M. meeting with the Leader. Thereafter the Spiritual Formation Group Facilitators will distribute copies of the questions for the "Interlude with God" at the end of their group discussion times.

DEBRIEFING: SOME THOUGHTS ON REENTRY

(Sunday 3:00 P.M.)

"Soaring as Eagles" (Isaiah 40:41)

Have the Retreat Leader share the following thoughts at the final group time on Sunday:

During this retreat we have waited on God and have soared like eagles in God's goodness. As we go back into the world, here are some suggestions to keep us soaring. In each session of our Spiritual Formation Groups we have focused on one of the great Christian virtues or disciplines.

1. **The Prayer-Filled Life:** focuses on intimacy with God. We need to set aside regular time for prayer, meditation, and spiritual reading as we seek to practice the presence of God.

2. **The Holy Life:** focuses on transformation of life. In God's power we need to strive against sin. In God's power we need to do righteous deeds of love and mercy.

3. **The Spirit-Filled Life:** focuses on the work of the Spirit in our lives and worship. We must continuously seek the gifts of the Holy Spirit and nourish the fruit of the Spirit so that we may experience the freshness of His joy.

4. **The Word-Centered Life:** focuses on the centrality of Christ and the importance of the Scriptures. We must regularly study the Scriptures and share our faith with others.

5. **The Compassionate Life:** focuses on justice and peace in human relationships. We must seek to serve others in love and mercy everywhere we can.

May this be our prayer as we return to our world.

EQUIPMENT/SUPPLIES (To be furnished by the event leaders)

- ☐ Cut-apart copies of Resource 3 (page 177) and Resource 4 (page 178).
- ☐ Extra Bibles, paper, pens/pencils
- ☐ Communion supplies
- ☐ Snack foods and drinks

WHAT TO BRING (To be provided by participants)

- ☐ Casual clothing
- ☐ Toiletries
- ☐ Bible, journal or notebook, pen/pencil
- ☐ Bedding (if requested by facility)
- ☐ A desire to make new friends and to grow spiritually.

PLANNING THE EVENT

PLANNING TEAM

For this event you will need an Event Director (possibly an Assistant Event Director) and coordinators for the event site, publicity, worship, budget, registration, food, audio/visual equipment, small groups (Spiritual Formation Groups), transportation, and materials/supplies.

In addition, you will need a Retreat Leader and Spiritual Formation Group (SFG) Facilitators (one for every 7–10 people). The leader does not need to be an outside speaker. It is possible that you have a very capable leader within your church or even within your group. Qualifications and responsibilities for the group facilitators are included on page 173 of the Planning Timeline.

❖ *The more people who have ownership and involvement in the planning, the greater success you will have.*

Planning Timeline

Event: *Community in Solitude*   **Date of event:** _____

Event Director: _____   **Phone:** _____

Thanks for agreeing to serve on our retreat Planning Team. Please check over this timeline for your assigned task(s). Adapt as needed and supplement with information in the generic job descriptions. Highlight your tasks (and due dates) and mark your calendar accordingly.

Date: _____   6 TO 9 MONTHS IN ADVANCE

Event Director (page 226)

☐ Recruit a Planning Team.
☐ Meet with the Planning Team to brainstorm ideas and adapt this event to fit your ministry goals and objectives.
☐ Distribute copies of this timeline and related job descriptions. Make sure team members understand their assigned responsibilities. Adapt timeline as needed.
☐ As a team, decide whether to look for an outside Retreat Leader.

Speaker Coordinator (page 250)

☐ With the team, recruit the Retreat Leader.
☐ Discuss retreat goals and the Retreat Leader's responsibilities before and during the retreat (see page 170).
☐ Send a contract outlining fees.

Event Site Coordinator (page 234)

☐ Search for a site that offers (1) a peaceful atmosphere, free from outside distractions; (2) places for small- and large-group community building, (3) room to roam; (4) quiet, solitary places for personal, uninterrupted "Interludes with God"; (5) complete meal service. A country retreat center is ideal. If none is available, use a site that meets as many of the criteria as possible.
☐ Visit potential sites to evaluate suitability before making reservations.
☐ Put the dates on the church calendar.

Budget Coordinator (page 229)

☐ Prepare a budget proposal.

Publicity Coordinator (page 238)

☐ Begin developing a promotional strategy.

Date: _____   5 MONTHS IN ADVANCE

❖ *For more ideas and help, refer to job description beginning on page 225.*

Event Director

☐ Meet with the Planning Team to check their progress.
☐ Order any books needed for the retreat reading list.

Budget Coordinator

☐ Finalize the budget with the team.

Publicity Coordinator

☐ When details are finalized for the location, dates, leader, registration fees and deadlines, etc., prepare promotional materials.
☐ With the Registration Coordinator, design the registration form (sample, page 245).
☐ Send materials to the printer.

Speaker Coordinator

☐ Send resource material (pages 175-178) for the Retreat Leader's review and input.
☐ Send a rough schedule and ask for a list of suggested readings and Scripture passages (see suggestions on page 168).

Food Coordinator (page 236)

☐ Make all meal and refreshments (including snacks and beverages) arrangements with the Event Site Coordinator.

Transportation Coordinator (page 252)

☐ Decide the best mode of transportation to the retreat site. If by bus, reserve it now.

Date: _____	**4 MONTHS IN ADVANCE**

Registration Coordinator (page 241)

☐ Encourage early registrations.
☐ If scholarship are being offered, make application forms available (see page 246).

Date: _____	**3 TO 6 MONTHS IN ADVANCE**

Event Director

☐ Meet with the Planning Team as needed to discuss progress of all details.
☐ Begin to finalize the retreat schedule.
☐ Make sure all suggested reading list books are available for participants to use.

Event Site Coordinator

☐ Confirm all details with the event site.
☐ Make sure a signed contract is on file at the site and at the church.

Registration Coordinator

☐ Continue registration.

Publicity Coordinator

☐ Continue all promotion.

Small-Group Coordinator (page 247)

☐ With the help of the Event Director, prayerfully select Spiritual Formation Group facilitators (one for every 7-10 participants). Their primary responsibility will be to facilitate small-group discussions. Facilitators should be skilled in guiding discussion without dominating; open to knowing God through prayer; and wanting to learn how to wait on God.

Group facilitators' responsibilities:

☐ Create an atmosphere of grace, mercy, love, and acceptance so small-group members will feel free to open their hearts to God and to one another for encouragement and challenge.

☐ Guide discussion of assigned questions.
☐ Distribute questions for individuals to use during personal "Interludes with God."

Date: _____	**2 MONTHS IN ADVANCE**

Event Director

☐ Call a Planning Team meeting to check progress.

Small-Group Coordinator

☐ Finalize the selection of Spiritual Formation Group facilitators.
☐ Coordinate the two training sessions with the Spiritual Formation Group Facilitators and the Speaker Coordinator.

Speaker Coordinator

☐ Ask the Leader to supply handouts or other resources that need to be copied.
☐ If the leader is from out of town, confirm all travel and lodging arrangements.

Publicity Coordinator

☐ Continue to promote the event.

Registration Coordinator

☐ Continue registration and collect fees.
☐ Collect scholarship applications, process approval, and inform recipients of funds granted.

Audio/Visual Coordinator (page 228)

☐ Determine audio/visual equipment needs.
☐ Fill out any necessary forms for use of church, rental, or facility equipment.
☐ Select someone to run the sound system at the retreat.

Date: _____	**1 MONTH IN ADVANCE**

Event Director

☐ Meet with the Planning Team to make sure all details have been arranged.

Creative Weekends © 1995 David C. Cook Publishing Co. You may photocopy this form for ministry use in your local church.   **173**

☐ Give registrants suggested reading lists and encourage them to read before the retreat.

Event Site Coordinator

☐ Send schedule to event site contact person.
☐ Check payment plan details.
☐ Create and maintain a list of all items/services needed while at the facility.
☐ Coordinate needs with the retreat facility.

Food Coordinator

☐ Confirm all food arrangements with the event site contact person. Confirm with the Event Site Coordinator what site will provide and what the group must provide.

Event Materials Coordinator (page 233)

☐ With the Registration Coordinator, prepare and photocopy the event schedule, all Resources, maps, letter to registrants, and any other material.

Worship Coordinator (page 251)

☐ With the Event Director, Retreat Leader, and volunteers of your choosing, plan the worship services (Friday, 10:30 P.M.; Saturday, 7:30 A.M.; Sunday, 8:00 A.M.).

Date:	**2 WEEKS IN ADVANCE**

Speaker Coordinator

☐ With the Retreat Leader and Small-Group Coordinator, hold the Spiritual Formation Group facilitators training session one.

Registration Coordinator

☐ Mail a final letter to all registrants (page 244 for sample), including time, date, and place to meet and want to bring. Include an emergency phone number and address.

Date:	**1 WEEK IN ADVANCE**

Event Director

☐ Confirm all plans for the retreat.

☐ Provide church staff with the retreat site emergency phone number and address.

Small-Group Coordinator

☐ Assign each participant to a spiritual formation group. This can be done in a variety of ways: by age, by sex, mixing "old-timers" and "first-timers," etc. Choose what is best for your situation.

Registration Coordinator

☐ Close registration.
☐ Make roommate assignments.

Transportation Coordinator

☐ Confirm all travel plans, drivers, etc.
☐ If carpooling, determine who can drive and the number per vehicle. Make sure all registrants are assigned to a carpool and that drivers have maps to the retreat site.

Speaker Coordinator

☐ Hold the second Spiritual Formation Group facilitators training session.
☐ Confirm all arrangements with the Leader.

Budget Coordinator

☐ Prepare all checks to be paid at the event (last event site payment, honorarium, etc.)

Worship Coordinator

☐ Purchase necessary communion elements and needed plates and cups for the presentation of the elements.

Food Coordinator

☐ Purchase any food items as needed.

Date:	**2 TO 4 WEEKS AFTER EVENT**

☐ See "Followup Guidelines" on page 254.

Community in Solitude

OVERVIEW

One of the most important aspects of this event takes place in small groups called Spiritual Formation Groups. The purpose of the groups, and thus of the facilitator of those groups, is to encourage and challenge each individual to get the most out of the experience.

COMMUNITY IN SOLITUDE "PROCESS"—WHAT IS IT?

A. Interludes with God (The following format is only a suggestion. Whatever format brings people closer to God is appropriate.)

  1. How to meet God in the "Interludes with God":
    a. Quiet your mind.
    b. Focus on Him by slowly reciting the Lord's Prayer, reading a psalm, or singing a praise song.
    c. Concentrate on God's goodness only. Focus on who He is.
    d. Ask for nothing.
    e. Wait patiently, delighting in His goodness.
    f. Allow the Holy Spirit to stir your soul.
    g. Be patient. Wait until you have met Him.

  2. Journal your thoughts during each interlude, writing them down as they come. Recording ideas about who you think God is can help you focus on Him. Then detailing your thoughts, struggles, and frustrations, as well as what you hear God telling you, will become an invaluable tool to use after re-entry into the world.

  3. Be willing to share your thoughts in the Spiritual Formation Groups, with those at the retreat, and with your roommate. This will help you integrate them into your life.

  4. Use your free time to meditate on what God is saying.

B. Spiritual Formation Groups

  1. These groups are for sharing and encouragement.

  2. Discussion questions will be provided to assist in sharing and to encourage you in your quest to meet God. Some questions are designed to help during quiet times with God.

The time spent in the Spiritual Formation Groups should be a time of growth, the birth of something new in each person's life—individually and collectively. Help each person realize and feel the Father God's love for them. Growth is a process. Anguish and frustrations are normal parts of the process.

  175

Training Bible Study

"Wait on God" (Psalm 37:1-7; Psalm 62:5; Isaiah 64:4)

Sometimes, when we haven't experienced the real power of God in our lives, we seek to manipulate or control God through our prayers. We begin to have personal problems.

Perhaps it can all be summed up with, "We want what we want when we want it, and we want it now!" Such thinking leads to powerless living.

The solution? To wait on God.

Turn to Psalm 37 and answer these questions: (Since this is a training Bible study, answers to Bible questions are provided in parentheses.)

1. What kind of things do you find yourself fretting about?

2. What do you find to be the best way to overcome worry?

3. What does Psalm 37 say to help us in our worries?

(Psalm 37 spells out the formula: "Do not fret [worry]" [v. 1]. How do we avoid fret? By "trust[ing] in the Lord" and doing good [v. 3]. Note that trusting in God brings about good works.)

4. Do you find it hard to trust? Why or why not?

5. How have you built trust before?

6. Does Psalm 37 give you new ideas on how to trust or what it means to trust? If so, what are they?

(We trust first, by "delight[ing] in God" [vs. 4] and experiencing and enjoying His presence. Secondly, by committing our "way" to God [vs. 5]. In other words, we seek *God's* best for our lives, rather than telling God what we think is best. Thirdly, we need to "be still" before God [vs. 7]. We need to clear our minds of those things that clutter them, to focus on the holiness and goodness of God. Lastly, we trust by waiting patiently for God to work [vs. 7].)

7. What happens if we fail to follow this pattern and wait on God? (Verse 8 says that we become angry at our circumstances, ourselves, and ultimately, God.)

8. What will be the results when we do trust?

(However, God promises to lift us up (vs. 23, 24) and "restore us to the land" if we wait on Him (vs. 34).

Read Psalm 62:5 and Isaiah 64:4.

What do these verses tell us about trusting in God?

(Psalm 62:5: When we trust in God alone we will find rest and hope.)

(Isaiah 64:4: We will receive blessings from God that are more than our ears have heard or our eyes have seen. In other words, the rewards are great.)

Close in prayer.

Interludes with God

Directions: Make enough copies for each retreat participant to receive one. Prior to the retreat, cut apart each sheet and distribute the questions just before each "Interlude with God."

Personal Interlude with God #1
(Saturday 9:00 a.m.) Remember to journal. Some suggested Bible verses to reflect upon: Psalms 51; 57:7-9; 92:1-5; 93:1-5; 97:1-12; 139:23, 24; I Corinthians 2:9-12; Ephesians 1:16-18

1. God, what is the number one thing You are trying to tell me today?
2. God, what keeps getting in the way so that I can't hear You?
3. God, forgive me for allowing self to get in the way.
4. Write four words or phrases that describe prayer (plan to share these later with your Spiritual Formation Group).

Personal Interlude with God # 2
(Saturday 1:00–2:30 P.M.)
Some suggested Bible verses to reflect upon: I Chronicles 16:8-36; I Corinthians 1:1-3; Ephesians 1:1-10; Colossians 3:1-17; I Peter 1:13-16

1. God, what am I doing to hinder my future?
2. God, what do You want for me?
3. God, forgive me for my shortcomings.
4. Make a list of what you need to do to be holy.

Personal Interlude with God #3
(Saturday 8:00–9:00 P.M.)
Some suggested Bible verses to reflect upon: John 17:5-15; Acts 10:34-48; Galatians 5:16-26

1. God, in what areas of my life do I need to experience You?
2. God, what is keeping me from experiencing You more?
3. God, forgive me when I keep trying to control my life.
4. Write down how you have seen, or not seen, the fruit of the Spirit in your life.

Personal Interlude with God # 4
(Sunday, 9:30–10:30 A.M.)
Some suggested Bible verses to reflect upon: John 1:1; I Corinthians 15:1-11; Colossians 3:15-17; II Timothy 3:14-17; I Peter 2:1-3

1. God, later today I will be back in the world. What can I do to strengthen my daily encounter with You?
2. God, I encountered You in a real and special way. Please help me keep that encounter alive.
3. Write down how the Scriptures can help you in your walk with God.

Personal Interlude with God # 5
(Sunday, 1:00–2:00 P.M.)
Some suggested Bible verses to reflect upon: Psalm 85; Isaiah 58:6-11; Amos 5:21-24; Matthew 5:23, 24

1. God, show me, as I reenter the world, what opportunities I have to give of myself so that I might experience your love more fully.
2. God, show me how I might give of myself to You through giving of myself to others.

Spiritual Formation Group Discussion Questions

Directions: Make enough copies for each retreat participant to receive one. Prior to the retreat, cut apart each sheet and distribute the questions just before each Spiritual Formation Group time.

Session 1—Prayer (Saturday 10:30 A.M.)

Group discussion questions:
1. What experiences of prayer and meditation have you had?
2. What difficulties or frustrations have you encountered with prayer/meditation?
3. What joys and delights have you experienced with prayer/meditation?
4. What are your expectations of prayer and meditation?
5. How did your "Interlude with God" go?
6. Did you learn anything that you would like to share?

Session 2—Holiness (Saturday 2:30 P.M.)

Group discussion questions:
1. What happened between you and God in the previous "Interlude with God"?
2. What is God saying to you?
3. What temptations did you face as you sought to meet God?
4. How did you respond?
5. What did you list as actions to take to be holy?
6. Did you learn anything that you would like to share?

Session 3—Holy Spirit (Saturday 9:00 P.M.)

Group discussion questions:
1. What happened with you and God in the previous "Interlude with God"?
2. What movements of the Holy Spirit have you experienced thus far in the retreat?
3. What fruit of the Spirit do you feel you need more of to live a life that is holy?
4. Did you learn anything that you would like to share?

Session 4—The Word (Sunday 10:30 A.M.)

Group discussion questions:
1. What happened with you and God in the previous "Interlude with God"?
2. How has the Bible been helpful to you in your walk with God in the past?
3. In what areas of your life is God working?
4. What is hindering His work?
5. What is God saying to do about it?
6. In what way have you encountered Christ during this retreat?

Session 5—Compassion (Sunday 2:00 P.M.)

Group discussion questions:
1. What happened with you and God in the previous "Interlude with God"?
2. What opportunities to serve others are available to you?
3. How can you work for justice and peace in others' lives?
4. Did you learn anything that you would like to share?

---

20 SILENCE FOR NOISY HEARTS

The Search for Simplicity and A Meaningful Prayer Life

Event Summary: A 24-hour spiritual retreat that includes quiet respite for study and prayer.

Teaching/Discussion Topics Included with This Event:

- A Meaningful Prayer Life
- The Components of Effective Prayer
- The Search for Silence and Simplicity

Length of Event: 24 hours

Suggested Theme Verse: "Be still and know that I am God. . . ." Psalm 46:10

Ideal Number of Participants: 20+

Estimated Cost Per Person: $25–$45

Facility Requirements: Retreat center, monastery, or hotel

Recommended Planning Team: 6–9 people

Advance Planning Needed: 6–9 months

INTRODUCTION

by Carol Sue Hutchinson
Associate Council Director
Florida United Methodist Conference
Lakeland, Florida

This retreat will be a breath of fresh air for your group—it offers busy single adults a chance to take a break, to reflect on their relationship with God, and to spend time with other like-minded singles. They will leave this retreat with a renewed sense of purpose and priorities for their life.

The focus of this 24-hour getaway is to learn how prayer is the path to simplicity and peace. Why do we pray? What are the hindrances to prayer? What are the components to effective prayer? This retreat is also an opportunity to become reacquainted with the Lord's Prayer, the model given to us by Jesus.

This retreat consists of three teaching sessions, along with several small-group exercises and discussions. It also includes quiet times, taking walks, reflection, play, and fellowship with others.

An event such as this requires minimal planning, yet it adds tremendous depth and life to those in your ministry. No outside speakers are required. Costs and time requirements are minimal. For the energy-expended, I've found this sort of 24-hour event to be one of the best investments possible in my singles ministry.

OBJECTIVES

- ❖ To take time from our busy lives to renew ourselves physically, mentally, and spiritually.
- ❖ To explore the power and purpose of prayer in our daily lives.
- ❖ To develop a more intimate relationship with God.
- ❖ To renew old friendships and initiate new ones.

THE BIG EVENT

SCHEDULE

Saturday

❖
Get as many people as possible involved in the planning of this event.

1:00 P.M.—Leave church
2:00 P.M.—Arrive at retreat center. Settle in, explore surroundings, take a quiet walk.
3:30 P.M.—Mixers/Icebreakers
4:15 P.M.—Session 1: A Meaningful Prayer Life
6:00 P.M.—Dinner
7:30 P.M.—Session 2: The Components of Effective Prayer

9:00 P.M.—Free time (snacks, table games, camp fire, etc.)

Sunday

7:00 A.M.—Morning devotions (individually)
8:00 A.M.—Breakfast
9:00 A.M.—Session 3: The Search for Silence and Simplicity
10:30 A.M.—Structured quiet time, Bible reading, personal reflection and prayer, etc.
12:00 P.M.—Lunch
1:00 P.M.—Worship
2:00 P.M.—Free time, quiet walks, Bible reading, personal reflection and prayer, etc.
3:30 P.M.—Depart for home

PROGRAM IDEAS AND SUGGESTIONS

STUDY GUIDES AND SMALL-GROUP SESSION MATERIALS

The following study guides are just that—guides. Take the ideas, quotes, Scriptures, and personal illustrations and translate them into your own experiences. Make them relative to your group. Read the given Bible references and, if possible, some of the book reference resources mentioned before presenting the material. This will provide helpful background for presenting the study.

❖
For a list of icebreakers, see the Table of Contents.

SESSION 1: SATURDAY, 4:15 P.M.
A MEANINGFUL PRAYER LIFE

Supplies Needed: Newsprint, chalkboard, or overhead projector; markers; index cards; and pens or pencils.

Large-Group Teaching Time
What Is Prayer?

On newsprint, a chalkboard, or an overhead projector, write the question, "What is Prayer?" Spend some time brainstorming and discussing the question and some or all of the following statements.

• Prayer is a means to build and develop a relationship with God.

• Genuine prayer does not strive after results, but arises out of a relationship.

• The kingdom of God is made up of right relationships. Right relationships with God and with others in the body of Christ produces purpose and freedom.

• "Prayer is the heart of religion." —George A. Buttrick in *Prayer*.

• "Prayer is nothing else but a sense of God's presence."—Brother Lawrence in *The Practice of the Presence of God*.

• "Though in its beginning, prayer is so simple that the feeblest child can pray, yet it is at the same time the highest and holiest work to which man can rise. It is fellowship with the unseen and Most Holy One. . . . It is the very essence of true religion, the channel of all blessings, the secret of power and life." —Andrew Murray in *With Christ in the School of Prayer*.

Small-Group Discussion Time

Divide into small groups of no more than five people per group. Keeping the same groups throughout the weekend enables participants to reach a deeper trust and sharing level. If it has not already been done, have the members of each small group spend a few minutes getting acquainted and learning something unique or unusual about each other.

Have each small group look up the following references and discuss what they say about prayer. (Another option would be to divide these Scripture references into two sections so that each group would only need to look up half of the verses listed.)

Romans 8:26, 27	Matthew 26:41
Ephesians 6:18	Psalm 91:15
I Chronicles 16:11	Luke 18:1
I Thessalonians 5:17	Isaiah 58:9
Matthew 7:7	John 16:24
Acts 4:31	Luke 11:9

Large-Group Teaching Time

Gather back together as a large group and discuss the findings of the above Scripture study. Have there been any new discoveries on the meaning of prayer?

Why We Pray

Read John 14:13 to the group, and then invite participants to discuss why they pray. (Write their answers on newsprint, a chalkboard, or an overhead projector.)

Next, discuss the following statements and quotations. (If possible, write these statements on newsprint, a chalkboard, or an overhead projector so that everyone can read them.) Does the group agree or disagree with these statements? Be sure they explain and discuss the reasons for their answers.

• Every answer to prayer will glorify God as its object. If there is no prospect of this end, there will be no answer to the prayer.

• Even in our requests, the chief end of prayer is to bring glory to God.

• Prayer is our best way to be in conversation with God.

• Prayer is a way to build a relationship with God.

• Prayer helps us share our needs and concerns.

• "Therefore, when you attempt to pray, see that it be your one design to commune with God, to lift up your heart to Him, to pour out your soul before Him. Any motive whatever on this side of eternity, any design

but that of promoting the glory of God, and the happiness of man for God's sake, makes every action, however fair it may appear to men, an abomination unto the Lord." What, according to this quotation of John Wesley, is the purpose of prayer? [Communion with God.]

Hindrances to Prayer

Draw a picture of a stick person praying. Above the person place an obstruction and the prayer lines bouncing off that obstruction. Write "God" in big letters above the obstruction. As a group, discuss the picture. Is it true that God sometimes cannot hear our prayers? If so, what are the things that might keep our prayers from getting through to God?

Discuss each of the following obstacles to effective prayer.

1. Sin. Read Isaiah 59:1, 2 to the group. The idea that God does not hear our prayers when we are sinning is misleading. However, when we are out of relationship with God, He may not act or respond because we are in no position to recognize His response.

2. Uncertainty. Read James 1:5-7 to the group. How are feelings of uncertainty reflected in our prayers?

3. Fear. Read II Timothy 1:7 to the group. With what attitude do we approach God? Fear focuses on the problem; faith focuses on the answer. "Fear knocked on the door, faith answered, no one was there."

What Are the Results of Prayer?

Read Matthew 6:33 to the group and discuss the results of prayer.

Small Group Discussion Time

Break into small groups again and have each group discuss the following Scriptures and ideas.

• What is the expected product of prayer? (See Job 42:7-9; Matthew 5:44-48; Luke 11:1-4; and John 16:24.)

• What are the factors in effective prayer?

• What role does fasting have in prayer?

(See Matthew 4:2; 6:16-18; 9:14-17.)

• What is the role of patience in prayer? (See Matthew 15:21, 22.)

• How do you typically respond when your faith is tested by God's silence?

Wrap up this session by having each person share in their small group one thing they have learned so far today that will help them have a more meaningful prayer life. Then ask that one person in each group close in prayer.

SESSION 2: SATURDAY, 7:30 P.M.

THE COMPONENTS OF EFFECTIVE PRAYER

Supplies Needed: Newsprint, chalkboard, or overhead projector; markers; index cards; pens or pencils; and a copy of Resource 1 (on pages 187-188) for each small group.

Large-Group Teaching Time

Write the following on newsprint, a chalkboard, or an overhead projector so that it will be displayed.

A – Adoration, praise

C – Confession

T – Thanksgiving

S – Supplication, intercession

Each of the above has its place and purpose in prayer. Each component needs to be part of our prayers.

Adoration/Praise

We adore or praise God for who He is.

Read Psalm 8 and Psalm 100 to the group. Praise and adoration is the movement of "taking off our shoes" as we stand on "holy ground". There is power in praise when we focus on the greatness, love, mercy, care, presence, and power of God. We are lifted above our own limitations. There is power in praise as our minds are directed to a source of strength beyond ourselves. Adoration and praise are a mixture of gratitude, reverence, and awe.

Confession

Through confession we experience cleansing and communion.

Read Psalm 66:16-20 to the group. Confession is a prerequisite not to God's forgiveness, but to our appropriating or receiving His forgiveness. Confession (or as Bill Bright puts it, "agreeing with God") opens the door to communion. As sin separates us from God, confession restores the relationship.

Thanksgiving

Thanksgiving is expressing gratitude to God for what He is doing.

Small Group Discussion/Exercise

Distribute a copy of Resource 1 (pages 187-188) to each group. Have them spend approximately 45-60 minutes completing the discussion and writing exercise.

Large-Group Teaching Time

Bring the group back together. If time permits, have a few people share their personal version of the Lord's Prayer with the whole group.

Supplication, Petition, Requests, Intercession

God is not a source of endless gifts. Prayer is putting ourselves in God's hands and will.

Read Philippians 4:6, 7 to the group. God wants what is best for us.

How do you test petitions to see if they are God's will (His best) for us?

• Do they conflict with Scripture?

• Do they build up or encourage us in the faith?

• Are they consistent with what you believe God wants?

• Are they in conflict with the way God works in the world?

There is no such thing as an unanswered prayer. When we pray believing, with faith, then God will assuredly respond to our prayer [Yes, No, Maybe, Later].

When we pray regularly, we move, almost instinctively, to lifting to God our concerns for other people (intercession). Results happen when people practice intercessory prayer. And praying for people increases our love for them.

Close this session by having everyone stand in a large circle to sing (or pray aloud) the Lord's Prayer.

SESSION 3: SUNDAY, 9:00 A.M.

THE SEARCH FOR SILENCE AND SIMPLICITY

NOTE: This entire session will be conducted in small groups or in solitary times of silence, prayer, and reflection. Distribute Resource 2 (pages 189-191) to each person for this session.

Supplies Needed: Copies of Resource 2 for each person. (Optional) Index cards for everyone plus one or two boxes to place cards in.

Worship: Sunday, 1:00 P.M.

As a part of the worship, consider having some of the participants share something about their quiet time before lunch—or have them read their paraphrased version of Psalm 23. What was meaningful to them about this time? How did God speak to them? What did they learn during their meditation on Psalm 23?

(Optional) At the conclusion of worship, have everyone place their name, address, and phone number on a index card, along with two or three specific prayer requests. Before participants leave the retreat, allow everyone to select one of these cards from a box. The name they select might become their prayer partner for the next year. If so desired, have the cards placed in two different boxes, divided by men and women, to team men with men and women with women.

RECOMMENDED RESOURCES

- Brother Lawrence, *The Practice of the Presence of God*. (Grand Rapids: Baker Book House/ Revell, 1958.)
- Jan Dargatz, *52 Simple Ways to Give Your Spiritual Life a Lift*. (Nashville: Oliver-

Nelson Books, 1991.)
- Richard Foster, *The Celebration of Discipline*. (HarperSanFrancisco, 1978.)
- Richard Foster, *Freedom of Simplicity*. (HarperSanFrancisco, 1981.)
- Richard Foster, *Prayer: Finding the Heart's True Home*. (HarperSanFrancisco, 1992.)
- Thomas Kelly, *Testament of Devotion*. (HarperSanFrancisco, 1941.)
- Andrew Murray, *With Christ in the School of Prayer*. (Greensburg, PA: Barbour and Co., Inc., 1988.)

EQUIPMENT/SUPPLIES (To be furnished by the event leaders)

- ☐ Copies of resource handouts
- ☐ Table games
- ☐ Items/props for mixers
- ☐ Newsprint/chalkboard/overhead projector
- ☐ Markers
- ☐ Index cards (plus two boxes to place cards in)

WHAT TO BRING (To be provided by participants)

- ☐ Casual clothes
- ☐ Bibles
- ☐ Notebook and writing pen
- ☐ Sleeping bag/bedding
- ☐ Toiletries
- ☐ Walking shoes

PLANNING THE EVENT

PLANNING TEAM

For this event, you need an Event Director (possibly an Assistant Event Director) and volunteers to take responsibilities for the event site, budget, publicity, printed materials, registration, food, worship, recreation, transportation, and audio/visual equipment and supplies.

❖ *The more people who have ownership and involvement in the planning, the greater success you will have.*

Planning Timeline

Event: *Silence for Noisy Hearts* **Date of event:** _____

Event Director: _____ **Phone:** _____

Thanks for agreeing to serve on our retreat Planning Team. Please check over this timeline for the task(s) assigned to you. Adapt as needed. Supplement this timeline with information on the reproducible, generic job descriptions found on pages 225-252. Highlight your tasks (and due dates) each time they appear. Mark your calendar accordingly.

Date: _____	**6 TO 9 MONTHS IN ADVANCE**

Event Director (page 226)

- ☐ Recruit a Planning Team. Brainstorm ideas and adapt this weekend event to fit your particular ministry goals and objectives.
- ☐ Make sure each team member understands his or her assigned tasks and responsibilities.
- ☐ Determine if this timeline will work for your area and make adjustments accordingly.
- ☐ Along with input from the Planning Team, determine who will be the retreat teacher. If someone other than the singles minister or a member of the group is being asked, contact that individual now. Suggested teaching materials are included with this event (see pages 180-183). However, when considering a possible teacher, look for someone who can synthesize material and communicate the thoughts and ideas without just reading the material to the group. In addition, the leader must have the ability to adapt, supplement, and apply Scripture and personal illustrations to the suggested thoughts and ideas included for this event.

> ❖ **For more ideas and help, refer to job descriptions beginning on page 225.**

Event Site Coordinator (page 234)

- ☐ With Planning Team input, secure the hotel, camp, or conference site.
- ☐ See that a deposit is paid, if required.
- ☐ Mark the date on the church calendar.

Budget Coordinator (page 229)

- ☐ Begin estimating per-person costs for this event.

Publicity Coordinator (page 238)

- ☐ Begin preparing a promotional strategy.

Date: _____	**5 MONTHS IN ADVANCE**

Event Director

- ☐ The retreat teacher should be in place. Provide this person with resource materials or suggested topics for the event.

Budget Coordinator

- ☐ In cooperation with the Planning Team, finalize a budget for the event.

Transportation Coordinator (page 252)

- ☐ Determine the best mode of transportation to the event site (i.e., car pool, church van, chartered bus, etc.).

Publicity Coordinator

- ☐ Once the event site, dates, registration fee, and other pertinent information have been determined, complete the promotional materials and begin promotion.

Registration Coordinator (page 241)

- ☐ If scholarship funds are available, prepare and supply the proper application forms.
- ☐ Determine all preregistration and registration deadlines.

Date: _____	**4 Months IN ADVANCE**

Event Director

☐ Hold a Planning Team meeting. Check on progress in each area of responsibility.

Event Site Coordinator

☐ Check to be sure a signed contract is on file at the event site and at the church.
☐ Make sure all details are correct.
☐ Verify that any required deposits have been paid and received at the event site.

Publicity Coordinator

☐ Continue promoting the event.

Date: _____	**3 Months IN ADVANCE**

Audio/Visual Equipment Coordinator (page 228)

☐ Determine audio/visual needs and fill out any request forms for using the event facility or church equipment.
☐ If church equipment is being used, arrange to reserve and transport it.

Registration Coordinator

☐ Continue registration.

Recreation Coordinator (page 240)

☐ Although recreational time for this event is limited, plan for a few games and activities.
☐ Make all necessary arrangements.

Food Coordinator (page 236)

☐ Begin making plans for refreshments and meals at the event site.

Publicity Coordinator

☐ Continue promoting the event.

Date: _____	**2 Months IN ADVANCE**

Event Director

☐ Hold another Planning Team meeting. Help resolve any problems that may exist and check on progress in each area of responsibility.
☐ Ask the retreat teacher to provide any handouts he or she will use, and arrange to have them copied prior to the event.

Registration Coordinator

☐ Submit scholarship applications for proper approval and inform recipients of funds granted.
☐ Continue registering participants.

Worship Coordinator (page 251)

☐ From the list of those planning to attend, ask musically talented people to lead the singing for the Sunday worship.
☐ With the help of the retreat teacher, make preparations for the Sunday worship time.

Publicity Coordinator

☐ Continue promoting the event.

Date: _____	**1 Month IN ADVANCE**

Event Director

☐ Hold another Planning Team meeting. Help resolve any problems that may exist and check on progress in each area of responsibility.

Registration Coordinator

☐ Collect any remaining scholarship application forms.
☐ Continue registering participants.

Transportation Coordinator

☐ Finalize transportation and drivers.

Event Site Coordinator

☐ Send a copy of the event schedule to the contact person at the event site.
☐ Check details of the payment plan, if needed.

Event Materials Coordinator (page 233)

☐ Have the event schedule, small group materials, maps, final letter to registrants (see page 244), and any other copied materials ready for assembly or mailing.

Equipment/Supplies Coordinator (page 233)

☐ Gather needed supplies for the icebreakers, activities, etc.

Audio/Visual Equipment Coordinator

☐ Double-check audio/visual equipment needs. Have all needs been met?

Food Coordinator

☐ Finalize all meal and snack plans. Coordinate details with the contact person at the event site.

Date: _____	1 WEEK IN ADVANCE

Event Director

☐ Meet with the Planning Team to be sure all plans are on track.
☐ Provide the church staff with a phone number and address at the event site, in case of emergency.

Registration Coordinator

☐ Send information letter to all participants. (A sample letter is found on page 244. Adapt the letter for your event.)

Budget Coordinator

☐ Prepare checks for payments as needed.

Date: _____	2 TO 4 WEEKS AFTER EVENT

☐ See the "Followup Guidelines" on page 254.

A–C–T–S

A—Adoration, praise
C—Confession
T—Thanksgiving
S—Supplication, intercession

As a small group, discuss the following:

1. Which of the A-C-T-S components are easiest for you when you pray? Why so?
2. Which are the hardest? Why so?
3. What component(s) do you need to practice more when you pray?

Jesus provided us an example—a model—of how to pray when He gave us the Lord's Prayer. As a small group, pray the Lord's Prayer together. Then find where each of the A-C-T-S components are in the prayer. In what order are they?

A MODEL PRAYER

Printed below is the Lord's Prayer (Matthew 6:9-13). To help you personalize this prayer, rewrite or paraphrase it in your own words—from your heart—in the space provided below. Be creative. Don't be afraid to color outside the lines. Write it the way you feel it. (See an example on page 188 as written by Carol Sue Hutchinson.)

Our Father in heaven,

Hallowed be your name.

Your kingdom come.

Your will be done on earth,
as it is in heaven.

Give us this day our daily bread.

Forgive us our debts,
as we also have forgiven our debtors.

(Continued)

And lead us not into temptation,
but deliver us from the evil one.

For thine is the kingdom, and the power,
and the glory, for ever. Amen. [KJV]

After each person has completed writing his or her own version, have volunteers read their personal Lord's Prayer to your group. Then read the Lord's Prayer (above) again, verse by verse. Reflect on its meaning. Discuss what it means to you. Share your thoughts with the group.

EXAMPLE: The Lord's Prayer
As written by Carol Sue Hutchinson

Daddy, You are everywhere that is good
    and are so very special to me.
You want the very best for me and have placed within me
    the ability and potential to be everything
You created me to be.
The victorious life You promised is mine right now,
    right here where I am.
Heaven—the time when I will live with You—is everything
    You have taught me and so much more
    than our human minds can comprehend.
You will see to my every need and I will want for nothing
    when I trust you.
Each day I do things that make You sad.
    I am not as considerate of others and
    I do not always live Your life.
Forgive me, I pray, even as I am right now forgiving
    those people who have hurt me.
Keep those things in my world that come between You and me
    unattractive, and give me the willpower to ignore them
So that my victorious life will be a blessing to You
    and a witness to others.
When I do fall, I know You are there
    to pick me up and dust me off.
Because all power, glory, and honor are Yours for ever and ever.
Amen.

In Search of Simplicity

(vs. Feeling Overwhelmed by Life)

Read the following poem and quotes aloud to your group. Then discuss the questions that follow.

> THE DIFFERENCE
> I got up early one morning
> and rushed right into the day;
> I had so much to accomplish
> that I didn't take time to pray.
>
> Problems came tumbling about me
> And heavier came each task.
> *Why doesn't God help Me?*
> I wondered.
> He answered, "You didn't ask."
>
> I wanted to see joy and beauty,
> But the day toiled on grey and bleak.
> I wondered why God didn't show me.
> He answered, "But you didn't seek."
>
> I tried to come into God's presence;
> I used all my keys at the lock.
> God gently and lovingly chided,
> "My child, you didn't knock."
>
> I woke up early this morning,
> And I paused before entering the day.
> I had so much to accomplish
> That I had to take time to pray.
> —Author Unknown

When we take time to pray our lives become simplified because we limit our hearing to only one voice—God's.

"We feel honestly the pull of many obligations and try to fulfill them all. And we are unhappy, uneasy, strained, oppressed, and fearful we will be shallow. We feel pulled into too many different directions, we begin to feel overwhelmed and unable to do anything well." —Thomas Kelly in *Testament of Devotion*

"What will set us free from the bondage of feeling overwhelmed and having to do things right? We are bound to the spiral of ever increasing bonds on us: work, family, world, and even our faith journey. The answer is found in simplicity. This virtue, once worked into our lives, will unify the demands of our life. It will prune and trim gently and in the right place." —Richard Foster in *Freedom of Simplicity*

"We have hints that there is a way of life vastly richer and deeper than all this hurried existence, a life of unhurried serenity and peace and power. If only we could slip over into that center." —Thomas Kelly in *Testament of Devotion*.

Read Isaiah 40:30-31, "Even youths grow tired and weary, and young men stumble and fall; but those who hope in the Lord will renew their strength. They will soar on wings like eagles; they will run and not grow weary, they will walk and not be faint."

Questions for Discussion

1. What is your biggest obstacle to finding time to pray?

2. Why are most of us so rushed and frazzled in our daily schedules? Why does everything seem to be going faster and faster, with less time to think, meditate, and pray?

3. Is it possible to get off this roller coaster and find more simplicity and peace in our lives? If so, how?

(Continued)

4. How would your life be different if you were living a more simplified, less hurried life? Describe it.

5. What is the price of simplicity? What will we have to sacrifice to find it?

6. What criteria do you use to decide what you will respond to and what you will let go? (How can you keep from being pulled in too many directions?)

7. What priority list do you use to make commitments of your time and talents?

These are important questions to ask if you want to simplify the demands on your life. If you have no criteria or priority list, then you have no way to evaluate all that is asked of you. The usual consequence is that you are in too deep and are pulled in too many directions.

When we do not take time for silence and operate without a priority list, we begin to feel like our friend the duck: above the surface we are composed and unruffled; below the surface we are paddling with all our might. Outwardly we are confident and in command, but inwardly we are tired and scattered.

The Discipline of Silence

One way to nurture simplicity is through the discipline of silence. We seem dominated by the notion that action is the only reality.

Read Psalm 46:10— "Be still and know that I am God; I will be exalted among the nations, I will be exalted in the earth."

"Silence is not native to my world. Silence, more than likely, is a stranger in your world, too. If you and I ever have silence in our noisy hearts, we are going to have to grow it. . . . You can nurture silence in your noisy heart if you value it, cherish it, and are eager to nourish it." —Wayne Oates in *Nurturing Silence in a Noisy Heart*

Coming into the divine center requires an attitude of silence, waiting—expectant waiting—a simplicity of heart and thought.

Questions for Discussion

Take time to think through, discuss, and share the following. Use personal experiences to illustrate your sharing when appropriate.

1. Describe a recent time when you experienced real silence. Was it a good or bad experience? Why?
2. Why is silence difficult for most of us?
3. Is "action" [or doing something] the only reality in your life? Explain.
4. How can you "nurture silence in your noisy heart"?
5. Is there a difference between "silence" and an "attitude of silence"? Explain.
6. What is the meaning of the verse, "Be still and know that I am God"? What does this require?
7. In order to develop a habit of silence, one needs a specific time and place. Based on your current life, when and where is the most likely time and place for you?

Finding God

Where do we go from here? What is the key that will unlock the mystery of spiritual awareness in the deepest part of our soul? How can we better realize that God is real and alive within us? The answer may well be different for each one of us!

According to Jan Dargatz, author of *52 Simple Ways to Give Your Spiritual Life a Lift*, some become aware of God's presence while reading a book of someone's experience of God's work in his or her life. Some experience the presence of God while listening to a speaker. For some, it is meditative prayer. For others, it is meditatively praying Scripture. For still others, it is quiet time alone with God. And some have not yet

(Continued)

awakened to God's presence in their lives. Not everyone is ready at the same time to be aware of God's presence.

Choose activities that will put you in a place to receive God's presence in your life: prayer, Bible reading, worship, Bible study. Ask for God's guidance on your journey.

A challenge for each of us this next week—and beyond:

Making God central is not adding God to my life, but integrating or making God part of everything I do.

Have you ever tried to fill each moment of the day with God—not ceasing your daily activity, but bringing God to everything you do and every person you meet? This is done silently as you meet people and enter events. This takes a conscious effort—beginning with your family or those closest and dearest to you, then the office staff as you enter your work, and each person you might meet along the way. It makes a day very happy and filled with joy. And for one reason: you are concentrating on God and others rather than being focused on yourself.

It changes the way we see people and relate to them. It's hard work at first because it is quite against our nature. But the rewards are immeasurable.

Frank Laubach, a writer of devotional and prayer materials, writes of his "Game with Minutes." The idea is to take a given hour each day and see how many minutes during that hour you can be conscious of God's presence. Begin with the hour of worship and then extend it to hours during the week.

Individual Exercise

Take the next hour to be alone, in silence. Go outside or to some other part of the building where you will be undisturbed.

Read Psalm 23 and reflect on each sentence. What does it mean? What does it say to you? Read the example of how it was paraphrased by Paul M. Petersen on this page, then spend time paraphrasing Psalm 23 in your own words.

EXAMPLE: The Twenty-third Psalm
As written by Paul M. Petersen

The Lord is my mentor, I will not quaver.
He gives me rest in the midst of my busy
    schedule,
He refreshes me with words of
    encouragement and puts my feet on solid
    rock.
He shows me right decisions that glorify Him
    in a world of gray questions.
Even when my day is black and confusion
    surrounds me,
I will not lose heart because I find comfort in
    Your guidance, admonition, and
    encouragement.
You take care of my physical needs,
    such as feeding me well,
      even where my enemies can see me.
He anoints me with oil to protect me from
    my opponents.
I know that Your good favor and protection
    will be with me at all times and Your
    hospitality will never wear out.

21 "NORTHERN EXPOSURE" RETREAT

A Winter Retreat with a Culturally Relevant Theme

Event Summary: A weekend retreat, ideal for winter, using ideas based on a popular television program. Food, activities, small-group sharing, and devotions are developed using the program themes. Scenes from the program are shown as discussion starters.

Length of Event: Friday evening to Sunday noon

Suggested Theme Verses: Proverbs 8:1-3

Ideal Number of Participants: At least 12, but the maximum is unlimited by virtue of the small-group nature of the sessions.

Estimated Cost Per Person: $40–$85 The videos generally are $3.00 to rent or $14.95 to purchase.

Facility Requirements: A nice retreat site. This is not a good theme for a camping retreat.

Recommended Planning Team: 6–10 people

Advance Planning Needed: Approximately 6 months.

INTRODUCTION

by Terry Fisher
Singles Pastor
First Baptist Church
San Mateo, California

Using various forms of familiar media is a great way to interest non-Christians and thus create open doors of opportunity to tell people about Jesus. Episodes of classic television programs such as "The Andy Griffith Show" and "Leave It to Beaver," contemporary series like "M*A*S*H*" and "Northern Exposure," and movies like the *Oh, God* series starring George Burns are wonderful visual aids as discussion starters about contemporary issues and biblical topics.

OBJECTIVES

❖ Attract non-Christians to an event by using a contemporary theme for a retreat.
❖ Stimulate discussions of issues through the use of media.

The response from non-Christians to this style of event has always been very positive. Most seem surprised to find Christians who have this "cultural awareness." I have found Christians in various churches and singles ministries to sometimes be a little more comfortable including their non-Christian friends when they see culturally appealing programs like this.

"Northern Exposure," even though it has been canceled, is a wonderful show to use for a variety of reasons. Although some people may struggle with its eccentricity, that characteristic is one reason it is so easy to use in a retreat setting to discuss contemporary issues. The human struggles presented become the basis for small-group discussions during the retreat.

It is true that "Northern Exposure" contains story lines that might endorse subject matter contrary to holy living. Find an appropriate time during the retreat to make it clear to those attending that using portions of the program is in no way an endorsement of every lifestyle presented on the show.

THE BIG EVENT

SCHEDULE

Friday

7:00–9:00 P.M.—Arrival at the retreat site and registration

9:00 P.M.—Introduction, get-acquainted character activity

10:30 P.M.—Snacks (Maurice's spicy chicken wings)

11:30 P.M.—To bed (big day tomorrow!)

❖ *Get as many people as possible involved in the planning of this event.*

Saturday

8:00 A.M.—Breakfast (Adam's German apple pancakes)

8:30 A.M.—First session, video 1

9:15 A.M.—Small-group discussion 1

10:00 A.M.—Large-group discussion 1

10:30 A.M.—Photo shoot

12:00 P.M.—Lunch (The Brick's Caesar salad and Maggie's gumbo)

1:00 P.M.—Second session, video 2

1:45 P.M.—Small-group discussion 2

2:30 P.M.—Large-group discussion 2

3:00 P.M.—Free time

6:00 P.M.—Dinner (lasagna, Chris's glazed carrots, Holling's lime chiffon pie)

7:00 P.M.—Third session, video 3

7:45 P.M.—Small-group discussion 3

8:30 P.M.—Large-group discussion 3

9:30 P.M.—The Marilyn Whirlwind Dance Hall

11:00 P.M.—The Ed Chigliak Theatre

11:30 P.M.—The Classic Movie Theatre, featuring *Citizen Kane*

Sunday

8:00 A.M.—Breakfast, The Brick's Special (eggs, home fries, toast, coffee, and juice)

8:30 A.M.—Fourth session, video 4

9:15 A.M.—Small-group discussion 4

10:00 A.M.—Large-group discussion 4, worship service.

11:30 A.M.—Pack up and head for home

THE FOOD FOR THE WEEKEND

All snacks and meals are ideas from the television program and give an important tie-in to the theme of the weekend. If you are unable to find a retreat site that will allow you to prepare your own food, sit down with the cook and see if he or she has any dishes that are similar to those from the show. All recipes are found in the *Northern Exposure Cookbook*. (See Recommended Resources on page 195.)

HOUSING

It is very important to have a comfortable lodge or retreat facility. If you have this retreat in the winter, make sure your facility is winterized, has comfortable beds, good showers, and adequate space for meals, large group meetings and several small group meetings at one time. Some of the people will have never experienced anything like this before. Inadequate facilities can ruin the experience for new guests.

PROGRAM IDEAS AND SUGGESTIONS

GET-ACQUAINTED CHARACTER ACTIVITY, FRIDAY 9:00 P.M.

Introduce the group to "Northern Exposure." It is a television show set in fictitious Cicely, Alaska, population 839, and is a celebration of loving eccentricity. The show is a blend of comedy, drama, fable, fantasy, and fact. Its residents are a quirky collection of personalities who combine into a wonderful example of community, showing strengths as well as weaknesses.

Divide the people into small groups. It is beneficial if the small groups remain the same throughout the weekend; it helps give continuity. Try to mix new people with those who have attended

❖ *For a list of icebreakers, see the Table of Contents.*

similar events before. Give everyone a copy of Resource 1 (page 199) and tell them to answer these questions:

1. What is your name, occupation, place of employment, and preference between Mac and IBM?

2. Which "Northern Exposure" character would your mother say is most like you?

3. Which character would you least want to be? Why?

4. Where have you experienced a similar mix of people? At your job? In college? In the cast of a play? At church? In your singles group?

"CHRIS IN THE MORNING" DEVOTIONS, SATURDAY AND SUNDAY AT THE BEGINNING OF BREAKFAST

Just as the people of Cicely are accustomed to hearing Chris in the Morning first thing each day, the people on your retreat will hear Chris-style devotions as a lead-in to the morning prayer for breakfast. These devotions need to be short and pointed, a combination of exhortation and observation. The following are given as examples, but feel free to use them. Appoint your "Chris in the Morning" well before the retreat so he or she has ample opportunity to prepare.

Saturday Morning

"Our brother Paul wrote in the first letter that he fired off to that church in Corinth, 'To the Jews I became like a Jew, to win the Jews. To those under the law I became like one under the law . . . so as to win those under the law. To those not having the law I became like one not having the law . . . so as to win those not having the law. To the weak I became weak, to win the weak. I have become all things to all men, so that by all possible means I might save some.' (I Corinthians 9:20-22)

Share: "We are here this weekend learning a little more about ourselves. That is an important thing. The philosopher said, 'To thine own self be true,' and how can you be true to yourself unless you know yourself? But let's not forget that sometimes it is important to deny yourself. Put yourself aside for the greater good of others. Frederick Buechner, a modern-day writer, poet, and philosopher wrote, 'To sacrifice something is to make it holy by giving it away for love.'

"Wise words from a wise man.

"To make a sacrifice, deny yourself for someone you love, even if you don't know the person.

"Let me lead us in a prayer of thanks for this wonderful food."

Sunday Morning

"Everything has its season and time. (Read Ecclesiastes 3:1-8.) American poet Pete Seeger made these words famous by using them for 'Turn, Turn, Turn,' a classic song recorded in the sixties by The Birds. Since then it has been recorded by many other musicians and bands because it is a timeless message. Life is filled with many things—birth, death, and birth again. That circle of life is represented so well in *The Lion King*.

"But life is also filled with pain and joy. Violence and loving. Tears and laughter. Planting and harvesting. These events or experiences all have a beginning and an end. They are temporal in nature, yet even so, are important pieces of life. And what is your life but a series of seemingly unrelated events that give you character and meaning and purpose?

"There is a time for everything. And now it is time to pray. And then it will be time to eat!"

VIDEO CLIPS AND SMALL-GROUP DISCUSSIONS

View each video as a large group, then divide into small groups to discuss the questions found on Resource 2 (page 200).

Saturday, 10:30 A.M.—Wildlife Photo Shoot

Holling and Ruth-Anne are lifelong bird-watchers who regularly leave in the early hours of the morning to spot and photograph birds. This activity, inspired by them, will send the small groups off with Polaroid cameras to capture all forms of wildlife on film.

Saturday, 9:30 P.M.—Dance the Two-Step

Marilyn is an avid dancer. Plan to have a two-step instructor for a few hours to teach the dance to your group. You might also include square dancing and country line dancing.

Saturday, 11:00 P.M.—The Ed Chigliak Theatre

Your "Ed" has been videotaping most of your weekend. Now it is time to view the results. Don't forget the hot buttered popcorn.

Saturday, 11:30 P.M.—Classic Movie Theatre

For the late nighters who refuse to sleep the second night of the retreat, have *Citizen Kane* on hand for viewing. In one episode of *Northern Exposure,* Maurice asks Ed to put together an Orson Wells Film Festival as a tourist attraction. The festival doesn't happen, but Ed spends a lot of time watching scenes from *Citizen Kane.*

RECOMMENDED RESOURCES

* *Northern Exposure Cookbook*, (Chicago, IL: Contemporary Books, 1993), $9.95. This cookbook is available in most bookstores or libraries.
* "Northern Exposure" videos can be found at most video chains. Or contact MCA/Universal Home Video, 100 Universal City Plaza, Universal City, CA 91608 (818-777-1000).

EQUIPMENT/SUPPLIES (To be furnished by the event leaders)

- [ ] VCR/TV
- [ ] Video camera
- [ ] Polaroid cameras and film, one for each small group.
- [ ] Video projector and screen (for large groups)
- [ ] Sound system with tape deck (for large groups if retreat site is not equipped)
- [ ] Copies of character descriptions (Resource 1, page 199)
- [ ] Copies of discussion questions (Resource 2, page 200)

WHAT TO BRING (To be provided by participants)

- [ ] Sleeping bag/pillow/toiletries
- [ ] Casual clothing for two days
- [ ] Bible

PLANNING THE EVENT

PLANNING TEAM

For this event, you need an Event Director and volunteers to take responsibility for the event site, audio/visual needs, budget, food, publicity, recreation, registration, and speaker/workshop needs.

❖
The more people who have ownership and involvement in the planning, the greater success you will have.

Planning Timeline

Event: *Northern Exposure Retreat*   **Date of event:** _____

Event Director: _____   **Phone:** _____

Thanks for agreeing to serve on our retreat Planning Team. Please check over this timeline for the task(s) assigned to you. Adapt as needed. Supplement this timeline with information on the reproducible, generic job descriptions found on pages 225-252. Highlight your tasks (and due dates) each time they appear. Mark your calendar accordingly.

Date:	**6 MONTHS IN ADVANCE**
_____	

Event Director (page 226)

☐ Recruit a Retreat Planning Team. Make sure everyone understands the uniqueness of this retreat. Brainstorm ideas, and adapt this weekend event to fit your particular ministry goals and objectives.

☐ Make sure each team member understands his or her assigned tasks and responsibilities.

☐ Determine if this timeline will work and make adjustments accordingly.

Event Site Coordinator (page 234)

☐ Find an adequate site.

☐ Lock in your date by sending a deposit to the lodge or camp.

☐ Communicate to the Budget Coordinator the per-person cost of using the site.

Date:	**5 MONTHS IN ADVANCE**
_____	

Food Coordinator (page 236)

☐ If preparing your own food, plan your menus, including snacks.

☐ Estimate the cost per person for the weekend. Communicate this amount to the Budget Coordinator.

☐ If the retreat site is preparing your food, meet with the site's cook to see if menus can be chosen to accommodate the retreat. Take your *Northern Exposure Cookbook* along so the cook can see the recipes.

Audio/Visual Equipment Coordinator (page 228)

☐ Secure the videos to be used for the small-group discussions either through purchase or making sure they are reserved at your local video rental outlet.

☐ Inform the Budget Coordinator of the cost of the videos.

Recreation Coordinator (page 240)

☐ If you are not a two-step instructor, look in the phone book under Dance Instructors. Find someone who teaches two-step, square dancing, and country line dancing to beginners. Schedule the instructor.

☐ Communicate to the Budget Coordinator the cost of this person, and how much must be sent as a deposit.

Registration Coordinator (page 241)

☐ Determine the registration deadline and means of registration.

☐ Communicate this information to the Publicity Coordinator.

Publicity Coordinator (page 238)

☐ Decide the types and extent of publicity.

❖ *For more ideas and help, refer to job descriptions beginning on page 225.*

Food Coordinator

- [ ] Unless your singles group is blessed with a trained chef, it will be best to have different people prepare each meal.
- [ ] Go over the menus with them and make sure they understand the recipes.

Audio/Visual Equipment Coordinator

- [ ] Collect the equipment needed to show the videos. If you need to rent a video projector, look in the phone book under Video Equipment Rental.
- [ ] Schedule the projector.
- [ ] Communicate costs to the Budget Coordinator, including any deposits that must be sent.
- [ ] Begin borrowing Polaroid cameras. Buy the right film.

Recreation Coordinator

- [ ] Make sure the retreat site has the proper sound equipment needed by your two-step instructor.

Budget Coordinator (page 229)

- [ ] Based on the costs provided by the team members, determine the per-person cost of the weekend.
- [ ] Give this information to the Publicity and Registration Coordinators.

Publicity Coordinator

- [ ] Begin distributing promotional materials.

Event Director

- [ ] Preview the videos with the Audio/Visual Coordinator, the Speaker/Workshop Coordinator, and any other interested team members. Determine if you will be showing entire episodes or just portions of episodes at the retreat.

Speaker/Workshop Leaders Coordinator (page 250)

- [ ] Write small-group questions if using episodes other than those mentioned in this book.

Audio/Visual Equipment Coordinator

- [ ] So you are not stuck behind a camera all weekend, recruit others to help you videotape portions of the retreat.
- [ ] Plan background music to be played during free times and meals.

Registration Coordinator

- [ ] Make copies of a map to the retreat site that can be given to each person who registers.
- [ ] Begin taking registrations.

Food Coordinator

- [ ] Determine who will purchase food, when it will be purchased, and how it will be transported.
- [ ] Visit the kitchen at the retreat site with your cooks to evaluate how well equipped it is and what cooking utensils might need to be brought.

Event Director

- [ ] Begin making contact with individual team members once a week.
- [ ] Schedule the final team meetings before the retreat.

Speaker/Workshop Leaders Coordinator

- [ ] Plan your morning devotions.
- [ ] Recruit others from your group to pray at various meals.
- [ ] Plan the Sunday worship time.
- [ ] Recruit the small-group leaders.

Food Coordinator

☐ Try out some of the recipes with your cooks.

Registration Coordinator

☐ Prepare name tags for all those registered.
☐ Send out a letter of confirmation with any balance due information (see sample on page 244).

Budget Coordinator

☐ Confirm with the retreat site when final payment must be made. If it's due upon arrival, draft a check to take with you.

Recreation Coordinator

☐ Confirm with the two-step instructor the location of the retreat, the date and time, and preferred payment method.

| Date: _____ | **1 WEEK IN ADVANCE** |

Event Director

☐ Meet with the team. Go over the schedule for the weekend. See that copies are printed to be given out at the retreat.
☐ Have each team member report on what each will do during the weekend.
☐ Confirm that all details have been taken care of.
☐ Pray together one final time for the weekend.

| Date: _____ | **2 TO 4 WEEKS AFTER EVENT** |

Event Director

☐ Send out notes of thanks to each team member.
☐ Schedule one more team meeting to evaluate the event. Find out how people felt about their responsibilities and the results as seen during the weekend. Notice which coordinators had a difficult time enjoying the event because of their responsibilities.
☐ See the "Followup Guidelines" on page 254.

Character Descriptions for Get-Acquainted Activity

Dr. Joel Fleishman: A fish out of water. New York-born Jewish doctor stuck in the Alaskan wilderness while he works off his debt to the state whose taxes paid his way through Columbia Medical school. Never feels like he fits in.

Maggie O'Connell: Bush pilot and Dr. Fleishman's landlord. Although she grew up in the suburbs of Detroit, her independent spirit drove her to the wilderness of Alaska. A mixture of styles, one scene has Maggie repairing her plumbing and the next planning a baby shower. Although very independent, Maggie has learned the importance of people.

Chris "In the Morning" Stevens: A man of many words. Poet, philosopher, morning disc jockey, and ordained minister (even if his ordination was purchased from an ad in the back of *Rolling Stone*). He's the narrative voice of the activities of Cicely. Always has a quote for any situation. Plays an eclectic mix of music styles. Presides over all weddings and funerals.

Ed Chigliak: Film-obsessed teenager with an IQ of 180. He sees things from a different perspective. Living moment to moment, he notices the sun come up each day with a childlike innocence. Has a tendency to invade private situations without realizing he has interrupted.

Holling Vincoeur: Reformed hell-raiser and drinker who has developed a strong instinct for right and wrong. Owner of The Brick, the local tavern/restaurant, Holling has incredible gifts of hospitality. He is passionately in love with his late-in-life wife, Shelly.

Shelly Tambo: The former Miss Northwest Passage, at 18, Shelly is wide-eyed and innocent. She has a slang expression for everything. Her days are spent waiting tables at The Brick while being near her "main squeeze, the Big H."

Maurice Minnifield: Crusty former astronaut who owns nearly everything in Cicely and is a gourmet cook and antiques expert. He has big visions for Cicely, where he sees a future metropolis of planned communities, resorts, roads, and mini-malls. Refers to Cicely as the "Alaskan Riviera."

Ruth-Anne: Owner of the local general store. Dispenser of practical wisdom. When asked her opinion, she usually begins, "I'll admit, I've never encountered anything like this, but if you want my advice . . ."

Marilyn Whirlwind: Dr. Fleischman's receptionist of few words. When she speaks, which is not often, her words are filled with the wisdom of her ancestors. She has natural insight into human nature. Marilyn dances a mean two-step.

Watching and Listening

SESSION 1: "THE PILOT"

Dr. Joel Fleishman, fresh out of his residency at Columbia Medical School, is on his way to Fairbanks, Alaska, to serve the people of the state for four years because their taxes paid for his schooling. Upon arrival, he learns that he is not needed in Fairbanks and is being sent to Cicely. Although he is assured it is paradise, he soon finds it is the opposite.

Discussion Questions

1. Joel experiences a major disappointment, thinking he will serve his time in Fairbanks but ending up in Cicely. What is a similar disappointment you have experienced? How has it affected your life?
2. The first time Joel orders a bagel, he is reminded of the vast cultural differences between his life in New York and Cicely. Describe a time when you have been a similar "fish out of water."
3. How could Galations 3:28 be a comfort to a person like Joel who might be at this retreat?

SESSION 2: "THE BAD SEED"

Marilyn becomes frustrated living with her mother and her rules. Marilyn wants a place of her own.

Discussion Questions

1. Describe the day you left home. Was it to go to college? To move into your own apartment?
2. What struggles have you had with your parents as you have grown into an adult?
3. What experiences have you had that show your parents' acceptance of you as an adult?
4. What do Proverbs 23:22 and 25 suggest about a proper relationship with one's parents as an adult?

Optional Questions for Single Parents

5. How are you planning for your children to leave home?
6. If your children are adults, how do you show them respect as adults?

SESSION 3: "THE BODY IN QUESTION"

Residents of Cicely find a body buried in ice. No one knows who it is, but the townspeople take a proprietary interest in making sure he has a proper funeral, presided over by DJ/Minister Chris Stevens.

Discussion Questions

1. A strong community has certain strengths. What strengths does Cicely exhibit in this episode?
2. What weaknesses?
3. In what ways is Cicely similar to the early church as described in Acts 2:44-47?
4. In what ways is your singles group similar to the church described in the same passage?

SESSION 4: "SEOUL MATES"

Joel buys his first Christmas tree. As a result, he struggles with his Jewish heritage and religious roots.

Discussion Questions

1. When you were a child, how did your family celebrate Christmas? What was your favorite part of the proceedings?
2. What changes have you made in the way you celebrate Christmas?
3. What was your religious heritage?
4. What changes have you made in your religious life when compared to your heritage?

22 A TIME FOR US

Single-Parent Family Vacation Retreat

Event Summary: A mini-vacation for single parents and their children. This is a time to relax and fellowship with others on the single-parent family journey and to be reminded of God's faithfulness. This event includes a children's carnival, crafts, outdoor games, and an inspirational "Discovery Walk."

Length of Event: Friday–Sunday

Suggested Theme Verse: "For I know the plans I have for you," declares the Lord,"plans to prosper you and not to harm you, plans to give you hope and a future." Jeremiah 29:11

Other Possible Theme Verses: Psalm 27:13, 14; Isaiah 55:12; Song of Songs 2:11

Ideal Number of Participants: 30+

Estimated Cost Per Person: $65–$115 per family

Facility Requirements: Campground or retreat center

Recommended Planning Team: 12–15 people

Advance Planning Needed: Approximately one year

INTRODUCTION

by Barbara Schiller
Executive Director
Single Parent Family Resources
St. Louis, Missouri

Most parents are required to spin a lot of plates. This is especially true with single parents—juggling work, cleaning the house, doing laundry, attending school functions, doing car maintenance or home repair, going to school, and paying the bills. And hopefully spending at least a little quality time with the children along the way.

Juggling all these responsibilities can become overwhelming, and single-parent families desperately need to occasionally "get away from it all."

This event, "A Time for Us," offers a mini-vacation retreat for single parents and their children. A change of pace. An opportunity for the children to have some fun. Time to connect and maybe relax with others on the single-parent family journey.

Although planning this retreat requires a considerable amount of preparation and organization, the results are well worth the effort. A young boy's story tells it all.

The young boy came running down the beach with his little feet kicking sand everywhere. Out of breath, he pounced on his mom's lap. "Mom, did you know that all those kids over there have only one parent just like me?" He didn't wait for his mom to answer. "Hey, Mom," he continued, "we're not alone, are we?" He flashed a wonderfully warm smile and ran down the beach to join his friends. His mom, with tears in her eyes, turned and smiled.

The single-parent families in your group will have similar experiences during this event. It will become one of the ways to remind those families that your church cares for them, and that they are special and loved.

OBJECTIVE

❖ To provide single-parent families time together to build new relationships, while being reminded of God's faithfulness and discovering they are not alone in their journey.

THE BIG EVENT

Most single parents have to work until 5:00 P.M. on Friday. To allow adequate time, do not start the evening's activities until approximately 8:45 P.M. Remember, the goal of the entire weekend's schedule is not to rush or pack the schedule too tight. The 8:45 P.M. time seems late, but most children are so wound up and excited that the lateness of the hour is generally not a problem. (But don't begin any later than around 9:00 P.M.) Friday night's activities are to be interactive, relaxing, and fun!

WHAT SHOULD IT BE?

❖ *Get as many people as possible involved in the planning of this event.*

Have a brainstorming luncheon to determine the real and felt needs of single parents. Every singles group has its own unique "personality," and consequently, it is essential to know and understand what your single parents most want to do on this event. Ask such questions as: What are the main topics you would like to see addressed at this retreat? Would you prefer to discuss a book or a chapter in the Bible? Or would you prefer an unstructured time of discussion with the other single parents? What kind of speaker would appeal to you, if any? Do you want a "structured" schedule or a flexible one? (Remember, people and their needs change. If this event becomes an annual retreat, the format and schedule may change due to changing needs.)

During this luncheon, ask each person to suggest five to ten possible discussion questions or topics that they would like to see addressed during the retreat. Then, before the retreat, the event leaders can select the best or most frequently ones submitted. Keep in mind that all the questions do not need to be concerned with single-parent issues. Any helpful topics should be considered if the single parents indicate a need or interest in them.

CHILDREN

Depending on the number of children under the age of four, who are too young to participate in the Saturday morning games and the Sunday morning crafts, it is important to recruit child care workers. Their responsibilities are to watch and care for toddlers in a designated place at the facility. Consider paying these workers.

COST

An event like this is especially dependent on scholarships. Oftentimes, individuals in the church will offer to underwrite the costs of one or two single-parent families for this retreat. A payment plan, although it requires extra work, helps make this event affordable for many single parents.

WELCOME PACKETS

Give a welcome packet to each family upon arrival at the event (in addition to their name tags and room key). This packet provides the families with all the information that is needed for a great retreat. See the Planning Timeline (pages 209-212) for details.

SCHEDULE

Friday

7:30–8:45 P.M.—Registration
8:45–9:00 P.M.—Overview of the weekend and announcements
9:00–10:00 P.M.—A carnival (with prizes!) for all ages

Saturday

7:30–8:45 A.M.—Breakfast
9:00–11:45 A.M.—Parents: a special walk together, followed by small-group discussions
9:00–11:45 A.M.—Children and teens: organized outside activities
12:00 P.M.—Lunch
1:00–6:00 P.M.—Free time!!!!

OR 1:30–3:00 P.M.—Organized games of
volleyball and/or basketball
3:00–6:00—Free time
6:00 P.M.—Dinner
7:00–8:30 P.M.—Hayrides
9:00 P.M.—Bonfire/Singing/S'mores
OPTIONAL—Nighttime hike or Kick the Can

Sunday

7:30–9:00 A.M.—Breakfast
9:00–11:00 A.M.—Children and teens: craft
workshops for all kids
9:00–9:30 A.M.—Parents' time to pack (without the kids)
9:30–11:00 A.M.—Parents: final small-group
discussion session
11:15–11:45 A.M.—Worship service for all
12:00 P.M.—Lunch
1:30 P.M.—Leave for home

MEAL TIME

It is important to provide plenty of time for
meals. Allow the parents at least one hour to
eat with their children.
Remember, their daily routine is
always hurried. Planning more
time in the schedule is one way of
showing you care, and it helps set
the tone for the weekend.

❖
*For a list of
icebreakers,
see the
Table of
Contents.*

PROGRAM IDEAS AND SUGGESTIONS

FRIDAY ACTIVITIES

• The Carnival

Children love this activity, and parents enjoy
helping out or just watching and visiting.
Three months before the event, the Children's
Coordinator needs to have a meeting to organize this activity with the help of other children's leaders. This meeting is required to
coordinate the following:

1. What carnival games will be offered to
accommodate the diverse group of children.
2. Selection of a leader for each carnival
game.

3. Selection of a leader to hang the decorations.
4. Selection of a leader to visit a carnival
supply store to get ideas, make purchases, or
rent games as needed.
5. Selection of a leader to build or create
simple carnival games and props as needed.

Carnival supply stores have a good selection of unique games. Make sure you have
enough games for all ages. A minimum of ten
games is needed (at least three games for children ages 2–5; three games for children ages
6–11; four games for children ages 12+). After
each game is played, a prize is offered to each
participating child. (Most carnival stores have
an ample supply of prizes.) Examples of three
possible games and prizes follow.

• *Fishing Pond Game (ages 2–5):* This game is
easy to assemble. It requires a large blanket to
create a "wall" to "fish" behind, two cane poles
with string, and some kind of weight tied to
the string. The kids toss their line over the
"wall" to "fish." Prizes, which are tied to the
weighted string by staff members hidden
behind the wall, could be sunglasses, a small
rubber ball, or crayons, as examples.
• *Milk Bottle Toss (ages 6–11):* A softball is
thrown to knock down three milk bottles.
Prizes could be colored pencils, small cars,
whistles, stickers, and so on.
• *Basketball Game (ages 12 and up):* The teens
stand back a designated distance to throw a
Nerf ball into the basketball hoop, which is
attached to the wall with a suction cup. The
winner makes the best out of five throws.
Prizes could be books, Frisbees, boomerangs,
and braided bracelets.

Helpful Tips for Organizing the Carnival

Give each child a large plastic grocery bag. In
the bag put "tickets" for each game. (If you
have ten games per age group, ten tickets are
placed in the bag.) One ticket is given by the
child to the leader who is working that game
booth. Only one prize is awarded to each
child at each game. This helps when purchas-

ing the prizes to know how many to buy. The bag can then also be used to hold the prizes.

Keep the room decorations simple. Use crepe paper and colorful balloons for a nice touch.

In most cases it is usually best to have two staff persons at each game booth to take tickets, distribute prizes, and help as needed.

When preparing for this event, go to a carnival supply store in your area for game ideas and supplies.

• Skits, Pantomimes, and Charades

Another idea for Friday night (if you choose not to do the carnival or if your schedule allows for time to do both) is to have the entire leadership team prepare skits, pantomimes, and/or charades. (The Event Director or Recreation Coordinator needs to have a meeting to organize these activities prior to the event.) Make sure these activities are designed to *include the parents and their children.*

You may want to ask some families ahead of time to come prepared to do their own skit or pantomime. Or have two or three families do a skit together. You might have several printed skits and pantomime ideas available as people arrive so they can pick one, spend a few minutes rehearsing, then perform it for the group.

Encourage people to write their own skits and pantomimes, have retreat leaders write them, or check with the local bookstore for books of skits that can involve kids, too. When participants get involved, skits, pantomimes, and charades are great icebreakers, —and fun, too.

SATURDAY MORNING ACTIVITIES

• Children's Activities

The purpose of these Saturday morning activities is to encourage team building through cooperation with each other. Divide all the children into teams, regardless of their ages (for example, first graders with third and seventh graders). Depending on the quality and

experience of your leaders, as well as the attitude of the kids, you can sometimes even include teenagers in these groups. If the teens hesitate to be in the groups, ask if they would be willing to serve as helpers.

To help create an atmosphere of cooperation, refer to the games book mentioned on page 207. This book contains numerous interactive, team-building activities without stressing competition.

Prior to the event, the Children's Coordinator is to meet with the children's workers to decided which games to use. Each leader is then responsible to gather supplies and lead the game.

• Parent Activities

In most cases, single parents say, "We just want to share together with other single parents during the retreat. We have so few opportunities to do this." To help kick the morning off and to help parents relax, take a short hike in the area. Then return for small-group discussions.

Prior to the retreat, small-group discussion leaders are recruited for each group. These discussion leaders need to be carefully selected, based on their maturity, experience, and ability to draw out and involve everyone in the group. The ideal group size is four or five people.

The goal of the parents' time together is to build new relationships, while discovering they are not alone in this journey. Often, these types of activities assist parents in gaining inner strength and learning to trust again.

SATURDAY AFTERNOON ACTIVITIES

This time slot is scheduled for free time, but do not assume that all parents will know what to do. For some, this may be the first time they have had undivided, uninterrupted, unscheduled time with their children, and it can be scary.

Consider offering options for part of the free time. (See the retreat schedule.) The Recreation and Children's Coordinators work together to organize two or three fun games. These games must be varied enough to accommodate all age groups. Games such as volleyball, basketball, and softball for the older children and "Simon Says" and "Freeze Tag" for the younger children are good examples. If a supervised swimming pool is available, it can also be fun for part of this time.

(Here's how to play "Freeze Tag": One person is It. When you are tagged by It, you become frozen. The object of the game is to get as many people frozen as possible in an allotted time period. The trick is that anyone playing who is not yet frozen can touch anyone who is frozen and unfreeze them.)

SATURDAY EVENING ACTIVITIES

Flexibility and knowing what parents desire for a single-parent family weekend must be the guiding rules. Generally, family-type activities such as an evening hike to watch the stars (don't forget the flashlight!), board games, a family movie (remember the popcorn and soda!), family "Talent Night," or a hayride are good choices. A bonfire with s'mores is a great way to end the day!

SUNDAY ACTIVITIES

On Sunday morning, the parents and children are again separated in their groups for another interactive time.

• Craft Time for Children

This is the children's last time together with their leaders, and it is important to make it memorable. One way to do this is to offer creative crafts at various tables.

Prior to the event, decide which craft ideas will be available. The number of children attending will determine how many crafts need to be created and organized. For a large group, plan twelve crafts. A medium group requires seven or eight crafts. A small group should be fine with four or five crafts. Assign one leader to each craft and each craft to a separate table.

Divide the children into groups, one for each craft. Give each group five to twenty minutes to do each craft. Have the children switch crafts a few times, moving from one table to the next, depending on the time allotted for each activity. The children love this part of the weekend!

Here are some craft examples:

• **Nature Collage Art** For the younger children (approximate grade level: preschool and kindergarten)

Items needed:
- [ ] 81/2" x 11" colored construction paper, one piece for each child
- [ ] glue
- [ ] aluminum foil
- [ ] cotton balls
- [ ] scraps of cloth
- [ ] colored felt
- [ ] nature items (from outdoors)
- [ ] pictures cut from magazines

This craft needs some advance preparation. Sometime before Sunday morning, the leader in charge of this craft needs to walk around the retreat facility (or a local neighborhood) and gather items such as pine cones, fallen leaves, small rocks, twigs, dandelions, and nuts. Place all the items on a table in the craft area. Also place items brought from home by the leadership team, such as aluminum foil, cotton balls, scraps of cloth, felt, and magazine pictures. Give each child a bright colored piece of construction paper (81/2" x 11"). Allow the children to glue the nature and "home" items to the construction paper to create any design or picture they like.

• **Design a Puzzle** For the older children (approximate grade level: first through third)

Items needed:
- [ ] 8" x 4" puzzles, one for each child
- [ ] colored markers (non-erasable)
- [ ] business-sized envelopes, one for each child

Depending on the number of children participating in this craft, purchase at your local craft supply store medium-sized blank puzzles (no picture or writing on them). The puzzles are divided up nicely and are made of durable cardboard. With non-erasable colored markers, have the children draw pictures on their puzzles—anything they want to draw! Then have the children break apart their puzzles and see if they can put them back together by following their pictures. Give each child a business-size envelope with his or her name on it to put the puzzle pieces inside.

• *Visor Painting* For the oldest children (approximate grade level: fourth through eighth)

 Items needed:
   ☐ visors, baseball caps, or large "clown-type" sunglasses, one per child
   ☐ colored paint pens (permanent)

Purchase at your local craft or carnival store the kind of visors that keep the sun (and hair) out of one's eyes. Give each child a visor. Place colored paint pens on the table. Have the children decorate the visors any creative way they want. Allow them to dry.

(Alternative 1) "Baseball Cap Painting." The activity is the same as above, but use plain baseball caps without any logos. (Sometimes local sports stores will give tremendous discounts when you state your purpose for purchasing the hats.)

(Alternative 2) "Sunglasses Painting."

The activity is the same as above, but done on large clown-type sunglasses, which can be found at your local carnival supply store.

• *Face Painting* Any age child
 Items needed:
   ☐ colored tube paints (enough variety to create fun pictures)
   ☐ painter's palette (optional, but it helps when mixing and changing colors)

Another activity most kids love, even though it is not considered a craft, is to have face painting at one of the tables. Purchase at your local craft or artist supply store colored tube paints for painting the face. A leader who has artistic ability needs to be in charge of this

activity. Have on the table a sheet of paper with examples of what designs the children might consider. (WARNING: Read all labels on tube paints. Some are NOT to be used on the face or near the eyes! When in doubt, don't.)

Parents' Activities

This last time together for small-group discussions needs to provide an opportunity for closure (sharing what they have learned from the weekend and what they have enjoyed).

SUNDAY MORNING WORSHIP

The closing worship activities are as follows and should take no longer than forty-five to fifty minutes.

1. Discovery Walk (See details below and Resource 1 on page 213.)
2. Mini-sermon (relevant and uplifting—and no more than ten minutes)
3. Sharing time by each family
4. Closing prayer and song(s)

• **The Discovery Walk**

As part of a unique worship experience, offer a Discovery Walk. This is a special time for parents and their children to walk together outdoors and find things in nature that are unique to their family. ("Find something that reminds you of God's Love.") It can be a wonderful time of sharing between family members as they walk and discuss together why they chose certain items.

The following are needed for the Discovery Walk to work effectively:

1. For each family, a Discovery Walk sheet listing five to seven sentences of what to find in nature that reminds the family of something about themselves. (See Resource 1 on page 213.)

2. For each family, a large brown paper bag with five to seven twist ties placed inside the bag.

3. One large wooden cross (about five or six feet tall) wrapped with chicken wire.

Give each family approximately fifteen to twenty-five minutes to gather their nature items. Ask each family to keep one item to talk about with the group, then attach all the others to the cross using the twists.

It is very moving to watch the families attach pinecones, leaves, flowers, and other things to the wire. These items eventually cover the cross in a very beautiful way. Observing the families as they decide which item to keep for the Sharing Time is also very meaningful.

Each family shares why this last item is so special to them. They then attach their last item to the wire. Be prepared for tears. It is a very spiritual and emotionally uplifting time.

Finally, all participants stand in a large circle, hold hands, and sing "Amazing Grace" and/or "Jesus Loves Me." Then one person closes in prayer.

(This activity was developed by Dorothy Fontana and the Texas Conference Task Force, United Methodist Church.)

EQUIPMENT/SUPPLIES (To be furnished by the event leaders)

- ☐ Craft items as needed (see pages 205 and 206)
- ☐ Items for activities (such as volleyballs, basketballs, etc.)
- ☐ Carnival game items and prizes
- ☐ Guitar
- ☐ Decorations (crepe paper, balloons, etc.)
- ☐ Suggested skits and charades (that both adults and children can play together)
- ☐ Board games
- ☐ Some family videos
- ☐ Wooden cross (five or six feet tall) wrapped with chicken wire
- ☐ Portable cassette player (for music at Discovery Walk closing)
- ☐ Large brown paper bag for each family
- ☐ Twist ties for each participant
- ☐ Plastic bag for each child
- ☐ Handouts and copied materials as needed

WHAT TO BRING (To be provided by participants)

- ☐ Snacks
- ☐ Flashlight
- ☐ Clock with an alarm
- ☐ Camera
- ☐ Notepad and pen
- ☐ Bible
- ☐ Walking shoes
- ☐ Casual clothes
- ☐ Personal items
- ☐ Raincoat
- ☐ Games
- ☐ Extra clothing for children
- ☐ Extra cash
- ☐ Guitar

RECOMMENDED RESOURCES

An excellent resource for games and activities:
Andrew Fluegelman, *More New Games and Playful Ideas*, (Doubleday, Inc., 1981).

Possible adult study/discussion books to consider:
Ramona Warren, *Parenting Alone,* (Elgin, IL: David C. Cook Church Ministries, 1993).
Barbara Schiller, *Just Me and the Kids,* (Elgin, IL: David C. Cook Church Ministries, 1994).

PLANNING THE EVENT

PLANNING TEAM

For this event, you need an Event Director (possibly an Assistant Event Director) and volunteers to take responsibility for the event site, budget, publicity, printed materials, registration, small groups, transportation, food, and equipment/supplies.

The position of Event Director should be filled by a

❖ *The more people who have ownership and involvement in the planning, the greater success you will have.*

member of the church staff, a remarried couple, an older, more "seasoned" single parent, or a single adult who has a compassionate understanding of single-parent families. The Event Director will receive ideas and suggestions from single parents during the planning of this event.

In addition to the above Planning Team, recruit a Children's Coordinator. This person should be experienced in working with and planning activities for children of all ages. This person should also be willing and able to recruit helpers to work with the children during the retreat. The Children's Coordinator and the child care workers should be aware of helpful information found on the Children's Information Forms (Resource 2, page 214).

If at all possible, do not ask a new single parent to fill this position. Single parents need the opportunity to participate, relax, and enjoy this event without any major responsibilities. Consider asking young single adults, young and older married couples, grandparents, and divorced or widowed singles to work with the children. Each worker must demonstrate love, patience, and understanding with children who are experiencing multiple losses and changes. (If possible, pay the housing and registration expenses for these workers, except for a small overhead fee such as $15–$25.)

The Children's Coordinator should plan activities that parents and children can participate in together. Check with the Event Site Coordinator for possible activities and supplies on site. Plan activities for Friday evening, Saturday, and Sunday morning. Selecting teams of workers to lead these activities may work best. If you have enough workers involved, you might try having one group of people do the activities and another group do the crafts.

Also determine if you will need a Recreation Coordinator, or if those responsibilities will be taken by the Children's Coordinator. If a Recreation Coordinator is involved, coordinate with the Event Director and the Children's Coordinator the specific responsibilities of each person.

Planning Timeline

Event: *A Time for Us*   **Date of event:** _____

Event Director: _____   **Phone:** _____

Thanks for agreeing to serve on our retreat Planning Team. Please check over this timeline for the task(s) assigned to you. Adapt as needed. Supplement this timeline with information on the reproducible, generic job descriptions found on pages 225-252. Highlight your tasks (and due dates) each time they appear. Mark your calendar accordingly.

Date: _____ **1 YEAR TO 9 MONTHS IN ADVANCE**

Event Director (page 226)

☐ Recruit a Planning Team for this event. Brainstorm ideas and adapt this weekend event to fit your particular ministry goals and objectives. Make sure each team member understands his or her assigned tasks and responsibilities. Determine if this timeline will work and make adjustments accordingly.

Event Site Coordinator (page 234)

☐ Try to find a location that includes hiking trails, plenty of trees, swimming, canoeing, and horseback riding. This will create a vacation-like atmosphere. June, July, or August are ideal times for families to participate. Time during the school year is simply too hectic.

   If reserving a recreational center is an impossibility due to budget constraints, have your Planning Team create a theme at your church for Friday and Saturday, such as an Hawaiian luau, and plan all the activities around that theme.

Date: _____ **6 MONTHS IN ADVANCE**

Event Director and Planning Team

☐ Invite at least twelve single parents to a "brainstorming" luncheon.

☐ Based on the facility and leadership involved, determine the maximum number of families who can attend and still experience an intimate time together.

☐ Begin planning the details of this event.

Budget Coordinator (page 229)

☐ Work with the Planning Team to determine the budget, including scholarship funds.

Publicity Coordinator (page 238)

☐ Develop an advertising game plan.

Registration Coordinator (page 241)

☐ Develop a plan for obtaining needed scholarship funds, as well as a monthly payment plan for interested participants.

Date: _____ **5 MONTHS IN ADVANCE**

Event Director

☐ Meet with the Planning Team to go over details as needed.

☐ Organize and plan all activities and events that do not involve the children (such as the parents' walk on Saturday morning).

☐ Prepare to lead the closing Discovery Walk on Sunday, or give someone that responsibility.

Publicity Coordinator

☐ Once the date, location, costs, and scholarship information are final, prepare promotional materials and begin advertising the event.

❖ *For more ideas and help, refer to job descriptions beginning on page 225.*

Registration Coordinator

- [ ] Remember to set a limit on the number of registrations allowed, based on the size of the facility and the number of leaders involved. For maximum benefit, you will need enough adults involved as helpers and leaders to maintain the following ratios: 1:5 with parents, 1:4-5 with children, and 1:3 with toddlers.
- [ ] Open registration. Parents with children should complete the "Children's Information Form" (page 214) for each child they plan to bring.
- [ ] Provide scholarship applications.

Speaker/Workshop Leaders Coordinator (page 250)

- [ ] If you plan to use a speaker or workshop leaders as a part of the event, begin securing these people now.

Date: _____ | **4 MONTHS IN ADVANCE**

Event Director

- [ ] Meet with the Planning Team to check on progress.

Children's Coordinator (page 232)

- [ ] Decide what activities and crafts will take place during the event.
- [ ] Arrange for supplies as needed.

Food Coordinator (page 236)

- [ ] Work with the contact person at the event site to arrange meals and refreshments. Develop a meal plan.
- [ ] Ask each family to bring snacks to share. (Or request that the retreat center provide the snacks.)

Publicity Coordinator

- [ ] Continue promoting the event.
- [ ] Regularly post brochures in public areas.

Registration Coordinator

- [ ] Continue to register families.
- [ ] Encourage families to stay on track with their monthly payment plan.
- [ ] Provide scholarship applications as requested (see sample on page 246).

Transportation Coordinator (page 252)

- [ ] Determine the best means of transportation to the retreat site.

Small-Group Coordinator (page 247)

- [ ] Carefully choose small-group facilitators for the adult discussion groups.

Speaker/Workshop Leaders Coordinator

- [ ] If a speaker and/or workshop leaders are being used, contracts should now be on file for each person.

Date: _____ | **3 MONTHS IN ADVANCE**

Event Director

- [ ] Meet with the Planning Team to make sure plans are on track.
- [ ] Check on adult-only activities and the Discovery Walk on Sunday.

Children's Coordinator

- [ ] Recruit child care workers.
- [ ] Meet with the workers responsible for the older children. Discuss specific plans for the three major time slots for which activities are planned. Arrange to supply materials and idea suggestions for these workers.

Speaker/Workshop Leaders Coordinator

- [ ] Contact speakers to verify their presentation topics for the event.
- [ ] Request any handouts they may have at this time.
- [ ] Send a schedule showing times and length of each session. Limit each session to forty-five minutes to one hour.

Small-Group Coordinator

☐ Meet with the small-group facilitators. Finalize with the Event Director the focus, theme, and small-group questions.
☐ Order any materials you need.
☐ Train small-group facilitators if applicable.

Event Site Coordinator

☐ Check to be sure a signed contract is on file at the retreat site and at the church. Make sure all details are correct.
☐ Verify that a deposit has been paid and received by the event site.

Audio/Visual Equipment Coordinator (page 228)

☐ Determine the audio/visual needs for the children's programs and activities.
☐ Check with various Planning Team members concerning any audio/visual needs they might have.

Date: _____	**2 Months IN Advance**

Event Director

☐ Meet with the Planning Team to make sure plans are on track.
☐ Work with the Registration Coordinator to make sure all needed scholarship funds have been secured.

Audio/Visual Equipment Coordinator

☐ Finalize equipment requests and/or rental forms as needed.

Registration Coordinator

☐ Turn in scholarship applications for approval.
☐ Inform recipients of the available funds.
☐ Continue registration.
☐ Seek additional scholarship funds if necessary.

Transportation Coordinator

☐ Have transportation decisions finalized and communicated to the Planning Team.
☐ Obtain a map to the event site.

Children's Coordinator

☐ All plans for activities and crafts and needed leaders should be in place.

Speaker/Workshop Leaders Coordinator

☐ Make any necessary lodging or transportation arrangements for speakers.

Date: _____	**1 Month IN Advance**

Event Director

☐ Meet with the Planning Team. Determine if all aspects of the event are on track. Make final plans.
☐ Contact individuals to assist with the unique Sunday morning worship time to conclude the event.

Transportation Coordinator

☐ Finalize all transportation details.

Children's Coordinator

☐ Meet with all children's workers. Be sure all the workers know what is expected of them and that they have the proper supplies to complete their assigned tasks.
☐ Review the Children's Information Forms.

Registration Coordinator

☐ Begin assigning housing.
☐ Recruit someone to prepare name tags.

Event Materials Coordinator (page 233)

☐ Work with other Planning Team members to prepare a Welcome Packet to give each family. This packet (which should be in a nice folder) contains the following:

1. The retreat schedule
2. The small-group discussion questions (for parents)
3. Late announcements and changes
4. A campsite map and rules
5. An evaluation form to use at the end of the retreat (see sample on page 255).
6. Emergency phone numbers
7. (Optional) A small gift for each person. This could be a bookmark, a book, an inexpensive toy, or a gift certificate.
☐ Have the small-group materials, handouts, and any other needed materials copied and ready for assembly and distribution.

Food Coordinator

☐ If you choose to not have the retreat site responsible for snacks (and to save money), recruit two teams to help with them for Friday night (two people) and Saturday night (two people). These people will organize the snacks for all participants. Each participating family will be asked to bring a snack item to share. The Friday Night team is responsible for organizing and arranging the food. (To keep the children from becoming too hyperactive, provide low-sugar snacks.)

The Saturday Night team should buy all the ingredients for s'mores. They are responsible for making sure a table, wires for roasting the marshmallows, and the ingredients for s'mores are at the bonfire. They are also responsible for seeing that a bonfire is prepared and lit when needed.

Equipment/Supplies Coordinator

☐ Check with the Children's Coordinator for supplies for children's activities and craft time. Buy supplies or coordinate your efforts with the Planning Team members.

Date: _____	2 WEEKS IN ADVANCE

Registration Coordinator

☐ Close registration and make final housing assignments.
☐ Have all the name tags ready.
☐ Send a letter to the registrants. (See sample on page 244. Adapt it for your group.)

Date: _____	1 WEEK IN ADVANCE

Event Director

☐ Meet with the Planning Team to make sure the final details are being completed. Give the church staff an address and phone number(s) at the event site in case of an emergency.

Budget Coordinator

☐ Write checks as needed.

Event Site Coordinator

☐ Check with the event site to confirm all plans and the number of people attending.

Registration Coordinator

☐ Work with the Event Materials Coordinator to make sure the Welcome Packets are ready.
☐ Be prepared to greet each family at the registration table and distribute their packets, name tags, room numbers, and keys.

Transportation Coordinator

☐ Assign all the registrants to a car pool or van and give all the drivers a map to the event site.

Date: _____	2 TO 4 WEEKS AFTER EVENT

☐ See "Followup Guidelines" on page 254.

Guide for the Discovery Walk

During this Discovery Walk with your family, look for the things listed below. (They should be fairly small and easy to bring back with you.)

When you return to the designated meeting area, select one item you wish to talk about as a family during the closing time of worship. You will be asked to tell why this one item reminds you of something in the list below. The remaining items can be attached to the wire-covered cross.

During your walk look for:

1. Something that reminds you of God's love.

2. Something that reminds you of your family.

3. Something that lasts.

4. Something that changes.

5. Something that promises new life.

6. Something that reminds you of hope.

7. Something that reminds you that God is always with you.

Find as many of the above items as you can during your allotted time. Let this be a special time for you and your family.

As you explore God's creation, be aware that He is always ready to help you "discover" how much He loves you, that He has "hope and a future" for you, and that you are very special to Him.

Children's Information Form

Please complete a form for each child who will be accompanying you.

Child's name _____

Child's nickname (if applicable) _____

Child's age _____

Parent's name _____

Medical information we need to know about your child: _____

    Medications (times and dosages): _____

    Allergies: _____

Special toys you plan to bring _____

_____

Please list any toys or other items that might be helpful for your child(ren) at the retreat (for example, really likes blocks, needs a walker, likes to color) _____

_____

Please offer any comments that would help the child care workers do their best with your child(ren) _____

_____

Items that would be helpful to have at the event
- ☐ Extra cot in room
- ☐ Crib
- ☐ Assistance with luggage upon arrival
- ☐ Other: _____

Comments

23 "PEACE AND LOVE" MUSIC FEST

A Nostalgic, 60s-Era Community Outreach

Event Summary: A mini-music festival, a David Letterman-like variety show, plus a community outreach—all designed around a 1960s Woodstock time period with a "Peace and Love" theme.

Length of Event: Friday or Saturday evening

Suggested Theme Verses: Ephesians 2:14-18

Ideal Number of Participants: The more the better

Estimated Cost Per Person: $3–$5 (to cover refreshments)

Facility Requirements: All-purpose room, activity center, or large meeting room. (This could also be done outdoors.)

Recommended Planning Team: 8 people minimum

Advance Planning Time Needed: 4–6 months

INTRODUCTION

by Kerry O'Bryant
Minister of Singles and Young Adults
Central Christian Church
Las Vegas, Nevada

"What could we do that would be new and exciting, something creative that would draw our singles and perhaps even bring in people from outside our church?"

This is a question we often ask in our singles ministry planning meetings. And we don't always have a good answer. But this mini-music festival—in a David Letterman-type show format—turned out to be one of our best received special events. Not only did it create interest among our own singles, but it also brought in many community and unchurched singles.

It can be difficult to find a common, uniting interest for the broad range of area singles. But nearly everyone enjoys good, live music, and each generation has associated with its respective music festivals (Woodstock for the Boomers; Lollapalooza for the Busters, etc.). Add to that an entertaining, fun show, attention-getting nostalgia, and some delicious snacks and you have a winning event. It can also become a creative approach to help build a bridge between a point of interest and some part of the gospel message.

If this event is well-planned, properly-promoted, and correctly-carried off, it can draw all kinds of singles (from within and outside of your church) and give you the opportunity to help focus them on the One who created music.

OBJECTIVES

❖ To create a seeker-sensitive event around an appealing nostalgic theme.

❖ To provide an evening of entertainment for area-wide singles.

❖ To become more familiar with the Christian bands and singers in the area.

THE BIG EVENT

SCHEDULE

6:55 P.M.—Doors open

7:00 P.M.—Band #1 plays two songs

7:25 P.M.—Host comes out to warm-up audience

7:30 P.M.—(Optional) Icebreakers

7:45 P.M.—Show Starts
- Musicians play "Amazing Grace"
- Musicians lead into theme song (à la

Letterman or "The Tonight Show" band)
- Host welcomes audience and makes introductions, then sits at desk (à la Letterman or Carson)
- Host chats with co-host, does Top Ten list
- Host does door prize giveaways
- Host introduces special guest
- Special guest sings song
- Host conducts light interview with special guest

❖
Get as many people as possible involved in the planning of this event.

8:30 P.M.—INTERMISSION
- Total Flower Child Contest
- Host interviews Band #1
- Kooky Kazoo Krew rushes stage and plays number
- Host introduces the singles ministry and does a short promo

9:00 P.M.—CLOSING SEGMENT
- Introduce Band #2
- Band #2 plays two songs
- Host interviews Band #2
- Chip and Pez comedy skit
- Host introduces Band #3
- Band #3 plays two songs
- Host interviews Band #3
- Host introduces Band #4
- Band #4 plays two songs
- (Optional) Show some video clips from Woodstock for segueway
- Host (or designated other) gives short, seeker-sensitive message based on the theme of the evening
- Host does announcements and wraps up show
- All bands play "Let the Son Shine In" to close program (with sing-along participation from the audience.)
10:00 or 10:30 P.M.—Show Ends

PROGRAM IDEAS AND SUGGESTIONS

FORMAT FOR THE SHOW

Plan this around a David Letterman, "Tonight Show" or Conan O'Brien variety-show format.

Include music, drama, and a brief closing message or challenge. The host sits behind a desk (or table) and interviews the guests, does a Top Ten list, participates in skits, and occasionally wanders into the audience for spoof games, conversation, or whatever seems to fit the theme of the evening. This format seems to be quite popular, especially with singles in their 20s and 30s.

With a format like this it is important to keep the program fast-paced and varied. For example, include icebreakers, skits, surprise-acts and door prizes between the various bands. The host must be comfortable and skilled with an audience, quick on his/her feet, and able to stay on time.

INVITE AREA BANDS

One of the highlights of an event like this is to become acquainted with some of the musical talent in your area. Find out who the best Christian bands and singers are in the community. Invite as many of them as possible to participate. (Limit each band to two songs, allowing several bands to perform.) It provides you an opportunity to become acquainted and create rapport with the local Christian bands—some you may want to invite back for a singles retreat or other event.

Although you may not be able to pay them for their performance, remind them that this is an excellent opportunity to familiarize others with their ministry. (During the event, do a brief interview with each band on stage to help everyone learn more about them.) Since some may be new, this event can be a real boost for their ministry.

A side benefit to involving several bands is that they may help promote the event within their own circle of influence. Many people may come to the event because of one of the bands.

Although this event is designed around a 60s theme, all the music does not need to be from then. For example, some music might be from newer bands who are quite young and much more contemporary sounding. It's nice to have some 60s sounds, but you will probably have a mixture of musical tastes represented. You can even have some fun with this wide variety (à la David Letterman). Just for fun, have a spoof "Kooky Kazoo Crew" band rush the stage for a "surprise" performance.

MEET AROUND TABLES

To create a more intimate, coffeehouse feel arrange the room so everyone sits at round tables. While not essential, this lends itself to meeting new people, small-group interaction, and sitting to munch on snacks while listening to the music.

WHY WOODSTOCK?

Woodstock was a defining moment for one generation. And more recently it has become a nostalgic interest even to those who weren't yet born in 1969. There will no doubt be Woodstock coattails to ride on for many more years. And using a Woodstock theme can be especially helpful in creating interest beyond the church walls.

However, it is not essential to use a Woodstock theme. It is more important to build around some nostalgic event that is familiar to a wide cross-section of people. You may find another type of event that works better for your community. Be creative. One idea would be to build it around Lollapalooza (a more recent music event very popular with the Buster generation)—or maybe even call it Churchapalooza.

HAVE FUN WITH THE NOSTALGIA

Encourage everyone to wear their best 60s outfit. Some will still have one in their closets. Others may need to go to a thrift shop or costume store and find the right garb. (Remember the tie-dyes, bell bottoms, Nehru jackets—and those wonderful hairstyles.) The more people who dress the part, the more entertaining the evening will be.

Decorate the host's desk with a lava lamp, peace signs, and daisies. If room allows, park an old Volkswagen bus on stage. Be creative.

Although this particular event is designed around a 60s theme, you may decide to do a 20s, 50s, or 70s theme. Consider all the possibilities.

TOTAL FLOWER CHILD CONTEST

During the show, invite people on stage who really went all out with their 60s look. Give each of them a large number to wear and have them parade across the stage. Invite the audience to vote on the "best flower child" outfit. Showcase those who have really played the part. Give prizes.

INVITE A SPECIAL GUEST

If possible, find a Christian in your area who was involved musically in the 60s (or even one who may have played at Woodstock). This can be a great opportunity for someone to share their faith with the seekers in the audience—someone who was "in the scene" but now has a new perspective on things because of their relationship with Jesus Christ.

(Editor's Note: As an example, Kerry O'Bryant, the contributor of this chapter, had James Smith participate in their program. James had been the lead guitarist for both Three Dog Night and Sly and the Family Stone, two very popular bands during the 60s and early 70s. He shared about his faith and how life had changed for him since he came to Christ.)

CONDUCTING INTERVIEWS

There are three primary reasons to conduct a few interviews during the program. 1) Interviewing band members helps the audience get acquainted with them, their ministry and, in the process, learn something about their faith and testimony; 2) Interviews can take place between sets, helping provide a natural transition while the next band is getting ready; 3) Interviews can lend some variety and interest to the program.

In addition to interviewing the various bands between sets, you may want to consider finding someone in the audience who was at the real Woodstock and interview them.

DOOR PRIZE GIVEAWAYS

Another part of the fun and variety of this evening can be the giving of door prizes throughout the evening. Work with area stores. Many will provide free giveaway items just for the publicity. Consider cassettes, CDs, books, and coupons for free meals, etc. If you have a T-shirt with your ministry name/logo on it, that can make a great prize too. Think of fun 60s memorabilia.

"MESSAGE THEME" FOR THE EVENING

As you plan this event, keep in mind that there might be several seekers in the audience. Prepare your message with that in mind.

The theme that runs throughout the evening

has to do with peace and love. Begin by looking at peace and love as two separate topics, then at the end tie them both together. Help people contrast the Woodstock version of peace and love with what it is according to God's word. What is it that God wants us to know about peace and love?

For the text, consider Ephesians 2:14-18 and Romans 12:18 through 13:8.

WOODSTOCK VIDEO

If your schedule and equipment allow, consider flashing on a large screen one or more short clips of video from one of the Woodstock documentaries. This could also be an excellent way to introduce the closing message at the end of the evening by helping set the scene for the mood and atmosphere during Woodstock.

One famous clip to consider is Jimi Hendrix playing the Star-Spangled Banner—possibly the single most memorable event of Woodstock.

However, if you choose to use some of the Woodstock video, be purposeful. Make sure it is clear to the people why you are using it and what it is intended to communicate. How does it help illustrate the message or theme of the evening?

(To get a copy of any Woodstock video contact your local public library, video store, or Public Broadcast Television station.)

(OPTIONAL) MAKE IT A WEEKEND EVENT

This Fest could quite easily be expanded to a half- or full-day event. Or to give it more of a weekend festival feeling, it could begin on Friday night and then run again from Saturday late morning until mid-afternoon. It would be quite easy to expand the format by simply allowing the bands to play 6, 8 or 10-song sets rather than limit them to two. This longer weekend version may lend itself better to an outdoor setting.

ICEBREAKERS

Keep in mind that the primary purpose of "breaking the ice" is to help people mix, laugh together, break barriers, and get to know the others at their table (or sitting nearby).

If you want to mix people by age, consider having all the "were-not-even-born-yet" people move to one side of the room.

• How many people attended Woodstock?
• What was the name of the farmer who provided the field where Woodstock was held?

❖ *For more icebreakers, see the Table of Contents.*

• Who were some of the musicians who played at Woodstock? Which would be closest to your favorite?
• Did you (or anyone you knew) attend Woodstock? If yes, describe the experience.
• If you were old enough to remember, what were your impressions of Woodstock? What memories does this event bring back?
• What hairstyle or clothing from the 60s do you wish would come back in style?
• What hairstyle or clothing from the 60s do you hope never comes back in style?
• What is the biggest festival/event you've ever attended? What do you most remember about it?
• What is there about Woodstock that appeals to you? What turns you off?
• What one image or photo of the 60s most stands out to you? Why?

Going Deeper

• What were people seeking at Woodstock?
• How (or where) are people seeking the same thing(s) today?
• Woodstock was a defining moment for a generation. What has been a defining moment for you personally?
• Why do you think Woodstock happened? What made Woodstock such a major event in the late 60s?
• What was the significance of Woodstock, in your opinion?
• Peace and love were sort of the theme of Woodstock. How has the idea of peace and love changed today as compared to then?
• How do you define peace and love? When do you experience them most?

TOP TEN LIST

Here's an idea for a Top Ten list. Feel free to adapt and use this, or develop one of your own.

THE TOP TEN DIFFERENCES BETWEEN WOODSTOCK AND THIS SHOW

10. *Woodstock:* Hell's Angels worked security and assaulted dozens of innocent fans.
    Our Show: Officer Hammond works security and assaults dozens of innocent donuts.
9. *Woodstock:* 300,000 people—and 5 Port-a-Potties.
    Our Show: 5 good jokes—and 300,000 bombs.
8. *Woodstock:* You can't remember attending.
    Our Show: Try as you might, you can't get this evening out of your mind. (The memory sticks in your head like a bad song.)
7. *Woodstock:* Jimi Hendrix intentionally set his guitar on fire.
    Our Show: The only way this show will become interesting is if our host sets his hair on fire.
6. *Woodstock:* Happened before our HOST was born.
    Our Show: Makes fans wish that our HOST had never been born.
5. *Woodstock:* Wild storms deposited several inches of rain during the weekend.
    Our Show: Wild fans deposited several inches of marshmallows during the evening.
4. *Woodstock:* Several people died of natural (and other) causes.
    Our Show: Several people died of boredom.
3. *Woodstock:* Lots of 'shrooms being passed around in the audience.
    Our Show: Lots of 'shmallows being thrown around by the audience.
2. *Woodstock:* Fans staged sit-ins to protest the war.
    Our Show: Fans staged walk-outs to protest that the show runs too long.
1. *Woodstock:* Mud, Drugs, and Rock 'n Roll.
    Our Show: Popcorn, soda, and the "Kooky Kazoo Crew" band.

EQUIPMENT/SUPPLIES (To be furnished by event leaders)

- [ ] Props for stage and Host desk
- [ ] Finger food snacks and refreshments (include marshmallows)
- [ ] (Optional) Name tags and writing pens
- [ ] Various door prizes and giveaways
- [ ] Awards for "Total Flower Child" Contest
- [ ] 60s decorations for the meeting room
- [ ] (Optional) Woodstock video clips
- [ ] Professional quality sound equipment

WHAT TO BRING (To be provided by participants)

- [ ] 60s wardrobe/hairstyles
- [ ] A friend

PLANNING THE EVENT

PLANNING TEAM

For this event, you need an Event Director (possibly an Assistant Event Director) and volunteers to take responsibilities for the event site, budget, publicity, at-door registration, speaker, music, food, audio/visual equipment, and equipment/supplies. In addition to the above Planning Team, recruit a photographer/videographer and a set designer.

❖ *The more people who have ownership and involvement in the planning, the greater success you will have.*

Planning Timeline

Event: *"Peace and Love" Music Fest*   **Date of event:** _____

Event Director: _____   **Phone:** _____

Thanks for agreeing to serve on our music fest Planning Team. Please read over this timeline for your assigned task(s). Adapt as needed and supplement with information in the generic job descriptions. Highlight your tasks (and due dates) and mark your calendar.

Date: _____ **6 MONTHS IN ADVANCE**

Event Director (page 226)

☐ Recruit a Planning Team. Brainstorm ideas, and adapt this event to fit your particular ministry goals and objectives.
☐ Make sure all team members understand their own tasks. Adapt timeline as needed.
☐ Discuss suggested possible locations, themes, special guests, musicians, etc.

Event Site Coordinator (page 234)

☐ Select and reserve the event location.
☐ Get the confirmed dates and site on the church calendar (notify the Planning Team).

Music Coordinator (page 237)

☐ Compile a list of all potential area bands and their fees. Check references for quality.

Budget Coordinator (page 229)

☐ Begin estimating costs and revenue.

Speaker Coordinator (page 250)

☐ Start special guest search.
☐ Coordinate with the Event Director who will be the Host and who will do the closing message.

Date: _____ **5 MONTHS IN ADVANCE**

Event Director

☐ Meet with the Planning Team to ensure that established goals and objectives are being incorporated into this event.
☐ Finalize program theme and details.
☐ Recruit person to put together the program script (to help keep the show on schedule and moving fast).

Music Coordinator

☐ Begin finalizing the bands for the event.

Publicity Coordinator (page 238)

☐ Begin developing a promotional plan.

Budget Coordinator

☐ Work with the Planning Team to finalize an operational budget

Date: _____ **4 MONTHS IN ADVANCE**

Event Director

☐ Check Planning Team's progress.

Music Coordinator

☐ Have all bands confirmed (in writing). Determine sound equipment needs.

Speaker Coordinator

☐ Confirm the special guest.

Audio/Visual Equipment Coordinator (page 228)

☐ Determine all audio/video equipment needs. Begin locating needed items.

Publicity Coordinator

☐ Once the event theme, location, special guest speaker, and the bands have been determined, begin preparing flyers,

❖ *For more ideas and help, refer to job descriptions beginning on page 225.*

brochures, radio spots, and other promotional material to advertise the event.
☐ Include info about the "Total Flower Child" contest so attendees can dress the part.

Set Designer

☐ Begin preparing a list of 60s items that could be used to decorate the event site.

Date:	**3 Months IN Advance**
_____	

Publicity Coordinator

☐ Begin promoting the event.
☐ Provide promotional material to each band so they can help promote too.

Program Script Writer

☐ Develop a minute-by-minute, first-draft program script.

Date:	**2 Months IN Advance**
_____	

Publicity Coordinator

☐ Continue all promotion.

Equipment/Supplies Coordinator (page 238)

☐ Coordinate with the Planning Team all props and miscellaneous equipment needs. Begin locating needed items.

Audio/Visual Equipment Coordinator

☐ Finalize all audio/video needs.
☐ Recruit one or two sound people.

Food Coordinator (page 236)

☐ Determine the snacks and refreshments to make available at the event.

Date:	**1 Month IN Advance**
_____	

Event Director

☐ Meet to check the team's progress.

Program Script Writer

☐ Finalize the show script.

Audio/Visual Equipment Coordinator

☐ Arrange for all audio/video equipment items to arrive at the event site as needed.

Music Coordinator

☐ Finalize all arrangements with musicians.
☐ Conduct pre-interviews with each band to help the host be better prepared.

Registration Coordinator (page 241)

☐ Have the at-the-door registration procedures established and ready to go.
☐ Order name tags.

Publicity Coordinator

☐ Make final promotional thrust.

Date:	**1 Week IN Advance**
_____	

Event Director

☐ Check in with the Planning Team.

Budget Coordinator

☐ Prepare checks to pay bills as needed.

Set Designer

☐ Collect all needed items to decorate the set/stage. Recruit help. Decorate.

Food Coordinator

☐ Recruit helpers as needed to prepare (or purchase) snacks and refreshments.

Photographer/Videographer

☐ Prepare to capture the event on film and/or video.

Date:	**2 TO 4 Weeks AFTER Event**
_____	

☐ See "Followup Guidelines" on page 254.

Comedy Skit

CHIP AND PEZ: "WHO'S ON STAGE?"

Written by Craig Sheeler
Running Time: 3-4 minutes

Recruit two people from your group to play Chip and Pez, a couple of rocker dudes (a la Wayne and Garth from the movie "Wayne's World"). This funny skit is a take-off from Abbott and Costello's famous "Who's on First?" sketch.

Caricatures:
Chip Chumley, a long-haired heavy metal British rocker with a confused outlook on reality.
Pez "Just Pez," a California Valley type with a party hearty attitude.
Both are on their way to becoming new Christians.

Chip and Pez enter from sides and set up lounge chairs and cooler for concert.

Music: Intro of hard rock metal lead and drums pounding with some senseless lyrics being screamed by Chip and Pez. (yeh, yeh, rock 'n roll, rock 'n roll)

Chip: Hey Pez, this spot looks ripping, man . . .
Pez: . . . But like Chip, man, we can hardly see the stage.
Chip: That's alright. I don't know any of the bands anyway.
Pez: Totally! (yeh, yeh, rock 'n roll, rock 'n roll)
Chip: Hey Pez, that was a righteous gathering after our last show.
Pez: Totally. That Christian band was way cool. Aye!
Chip and Pez: Hey, headbangers salute! (yeh, yeh, rock 'n roll, rock 'n roll)
Pez: Dude! Break's over . . . they're starting the show back up!
Chip: Alright. Hey Chip, who's that on stage?
Pez: The Who.
Chip: You know, the band on stage.
Pez: What?
Chip: Who's the band on stage?
Pez: Right.
Chip: Right what?
Pez: Who is the band on stage.
Chip: That's what I'm asking. Who's on stage?
Pez: . . . and that's what I'm telling you, dude. Who is the band on stage.

Chip grabs Pez's face and points him toward the audience.

Chip: Pez, do you see the stage?
Pez: Barely.
Chip: And who's playing now?
Pez: Absolutely.
Chip: Okay, so Absolutely is the band on stage.
Pez: No, dude.
Chip: Then who's on stage?
Pez: Absolutely!
Chip: That's what I said. So Absolutely is the band on stage.
Pez: No, Who.
Chip: WHO?
Pez: Yes!
Chip: YES is the band on stage!
Pez: No, dude. YES isn't even at this concert!

Chip responds with frustration.

Chip: What is the name of the band on stage?
Pez: WHO.
Chip: The band on stage.
Pez: WHO!
Chip: That's what I'm trying to find out
Pez: WHO is the band on stage.
Chip: That's what I'm asking you.
Pez: I'm telling you WHO's on stage.
Chip: I'm listening!
Pez: The Band on stage is The Who.
Chip: Right! WHO is the band on stage?
Pez: Yes! Yes! Yes!
Chip: Oh great, they're about to finish playing. Who's on next?
Pez: No, dude. Who's on now. The BAND is on after them.
Chip: What's the name of The band?
Pez: The Band!
Chip: Yes, what's the name of The band?
Pez: You know, The Band!
Chip: No I don't know The band. That's why I'm asking names of who just finished playing and The Band who's getting ready to play.
Pez: Yeh, you got it dude!
Chip: I don't even know what I just said. Pez, if you keep this up, it's gonna mean war!
Pez: No way, dude. They're not on till later.
Chip: Alright, that did it!

Chip then chases Pez off the stage.

23½ CREATIVE WEEKEND IDEA

Have you been wondering about the 1/2 idea in the title of the book?

Well, now that you have on hand the helpful resources in this book, we would like to challenge you to develop some creative ideas of your own.

Using the "Basic Steps to a Successful Event" section in the front of the book and the "Planning Team Member Job Descriptions and Resources" section in the back of the book, take one of the ideas suggested on this page (or one of your own) and develop an event to use with your own single adult group. Or take one of the ideas in this book and change or adapt it significantly so that it becomes a completely different idea. (Be sure to let us know about what you come up with. We may want to include it in our next Creative Weekends book!)

Possible Event Ideas to Develop for Your Ministry

What would you do to make these ideas into a meaningful weekend event for your singles? What are the Bible study/discussion possibilities that come to mind? Who are the kinds of resource people that could help make any of these ideas a success? How could these events help your singles grow in their relationships with God and with each other? Let your creativity and imagination go to work! Think of all the fresh and exciting possibilities!

- ☐ Tacky Roller-Skating Night
- ☐ A Robin Hood Weekend (surprising people with good deeds—anonymously)
- ☐ River Boat Cruise (with a study/discussion that fits the water or boating theme)
- ☐ Water Park Follies
- ☐ A Day at the Zoo
- ☐ Cross-Country Skiing
- ☐ A Day at the Beach
- ☐ Movie Marathon (selecting specific movies to watch and then discuss)
- ☐ *Gone with the Wind* Weekend
- ☐ Let's See the Colors (fall leaves)
- ☐ Make a Movie with a Message (form a cast and production crew and do something creative on video)
- ☐ Ropes Course Team-Building Weekend
- ☐ The Dude Ranch Event
- ☐ A Weekend on the Farm (or Sheep Ranch or Cattle Ranch) (lends itself well to a wide variety of Bible lessons/studies/discussions)
- ☐ Atten-Shun! A Military Base Retreat
- ☐ Weekend Book Discussion (requires reading a book ahead of time)
- ☐ A Weekend from the 40s (or 50s or 60s) (dress the part, play games that were popular then, etc.)
- ☐ Cookie Bake-off (where everyone helps make and/or decorate cookies, then helps deliver them to a nursing home, child care center, etc.)
- ☐ Bicycle Tour Weekend (or Mountain Biking)
- ☐ Houseboat Weekend
- ☐ Weekend Hospice Care (spending a weekend visiting with and caring for the terminally ill)
- ☐ The One That Got Away Weekend (based on fishing, lends itself well to a wide variety of Bible lessons/studies/discussions)
- ☐ Weekend Outing for Single-Parent Children
- ☐ Habitat for Humanity Weekend
- ☐ Over at the Nursing Home (visit with and help care for the residents—even stay overnight if possible)
- ☐ Silent Retreat
- ☐ The Fruit Farm Volunteers (pick fruit and deliver to the needy; lends itself well to a wide variety of Bible lessons/studies/discussions)
- ☐ A Weekend of Art (everyone participates with the art of their choice—sculpting, painting, pottery, etc.)
- ☐ Teaching English As a Second Language
- ☐ An Archeological Dig
- ☐ History in the Making (writing each other's history)
- ☐ A Star Trek Weekend
- ☐ A "What Color Is My Parachute" Weekend
- ☐ A Day with the Mayor (or the Governor, the Senator, or the Congressman)
- ☐ Megabyte Weekend: Surfing the Internet

Now that your mind is on a roll, jot down some of your own magnificent ideas! What are some creative weekend ideas you'd like to plan for your group?

The following outline may be helpful in planning an event. Also refer to "Basic Steps: How to Create a Successful Event," starting on page 9.

Objectives

Length of Event

Desired Cost Per Person

Program Ideas and Suggestions

    Topic or Theme

    Theme Verse

    Icebreakers

    Activities

    Small Groups

    Speaker

Schedule

Equipment/Supplies

What to Bring

Planning Team

Advance Planning Time Needed

Planning Timeline (by months and weeks in advance)

APPENDIX

PLANNING TEAM MEMBER JOB DESCRIPTIONS AND RESOURCES

Following are reproducible job descriptions, checklists, and related sample resources for Planning Team members. This information is to supplement the Planning Timeline provided with each event. Ask Planning Team members to adapt the following information to the specific needs of your event.

Event Director

The Event Director can either be the Singles Ministry Pastor/Leader or someone appointed by the Pastor/Leader to be in charge of only one event or to serve a one-year term.

QUALIFICATIONS

A spiritually mature Christian who

- [ ] is active in the church and in the singles ministry.
- [ ] is trustworthy, dependable, and a person of good repute.
- [ ] subscribes to the stated beliefs and policies of the church.
- [ ] possesses strong leadership, time-management, and organizational skills.
- [ ] has a servant's heart.

OBJECTIVES

- [ ] To encourage new ideas and creative thinking as part of the planning process.
- [ ] To get as many people as possible involved in the planning of this event, realizing that some of the best relationship-building and most effective ministry occur when people work together.
- [ ] To provide an atmosphere at the event in which good, healthy interpersonal relationships can be developed and community-building can happen.
- [ ] To provide a place where adults can begin or nurture a personal relationship with Christ.
- [ ] To create opportunities where participants can exercise their ministry gifts with others.
- [ ] To equip and empower event Planning Team members to accomplish their respective tasks.
- [ ] To support Planning Team members through prayer and encouragement.
- [ ] To choose leaders who represent most groups within the single adult community. Include both newcomers and oldtimers, men and women, and a variety of backgrounds and gifts.
- [ ] To select leaders who delegate and get others involved.

KEY RESPONSIBILITIES

- [ ] Report to the Single Adult Ministry Pastor/Leader.
- [ ] Oversee the planning, execution, and follow-up of a specific event.
- [ ] Recruit Planning Team members to coordinate various areas of responsibility as needed.
- [ ] Provide Planning Team members with training, clear instructions, and deadlines for their areas of responsibility. (See reproducible event Planning Timeline and related Job Descriptions.)
- [ ] Encourage each Planning Team member to prepare for the event with prayer.
- [ ] Closely follow the Planning Timeline and help all Planning Team members to do the same.
- [ ] Determine with the Planning Team if an outside speaker is needed. (A special guest speaker can sometimes add to the success of an event. But also keep in mind that may you have very capable people in your own church and city who could provide just what you need.)
- [ ] Attend all applicable scheduled meetings.
- [ ] Help single parents attend events by suggesting (or organizing) child care options.
- [ ] Get approval, as necessary, from the appropriate church official(s).
- [ ] Provide the church office and critical staff members with the telephone numbers of where the group can be reached during the event.
- [ ] Assist in helping raise scholarship funds as needed.
- [ ] Prepare an evaluation to be used during or following the event (see sample on page 255).

Assistant Event Director

The Assistant Event Director is appointed by the Event Director (in consultation with the Pastor/Leader). This person may serve a one-year term or be an assistant for only one event.

QUALIFICATIONS

A spiritually mature Christian who

- [ ] is active in the church and in the singles ministry.
- [ ] is trustworthy and dependable.
- [ ] subscribes to the stated beliefs and policies of the church.
- [ ] possesses strong leadership, time-management, and organizational skills.
- [ ] prefers to accomplish tasks by involving others rather than trying to do it all alone.
- [ ] is a team player and a person of good report.
- [ ] has a servant's heart.

KEY RESPONSIBILITIES

Report to and assist the Event Director as requested. Tasks are unique with each event, depending on how the Director delegates responsibility.

Hospitality Coordinator

Serves as a member of the Planning Team and reports to the Event Director.

KEY RESPONSIBILITIES

- [ ] Help participants feel welcomed and relaxed, especially upon arrival.
- [ ] Recruit a team of greeters.
- [ ] Where needed, arrange for information and welcome signs to be displayed.

QUALIFICATIONS

A people person who is caring, outgoing, dependable; an encourager; has a servant's heart.

RESPONSIBILITIES CHECKLIST

- [ ] Recruit a team of greeters to help welcome people as they arrive.
- [ ] Assist the Registration Coordinator, as needed, with on-site registration.
- [ ] Work with the Food Coordinator to maintain a "hospitality table," keeping it clean and filled with a variety of snacks and beverage options (ice tea, lemonade, water, coffee, etc.).
- [ ] Arrange for information and welcome signs as needed. (Don't assume people know where anything is located in the facility you are using, even your church building.)
- [ ] Make and display banners and other attractive displays to help people feel welcome and to set a warm and inviting atmosphere.

Audio/Visual Equipment Coordinator

Serves as a member of the Planning Team and reports to the Event Director.

KEY RESPONSIBILITIES

Coordinate acquiring, setting up, running, and returning all audio/visual equipment as needed by speakers, musicians, and event personnel. (A/V equipment includes any mikes, speakers, soundboards, amps, audiocassette players, videocassette players or cameras, televisions, overhead projectors, slide projectors, slide or movie screens, etc.)

QUALIFICATIONS

Skilled in use of audio/visual equipment, responsible, and resourceful; has a servant's heart.

RESPONSIBILITIES

☐ Determine audio/visual needs for the event, taking into consideration the size of your group, what the speaker and music needs are, etc.

☐ Check with the Event Site Coordinator to find out what A/V equipment is available to you at the event site. Determine if it is sufficient for your needs. If not, make arrangements to borrow or rent equipment as needed.

☐ During the early stages of planning, provide estimated cost/person to Budget Coordinator.

☐ Complete any necessary request forms for the use of event site equipment.

☐ Select someone to run the sound system at the event if needed.

☐ If you plan to tape any sessions, confirm that permission has been received from speakers/musicians as needed.

☐ (Optional) As people arrive and during suitable breaks, play soft background music that fits the theme and setting.

If borrowing or renting equipment . . .

☐ Get permission from the event site facility—**in writing**—that you are allowed to bring your equipment into the facility.

☐ Complete any necessary request forms for the use of church or rental equipment.

☐ Arrange for safe transportation of equipment to the event site.

☐ Arrange for the safe return of all borrowed or rented equipment following the event.

☐ Confirm that all deposits and payments are made on time.

Budget Coordinator

Serves as a member of the Planning Team and reports to the Event Director.

KEY RESPONSIBILITIES

- ☐ Prepare budget.
- ☐ Estimate costs per person.
- ☐ Help raise scholarship funding as needed.
- ☐ Pay bills and honorariums.

QUALIFICATIONS

Experienced accountant or treasurer, reliable, honest, prompt; has a servant's heart.

RESPONSIBILITIES CHECKLIST

- ☐ Prepare a budget proposal. Based on initial plans, ideas, recommendations, and input from the Planning Team, prepare a preliminary budget proposal for the Planning Team's approval. (Refer to "Budget Worksheet" on page 230.)
    - •One quick planning tip: In most cases, lodging and meal costs will be the largest portion of the budget. Once you've determined these costs, add approximately $30-$50 per person to cover all other costs. For example, if the lodging/meal cost per person is $100.00, charge between $130-150 for the event. Adjust this guide as needed for your situation.
- ☐ Once the budget has been approved, provide regular reporting to the Planning Team on the status of expenses. (Are you over or under the budget?) Make adjustments as needed.
- ☐ Meet with the church treasurer/business manager to learn about church policies and procedures pertaining to the handling of funds.
- ☐ Determine all deposit due dates and payment deadlines.
- ☐ Make payments as needed to Planning Team members for purchasing necessary supplies and equipment for the event.
- ☐ Make deposits in the approved bank account on a timely basis.
- ☐ Assist as needed in raising scholarships for those needing help to attend the event. Establish a scholarship fund.
- ☐ Work with the Registration Coordinator to develop a payment plan for participants, allowing them to pay in weekly/monthly installments prior to the event. (See sample payment plan coupons on page 243.)
- ☐ Arrange for a petty cash fund if needed during the event.
- ☐ Arrange for a lock box, if needed, at the event site to secure funds received on site.
- ☐ Develop a system of accountability for all income and expenses associated with this event. (How is cash handled? Are there two signatures on each check? How is registration income accounted for and transferred from the Registration Coordinator to the Budget Coordinator? What safeguards are in place to insure integrity with all funds?)
- ☐ Check on insurance coverage. Does your church have a policy that already covers any church-sponsored events? What insurance coverage is required by the event facility, if any? Make sure your event is adequately covered.
- ☐ Following the event, produce a report for the Event Director of total income and expenses.

Budget Worksheet

Event Name _____ Date of Event _____

Event Director/Person in Charge _____ Phone # Home _____
Work _____

Assistant Director _____ Phone # Home _____
Work _____

EXPENSES

$_____ Speaker/workshop leaders/musicians
_____ honorarium(s)
_____ travel
_____ lodging
_____ food
$_____ Group transportation (gas/tolls/tips for bus)
$_____ Event facility rental
$_____ Other/miscellaneous lodging costs
_____
$_____ Food (meals and snacks)
$_____ Books
$_____ Tapes
$_____ Publicity
_____ printing
_____ postage
_____ radio/TV
_____ other_____
$_____ Decorations
$_____ Miscellaneous costs for activities, etc.
$_____ Scholarships
$_____ Complimentary registrations (for staff/workers)
$_____ Prizes/thank-you gifts
$_____ A/V equipment
$_____ Other/Miscellaneous equipment rental or purchase
$_____ Child care
$_____ Photographer/videographer
$_____ Tax/gratuities/tolls/fees
$_____ Insurance
$_____ Deposits
$_____ Games/mixers/icebreakers
$_____ Other _____
$_____ **TOTAL ESTIMATED EXPENSES**

INCOME (not including registration)

$_____ Church budget
$_____ Gifts
$_____ Fund-raising
$_____ Other
$_____ **TOTAL ESTIMATED INCOME**

COST PER REGISTRANT

$_____ Total estimated expenses
$_____ Total estimated income
$_____ **TOTAL EXPENSES NOT COVERED** (subtract estimated income from estimated expenses)
_____ Anticipated number of registrants

$_____ **ESTIMATED COST PER REGISTRANT** (divide expenses not covered by anticipated number of paying registrants)

NOTE: To cover unexpected expenses or shortfalls in income, you may want to consider increasing this amount by 10 to 20 percent.

Bus Captains Coordinator

Serves as a member of the Planning Team and reports to the Event Director.

KEY RESPONSIBILITIES

- ☐ Recruit and instruct captains for buses (or vans) used to transport people to the event.
- ☐ Equip captains to help participants have fun and begin building relationships enroute.

QUALIFICATIONS

Organized; a good communicator; a "people person"; an encourager; has a servant's heart.

RESPONSIBILITIES CHECKLIST

- ☐ During the early stages of planning, provide estimated cost per person to Budget Coordinator.
- ☐ When buses (or vans) are chartered, recruit bus captains to count people on the buses, help "first-timers" feel welcome, make the trip enjoyable, and provide pertinent information.
- ☐ Encourage each captain to mingle with the people and be an encourager.
- ☐ Send a letter to the bus captains, spelling out their responsibilities (see sample below).
- ☐ On the day of the event, supply everything each bus captain needs. For example:
  - ☐ Sign-in sheet and pen
  - ☐ Name tags
  - ☐ Stickers for tags of first-timers
  - ☐ Sheet of any final announcements
  - ☐ Two trash bags (one for pop cans only)
  - ☐ Driver tip money in envelopes ($20 each way)
  - ☐ Supplies for icebreakers/songs/games on the bus
  - ☐ Box lunch for each person

Attention Bus Captains

Thanks very much for "volunteering" to help make this event a success by being a bus captain. For the participants you are often the first contact and official greeter—so your role is very important.

PLEASE DO THE FOLLOWING ON YOUR BUS:

- ☐ Welcome everyone and pray before the bus leaves!
- ☐ Count how many people are on board.
- ☐ Have everyone sign in.
- ☐ Head count = sign-in sheet count?
- ☐ Distribute name tags.
- ☐ Identify first-timers with special stickers.
- ☐ Do planned icebreakers/songs/games.
- ☐ Play "tour guide" if appropriate.
- ☐ Review the event schedule, especially the first part.
- ☐ Explain any important arrival/registration details (check-in, room keys, etc.).
- ☐ Place trash and pop cans in separate trash bags.
- ☐ Tip the driver upon arrival at the event site and back home.
- ☐ Repeat head count after any stops.

Thanks—and see you soon!

Children's Coordinator

Serves as a member of the Planning Team and reports to the Event Director.

KEY RESPONSIBILITIES

☐ To organize and schedule activities for children who attend the event. This includes recruiting a team of qualified individuals with a heart for children of various ages and an ability to work well with them.

☐ If children do not attend the event, to help coordinate child care as needed to make it possible for single parents to attend. This includes compiling a list of families and empty-nesters who might be willing to care for a child or two during the event.

☐ During the early stages of planning, provide estimated cost per person to Budget Coordinator.

QUALIFICATIONS

Knows and understands children, has strong organizational and communication skills, is resourceful, is familiar with many people in the church, has a servant's heart.

Drama Coach

KEY RESPONSIBILITIES

☐ To teach and demonstrate various techniques involved in acting: Improvisation, Characterization, Relaxation, and Presentation

☐ To perform a short monologue for demonstration purposes; if appropriate, lead the devotional times.

QUALIFICATIONS

Committed to this retreat project. Can teach by demonstration, be understanding and patient, work well with people, and be able to give direction and feedback. It is most helpful if this person is able to speak from acting experience.

RESPONSIBILITIES CHECKLIST (DURING THE EVENT)

☐ Help group people into teams of four or five each. Assist everyone through readings of the selected scripts. Offer ideas and suggestions for character development. Critique and encourage.

☐ Cast each of the one-act plays, giving those with more confidence and talent the more challenging roles. Offer the smaller roles to those who are less confident or less experienced.

☐ After the first meeting where scripts are handed out, meet with each small group. As they practice their one-act plays, coach them on their progress and use of new skills learned.

☐ Make notes and critique the small group "performances." Help the group at large see and experience the improvements each group is making.

☐ Encourage those who are struggling and ensure a safe, non-threatening environment in which everyone can learn, play, and have fun learning new skills!

Equipment/Supplies Coordinator

Serves as a member of the Planning Team and reports to the Event Director.

KEY RESPONSIBILITIES

☐ Work with all other Planning Team members to determine what items are needed.
☐ Coordinate the borrowing/rental/purchase, setup, and return of all equipment and supplies.

QUALIFICATIONS

Handy with equipment, tools, etc.; responsible and resourceful; has a servant's heart.

RESPONSIBILITIES CHECKLIST

☐ Check with all Planning Team members and keep a running list of all needed supplies (i.e., camping gear and equipment, icebreaker props, on-site registration supplies, etc.).
☐ Check with the Event Site Coordinator about equipment/supplies available at the event site. If not sufficient for your needs, secure items as needed. (Borrowing will save you money.)
☐ Arrange to transport all equipment/supplies to and from the event site.
☐ During the early stages of planning, provide estimated cost per person to Budget Coordinator.

If borrowing or renting equipment . . .

☐ Get written permission from the event site facility to bring your equipment, etc.
☐ Complete any necessary request forms for the use of church or rental equipment.
☐ Arrange for the safe return of all borrowed or rented equipment following the event.

Event Materials Coordinator

Serves as a member of the Planning Team and reports to the Event Director.

KEY RESPONSIBILITIES

Works closely with the Registration Coordinator and the Speaker/Workshop Coordinator in preparing all materials to be distributed before, during, or after the event.

QUALIFICATIONS

Organized; detail-oriented; computer-friendly; familiar with writing, editing, and printing process; has a servant's heart.

RESPONSIBILITIES CHECKLIST

☐ During the early stages of planning, provide estimated cost per person to Budget Coordinator.
☐ Plan, as needed, to help prepare, copy, collate, and assemble the following:

☐ Registration materials
☐ Scholarship application forms
☐ Confirmation letter to registrants
☐ Event schedule
☐ Welcome packet
☐ Small group materials/resources
☐ Song/music sheets or books
☐ Bibliography of suggested reading
☐ Map to the facility
☐ Diagram/map of facility
☐ Evaluation forms
☐ Any other needed materials

Event Site Coordinator

Serves as a member of the Planning Team and reports to the Event Director.

KEY RESPONSIBILITIES

☐ Acquire the best event site available that fits the budget and other needs of the event.

☐ Coordinate all arrangements related to the site (including confirmation, deposits, lodging, meals, facilities, and equipment).
Note: Whenever possible, it is best if *only* the Event Site Coordinator has direct contact with the facility. This helps facilitate communication and minimizes possible frustrations that can be caused by the facility being contacted by multiple members of the Planning Team.

QUALIFICATIONS

Highly organized; detail oriented; strong, capable negotiator; able to find the right facility for the particular event; has a servant's heart.

RESPONSIBILITIES CHECKLIST

☐ Choose/confirm the event site. In choosing a site, determine with the Planning Team the kind of facility needed to best accomplish event goals—hotel, conference center, campground, church building, large private condo, etc. The following questions for the facility will help you narrow the choices for your group.
• How long does it take to drive to your facility? (Keep in mind that people are generally willing to drive three to six hours for a long weekend event. However, for a short weekender, that will usually be cut to one to three hours.)
• Can you facilitate a group of _____ people during ___month? ___date? What is the maximum and minimum number of registrants your facility can accommodate?
• What room accommodations are available? Can you provide sleeping rooms for the number of people expected? Are bathrooms private?
(Note: Will attendees be willing to share a room with one or more persons or bathrooms with people in other rooms?)
• What is the size of your largest meeting room? How many "break-out" rooms do you have available? How many people does each room accommodate? Cost?
• What food services can you provide and at what cost? (Obtain prices for snacks and meals; find out if gratuity is included in the price.) Are vending machines available? May we bring our own food, beverages, and/or snacks?
• What meeting equipment is provided (tables, sound system, podium, overhead projector, etc.)? Will using this equipment cost extra? May we bring our own equipment?
• What recreational facilities do you have? When are they open? (Once the facility is confirmed, share this information with the Publicity Coordinator so it can be included in the promotional material.)

☐ Obtain an agreement **in writing** from the facility specifying that you may bring in your own refreshments and equipment.

(Continued)

Note: To make final approval of the site, check to see if the facility management will provide free accommodations to "scouts" who are planning an event. Also ask about reduced or waived costs for meeting rooms if a minimum number of guest rooms is guaranteed.

After the site is reserved:

☐ Provide any estimated per-person costs to the Budget Coordinator.

☐ Record basic information for future contact: Write down and file the convention site name, address, phone and fax numbers, and the name of the contact person.

☐ Ask for a written confirmation or contract that includes everything you discussed—food cost, tips, meeting rooms, payment arrangements, room types and prices, etc. Check to be sure a signed contract is on file at the convention site and at the church. Make sure all details are correct.

☐ Ask for a map of the facility and a list of the lodging rooms and sleeping accommodations you will be using. (The map can be duplicated and distributed to those attending.)

☐ Request brochures of the event facility, plus tourist sites of interest in the area. (Ask for enough brochures so they can be distributed to each registrant with the confirmation letter.)

☐ See that a deposit check is sent to hold the facilities.

☐ Confirm when the final payment is due.

As the event date draws closer:

☐ Verify that a deposit has been received by the convention site and that all arrangements are clear.

☐ Send a copy of the event schedule to the contact person.

☐ Communicate all details and requests concerning your event: meal times, refreshments in conference rooms, rooms needed for small group meetings, firewood, overhead projector and screen, where to pick up keys, etc.

☐ Work with the Audio/Visual Equipment and Equipment/Supplies Coordinators to create and maintain a list of all items/services needed while at the facility (microphones and stands, stage, flip charts, sound system, overhead projector, chalk boards; number of chairs in specific rooms; requests for refreshments; and tables in hospitality area.) Confirm with the facility what items they have available for your use.

☐ Work with the Registration Coordinator to identify which meetings/workshops will need the largest rooms. Make facility room assignments accordingly. (Coordinate information regarding room assignments with the Planning Team.)

☐ Keep the facility apprised periodically of changes (+/-) in estimated numbers of people who will be attending so they can plan accordingly.

☐ Coordinate with the facility the number of chairs and the equipment needed in each meeting room, any preferred seating rearrangements, etc.

☐ Confirm times and places for refreshments, etc.

Food Coordinator

Serves as a member of the Planning Team and reports to the Event Director.

KEY RESPONSIBILITIES

- ☐ If the facility is not providing meals, recruit assistants and organize all meal and snack preparation and related cleanup; oversee the purchase of all food items for the event. Arrange for necessary cooking utensils.
- ☐ If the facility is providing meals, coordinate any necessary details and menu selections with the Event Site Coordinator.

QUALIFICATIONS

Has experience in organizing and preparing meals and snacks for medium to large groups; can effectively recruit help as needed and can negotiate details with facility personnel; has a servant's heart.

RESPONSIBILITIES CHECKLIST

- ☐ During the early stages of planning, provide estimated cost per person to Budget Coordinator.
- ☐ If your event is a weekend event and a long bus ride is planned during a regular mealtime, arrange to have box lunches prepared and delivered to the buses about one hour before departure.
- ☐ Enlist cleanup crews to ensure the event site is left clean, trash is collected and disposed of properly, and any campfires are thoroughly doused.
- ☐ If snacks are not included by the event facility, consider asking participants to bring items to share (cookies, chips, fruit, etc.) throughout the weekend. Secure someone to be responsible for keeping the area clean and snacks available.
- ☐ Good break and refreshment choices include coffee, pop, and juice; cheese and crackers; cut fruit; and baked goods—these go a long way for less money.
- ☐ When help is needed with cleanup it is always best to recruit helpers beforehand. Never wait to ask people at the event to help clean up afterwards.

If the event facility is providing all meals:

- ☐ Based on the interests of your group and/or the theme of the event, suggest menu ideas for the facility kitchen staff. (Coordinate this with the Event Site Coordinator.)

If the group members are providing and preparing all meals:

- ☐ Begin planning the menus and collecting needed supplies.
- ☐ Determine what cooking utensils, if any, are available for use at the event facility.
- ☐ Coordinate cooking and cleanup teams for each meal. Select a cook captain and a cleanup captain for each meal time. Then develop a schedule for who will serve in meal preparation and cleanup with each captain. Get everyone involved on either a cooking or cleanup team.
- ☐ Coordinate the transportation and safekeeping (including refrigeration) of all food, supplies, and utensils.

Music Coordinator

Serves as a member of the Planning Team and reports to the Event Director.

KEY RESPONSIBILITIES
Coordinate the recruitment, selection, and confirmation of all music/musicians for the event.

QUALIFICATIONS
Organized; has knowledge and experience in leading singing and worship; has a sensitivity to how music can best be used in a variety of settings; is versatile with music that appeals to both the young and not-so-young; has a servant's heart.

RESPONSIBILITIES CHECKLIST
☐ During the early stages of planning, provide estimated cost per person to Budget Coordinator.
☐ With input and direction from the Planning Team, determine what type of musicians are needed for the event. (For example, do you want performance only or audience involvement? Do you want a song leader who sets the atmosphere before the speaker? Do you want "live" music or is a taped soundtrack acceptable?
☐ Research the musically talented people in your group. What do they have to offer this event?
☐ Clearly outline what is expected of the musician(s).

When scheduling outside musician(s):
☐ Get a signed contract that spells out specific expectations, honorariums, fees, etc.
☐ See that any required deposit has been sent to and received by the musician(s).
☐ Determine the type of sound equipment needed at the event. If needed equipment isn't available, arrange with the A/V Coordinator for necessary equipment.
☐ Arrange for lodging, airport pickups (if applicable), and transportation to the event site. If lodging is needed, prepay the hotel.
☐ Have check(s) prepared to give the musician(s) at the event. Include approved reimbursement of expenses for transportation costs, etc.
☐ As the event draws near, send an updated event schedule to the musician(s), clearly indicating their scheduled times.

Publicity Coordinator

Serves as a member of the Planning Team and reports to the Event Director.

KEY RESPONSIBILITIES

To promote the event in every way possible in the church and/or the community. To oversee the development and production of all promotion (i.e., flyers, brochures, posters, etc.).

QUALIFICATIONS

Knowledge of marketing, promotion, desktop production, printing, etc.; organized, detailed, creative and resourceful; has a servant's heart.

RESPONSIBILITIES CHECKLIST

☐ During the early stages of planning, provide estimated cost per person to Budget Coordinator.

Ideas to help your promotion be successful:

☐ As a general rule of thumb, people will need to see or hear at least seven different promotions. In other words, the same flyer sent seven times isn't enough. Flyers, posters, newsletter articles, personal invitations, phone calls, etc., combine for an effective promotion.

☐ Promotional information should give complete details about the event (such as dates, registration information, cost, schedule, special speaker/music, unique aspects of the event, details about scholarships and monthly payment plans, and a map to the facility). A detailed and creative brochure goes a long way toward enticing single adults to join the activities.

☐ Always have a few names written on any sign-up sheets that are passed around. (Seeing that others are interested helps motivate people to become involved.)

☐ If this is an annual event, announce next year's date, place, and theme at this year's event so people can plan ahead.

☐ Recruit someone who will go on this event to serve as the official photographer and record the event in pictures. Arrange for the photographer to take a group photo during the event and make copies available to all attendees. Photos of this event will stimulate people talking about how much they enjoyed it and will help promote your next event.

☐ When a speaker is involved, provide a brief biographical sketch and explanation of the speaker's specific qualifications. Even if the name is familiar to your audience, a brief description can help a single adult decide whether or not to attend.

☐ Get promotional items printed as early as possible. It can never be out too early. Repeat sending or handing out brochures/flyers as often as possible.

Ways to promote your event:

☐ Radio and TV public service announcements.
☐ Brochures distributed to all known single groups in your area.
☐ Announcements at your meetings and in your single adult Sunday school class(es).
☐ Flyers/brochures/posters distributed
    • throughout your church.
    • in public areas (public library, health clubs, singles' organizations, Laundromats, schools, grocery stores, and other key locations.) Remember to obtain permission first!
☐ A mailing to all singles on your church mailing list.
☐ The church bulletin and newsletter.
☐ Press releases to all area media.
☐ Radio and newspaper interviews.

(Continued)

☐ Place flyers on windshields in area shopping malls, etc.
☐ Encourage your group to invite their friends to this non-threatening, fun event.
(Note: distribute the form below to all the singles in your group. Ask them to complete it and return it to a member of the event Planning Team.)
☐ Since singles often live in apartment complexes, determine if a complex newsletter is published. If so, advertise the event.
☐ Show slides, pictures, and videos from previous trips if applicable.
☐ Encourage your singles to take brochures/posters to clubs and organizations where they belong (health clubs, professional organizations, singles organizations, etc.).
☐ Have a representative at all major singles functions in the area to promote the event.
☐ Use skits/drama to help promote your events in your church/group.

After the event:

☐ Send a photo/news release to the media after the event is over.
☐ Use event photos to develop an attractive display in a visible place where your singles meet. (This helps promote future events.)
☐ Use a video of the event to show at one of the singles functions.

Spread the Word

WOULD YOU HELP US TELL OTHERS ABOUT THE UPCOMING _____ EVENT?

The best way to spread the word is always by word of mouth. We depend heavily on those in our group to help spread the word about this event. We need you to help us by agreeing to hand out brochures/flyers and by personally inviting your friends and associates to attend.

If you sign below, you will receive a packet of brochures and information that will help you advertise this event. Since our budget is limited (and since you have contacts that we do not have), this can be one of our most effective methods of getting out the word.

Let's make this event all that we can—together. Thanks in advance for your great help!

Please sign below. You will receive the promotional information packet soon.

NAME: _____

ADDRESS: _____

CITY: _____ STATE: _____ ZIP: _____

PHONE: HOME _____ WORK _____

CHURCH: _____

Recreation Coordinator

Serves as a member of the Planning Team and reports to the Event Director.

KEY RESPONSIBILITIES

- [ ] Oversee, promote, and provide schedules and instructions for games.
- [ ] Motivate and challenge people to participate in various activities and sports, such as volleyball, basketball, ping pong, etc.
- [ ] Organize and coordinate all details and equipment as needed.

QUALIFICATIONS

Organized, active, playful; a natural "coach"; good with people; has a servant's heart.

RESPONSIBILITIES CHECKLIST

- [ ] During the early stages of planning, provide estimated cost per person to Budget Coordinator.
- [ ] Check with the Event Site Coordinator about on-site equipment for games and activities.
- [ ] Encourage people to bring a variety of board games, and sports and other equipment, as needed.
- [ ] Where appropriate, make arrangements for any event bonfires/campfires.
- [ ] Plan to include both physical and non-physical activities.
- [ ] Prepare to assist in (or lead) all mixers and icebreaker activities.

Retreat Leader

KEY RESPONSIBILITIES

Train Spiritual Formation Group Facilitators and guide the "Community in Solitude" process throughout the event.

QUALIFICATIONS

Spiritual leader; skilled speaker; able to train others, facilitate group process, and spend reflective time alone with God; available for conducting pre-event Bible studies and training sessions.

RESPONSIBILITIES CHECKLIST

- [ ] Review/adapt the Spiritual Formation Group questions (pages 175-178) to suit the group.
- [ ] Provide a list of optional suggested pre-event readings for participants: a bibliography of selected readings from books and Scripture passages (pages 168-169).
- [ ] Train the Spiritual Formation Group Facilitators, which includes leading a Bible study on reflective time with God prior to the event (page 176).
- [ ] Introduce the event on Friday night and be available to answer related questions.
- [ ] Share devotional thoughts at Worship (5-10 minutes on Friday evening, Saturday morning and evening, and Sunday morning). Suggested topics/Scriptures are on page 170.
- [ ] Lead the final day's sharing time.

Registration Coordinator

Serves as a member of the Planning Team and reports to the Event Director.

KEY RESPONSIBILITIES

Oversee, manage, and coordinate the registration and confirmation process.

QUALIFICATIONS

Organized, detail-oriented; works well under pressure; good with numbers; has a servant's heart.

RESPONSIBILITIES CHECKLIST

- [ ] During the early stages of planning, provide estimated cost per person to Budget Coordinator.
- [ ] In cooperation with the Publicity and Budget Coordinators, develop a registration form that can be included in publicity brochures and/or passed out or mailed to potential participants. Also develop a scholarship application form (see sample forms on pages 245-246).
- [ ] Determine all preregistration and registration deadlines.
- [ ] Provide incentives for early registration (better price, free book, etc.). However, it is recommended that registration always be open for walk-in traffic if possible.
- [ ] As the event approaches, adjust attendance figures as needed with the Event Site Coordinator. Some facilities require a guaranteed number two to three weeks in advance. This often includes a +/– 5 to 10% clause. Keep this figure in mind during the last few days.
- [ ] Provide the Event Director and all Planning Team members with a regularly updated list of those registered to date. This helps the team know who's coming and to plan accordingly.
- [ ] With help from the Hospitality Coordinator, recruit a team of people who are willing to serve as greeters at the registration table and to assist people with parking, luggage, rooms, etc. Many may be attending this event without knowing anyone else. It is very important that each attendee be greeted at registration and made to feel comfortable and welcomed. This need increases with those who are new and/or arriving after dark. If it is necessary to carry luggage, consider using dollies and luggage carriers to assist people to their rooms.
- [ ] Set up a roommate list. People generally request who they would like to room with. Look over the requests. Match where possible and assign the others.
- [ ] To aid follow-up on all newcomers, prepare a list of every attendee's name, address, and phone number (either before or during the event).
- [ ] During promotion, encourage people to sign a preregistration list and to reserve the dates. To build interest, make sure that all sign-up sheets include a few names before circulating.
- [ ] Consider including a "no refund" policy on the registration form. This way, participants will not be able to easily back out at the last minute and expect a refund, leaving the ministry to pay the financial difference. Include this "no refund" information on the registration form.
- [ ] If desired, ask for a registration deposit. This provides funds to use when making deposits for the event. It also helps to ensure that people who register actually attend.
- [ ] Make it very clear on the registration form what is included in the registration fee. For example, are all meals included or are they the responsibility of each participant? Clearly communicate what each person gets for their registration fee—and what is not included (see page 245 for a sample registration form).
- [ ] Be prepared for last-minute requests to attend, as well as last-minute cancellations. The following criteria may be helpful when handling these requests:

(Continued)

- Cancellation refunds are made if someone has experienced health problems or a personal crisis, or if there is someone who can fill their spot.
- Last-minute registrations are accepted if an appropriate rooming situation is available.

Name Tags

☐ Name tags are very important since up to one-half of those attending may be newcomers.

☐ Order name tags and name tag holders (found at any office supply store).

☐ There is a space limitation on what can be put on each name tag. However, putting first names in large, easy-to-read letters is especially important.

☐ Recruit someone who will be responsible for preparing the name tags. Find someone with lettering talents (calligraphy or professional-looking laser printing is nice) to print each person's name on a name tag prior to the event.

☐ If desired, identify Planning Team members and other resource persons with different colored name tags and identify newcomers with fun stickers on their tags.

☐ In addition to names, the name tags could also include room and small-group assignments. Be creative.

☐ Distribute name tags as people arrive at the event site. Or consider using them for check-in, distributing them as people get on buses/in cars for departure to the event site.

☐ For large events consider printing a picture and the theme of the event on each name tag.

☐ Take an extra supply of blank name tags for last-minute registrants or to replace lost ones.

☐ Require that name tags be worn throughout the weekend. This helps everyone remember each other's names and enables you to control walk-in traffic.

Confirmation letter:

☐ Send a confimation letter to all registrants no later than 7–10 days prior to the event (see page 244 for a sample registration letter).

☐ This letter should include the following (adjust as needed for your particular event):
  - Location and emergency phone numbers of the event site
  - Map to the location
  - Departure time and place
  - Arrival time and place
  - Return information (approximate time of return and stops along the way)
  - Time of first activities
  - Event schedule
  - List of what to bring and what to wear
  - Date and time of any informational meetings prior to trip
  - Room/tent assignments (so people can contact their roommates, if desired, for car pooling purposes, etc.)
  - Information about event site/campground facilities (private or shared rooms, private or shared restrooms and showers, and, if camping, flushable toilets)
  - Description(s) of optional side trip(s) and activities at the event site
  - Appropriate promotional brochures/materials of the event facility
  - Reminder that all "Liability Release Forms" need to be turned in before departure (see page 253 for a sample form)
  - Balance due, if any
  - Reminder that this is an alcohol- and smoke-free adventure

(Continued)

Scholarships

☐ Prepare a scholarship application form and include information about possible scholarships on the registration form. Include a deadline for the return of the form. This date should be about one to three months prior to the event (see page 246 for a sample form).

☐ Offer partial scholarships first. Offer full scholarships only in "dire need" situations.

☐ Once scholarship forms have been completed, get the necessary approval (usually from the Event Director). Call and let each scholarship applicant know as soon as possible if the request has been approved and for what amount.

☐ If needed, assist the Event Director and the Budget Coordinator in raising scholarship funds.

"LAYAWAY PAYMENT PLAN"

Offering this payment plan, although it requires extra work, is well worth it. Without a payment plan, many single adults, especially single parents, might be unable to attend. The payment plan is similar to a "layaway plan" uséd in department stores. Those who wish to use the plan pay a specified amount each month up until the event takes place. This method helps make it more affordable for many interested participants.

Here's a look at a set of payment plan coupons for a June event. These coupons make it easier for each participant to keep track of payments.

INSTALLMENT PAYMENT PLAN

$30.00 payment #1: Due March 1

for the _____
                    (Event)
Name: _____

Make payable to _____

INSTALLMENT PAYMENT PLAN

$30.00 payment #2: Due April 1

for the _____
                    (Event)
Name: _____

Make payable to _____

INSTALLMENT PAYMENT PLAN

$30.00 payment #3: Due May 1

for the _____
                    (Event)
Name: _____

Make payable to _____

INSTALLMENT PAYMENT PLAN

$30.00 payment #4: Due June 1

for the _____
                    (Event)
Name: _____

Make payable to _____

Confirmation Letter
(Sample)

Date

Dear <u>write in name</u>:

    Welcome to our SPRING RETREAT. I am looking forward to having you as a participant in this wonderful weekend filled with fun, fellowship, and time for spiritual growth.

    We will begin check-in procedures on FRIDAY, MAY xx, xxxx at 4:00 P.M. in the <u>(location)</u>. We have been asked to park our cars at the WEST end of the lot beginning with the THIRD ROW. We will notify the Police Department that our cars will be left there throughout the weekend. If you can carpool with another retreater to reduce the number of cars, it would be appreciated. When you arrive, please stop by the registration table by the buses to check in and pick up your name tag, then choose the bus you wish to ride, store your luggage, take a seat on the bus, and remain on the bus. This will make distribution of box dinners and counting of people much easier. Your cooperation will be (and is) greatly appreciated.

    Your name tag will have your room number at <u>the event site</u> on the back and your small-group number on the front (left corner). Upon arrival, YOU DO NOT NEED TO CHECK IN. YOUR ROOM KEY WILL BE IN YOUR ROOM!

    The buses will be departing at 5:00 P.M. SHARP! Dinner will be provided for everyone on the bus. EVERYONE WHO ATTENDS THE EVENT MUST RIDE THE BUS. Please allow yourself enough time to arrive on time.

    You should plan to bring your Bible and pen, notebook or journal, casual clothing (warm clothes for evening), personal toiletries, money for the dinner stop on the way home Sunday, and a great attitude, wanting to grow and be blessed. You should also bring a flashlight for our bonfires on Friday and Saturday night.

    You will have free time on Saturday and Sunday afternoons. Activities you may choose from include tennis (bring your own racket), softball, jogging, canoeing, or walking the beaches and dunes. Make sure you bring appropriate clothing and shoes.

    The phone number at <u>the event site</u> is (xxx) xxx-xxxx. Give this number to your family/friends in case of an emergency. If you need to call home, plan to use a credit card or pay phone as phone calls may not be charged to your room.

    On the way home we will stop for dinner at <u>(location)</u> around 7:30 P.M. We will be returning at approximately 9:30 P.M. on Sunday, May xx.

    As a reminder, if you have not yet paid your FINAL BALANCE, please do so.

    My prayer is that this will be a special time for you. I hope that you will have the opportunity to relax and be renewed through the love and friendship of this terrific group of people. Feel free to call me (xxx-xxxx) if you have any questions. I'M LOOKING FORWARD TO SEEING YOU ON MAY XX at 4:00 P.M.

Sincerely,

Event Director
(or Registration Coordinator)

Registration Form
(Sample)

(Modify for your needs, add and subtract elements as your event requires.)

Event Date

Cost: $210.00

Scholarships and payment plan available
Cost includes: 5 meals, 2 nights lodging, transportation,
all materials and loads of fun

Early Bird Registration due 1 month in advance (receive gift book, or discount)
Regular Registration due 2 weeks in advance

Deposit of $42.00, due with this form, is non-refundable.
Other deposits refundable for cancellation up to 2 weeks in advance.

Name: _____

Street: _____ Apt.: _____

City: _____ State: _____ Zip: _____

Phones: (home) _____ (work) _____ (fax) _____

Can you provide rides? _____ If yes, how many (including self)? _____

Roommate preference: _____

Will you need child care? _____ If so, for how many children and what ages?

_____

Which workshop(s) do you plan to attend? _____

I would like to speak with someone about a confidential scholarship. _____

office use: Payment #1 (deposit) made: _____
Payment #2 made: _____
Payment #3 made: _____
Payment #4 made: _____
Payment #5 made: _____
Paid in full? _____

Send or give this form to: _____
Name, address, phone

Scholarship Application
(Sample)

(Modify for your needs, add and subtract elements as your event requires.)

Due Date:_____

Name: _____

Street: _____ Apt.: _____

City: _____ State: _____ Zip: _____

Phones: (home) _____ (work) _____ (fax) _____

Event for which scholarship help is requested: _____

Total cost of event: $ _____
Scholarship amount requested: $ _____

(Please be aware that our policy is to provide a maximum scholarship of 50% of the cost of the event.)

Please provide below any information regarding your need that will guide the scholarship committee. (All information is confidential.)

_____
Signature   Date

Send or give this form to: _____
                          Name, address, phone

Small-Group Coordinator

Serves as a member of the Planning Team and reports to the Event Director.

KEY RESPONSIBILITIES

☐ Organize and coordinate all small-group participation and discussions.
☐ Recruit and train small-group leaders/facilitators.
☐ Prepare small-group discussion materials/handouts.

QUALIFICATIONS

Experienced in facilitating small-group interaction; organized; ability to train others; encourager of people; good interpersonal skills; sensitive; has the gift of hospitality, the ability to draw others out, the ability to stimulate discussion, and a servant's heart.

RESPONSIBILITIES CHECKLIST

Generally the greatest amount of growth occurs in small-group discussions, where the risk factor is low and everyone gets a chance to share and listen. When appropriate, plan a variety of discussion groups with topics that are coordinated with a general theme and/or the speaker's topic.

☐ During the early stages of planning, provide estimated cost per person to Budget Coordinator.
☐ Before the event, become familiar with any prepared discussion questions.
☐ Recruit and train Small-Group Facilitators (See guidelines on pages 248 and 249).
☐ Help create discussion questions if needed.
☐ Remind facilitators that they are not to lecture or to steal the spotlight, but to facilitate and encourage discussion.
☐ With the assistance of the Speaker Coordinator, become familiar with the focus, theme, Scriptures, and small-group questions for the event.
☐ Work with the Event Materials Coordinator to obtain supplies/materials as needed.
☐ When needed, develop some creative, fun ideas for dividing participants into small groups.
☐ Have leaders begin praying for their group members today! Prayer will help make them more effective leaders and prepare their hearts for this special time.

Recruiting small-group leaders/facilitators:

☐ As much as possible, recruit those who have been previously active in leadership of small groups or in other areas of the ministry (i.e., divorce recovery, grief support, Bible study groups, single-parent family ministry, etc.)
☐ Recruit a mix of both men and women as evenly as possible.

Small-Group Facilitator Guidelines and Suggestions

- ☐ Open the group with introductions and a short instructional talk on small-group guidelines including:
  - keeping confidences
  - listening to each other
  - praying for each other
  - not giving advice (unless it is requested)
  - not comparing your problem with another's
  - being considerate—allowing time for each person to share
  - not forcing anyone to share
  - not allowing condemnation
  - creating a safe place where each person is accepted and loved
- ☐ Leaders need to be alert to draw out shy people.
- ☐ Do not let one person monopolize the conversation. Tactfully move on by offering to meet one-on-one at a later time or ask someone else to give a response.
- ☐ Where needed, stimulate discussion with questions or sharing problems and concerns. This often requires you to take a risk and share before others feel safe enough.
- ☐ Your role is a moderator—you are not there to "fix" anyone or to lecture.
- ☐ End the discussion on a positive, encouraging note. Use Scripture or a song as appropriate.
- ☐ Make sure discussions aren't too serious. Include light, fun, humorous discussions too.
- ☐ Take time in your group each day to pray for each other's needs.
- ☐ Strive to ask "non-threatening" questions so that each person feels comfortable in sharing.
- ☐ At the end of the event, invite each member of your small group to share addresses and phone numbers with one another, encouraging them to stay in contact and to build on their time together.
- ☐ Address people by name as much as possible. The frequent use of names gives people a sense of belonging and connectedness.
- ☐ Remember that not everyone in your group may be a Christian, so be sensitive to all.
- ☐ Encourage everyone to have fun, get involved, and enjoy the fellowship of the event!
- ☐ Should a member of your group need additional time to talk, schedule it for another convenient time and place.
- ☐ Be sensitive to the Holy Spirit and remain open to His leading and direction.

Understanding the three different levels of sharing[1]

1. Sharing of information and facts is a relatively safe level of sharing, but doesn't communicate a lot about the individual.
2. Sharing of ideas and opinions takes a little more risk as people start to share information about themselves. As more people share opinions and ideas, differences emerge and members test the limits of diversity. If these differences are handled in a positive way, members will feel safe in risking more honesty in the expression of their ideas. Remember—there is no such thing as a "wrong" opinion or idea!
3. Sharing of feelings is the level of communication where people are taking the greatest risk. Members risk self-disclosure because they value the benefits of being known for who they really are. At this level members are less hidden and more open to each other.

(Continued)

Communication Skills for Leaders[1]

- ☐ Listen attentively to the person who is sharing. Face the speaker and use nonverbal communication to let them know that you value what they are sharing.
- ☐ Asking someone's opinion helps involve those who tend to be less active group members. It also lets them know that you value their opinions and input to the group.
- ☐ Ask for clarification if there seems to be confusion on the part of the group. Again, this reaffirms that you value their sharing and want to understand what they are really saying.
- ☐ Paraphrasing allows for opportunities to reflect back on what a member has shared, as well as to summarize the main point of a particular discussion.
- ☐ Extending allows you to take a certain thought and "extend" it into a discussion. (i.e., "Does anyone have something to add to what was just said?" "Is there anything else that comes to mind regarding this topic?")
- ☐ Personal implication questions allow the leader to take a discussion that seems too vague or general and to ask the group members how that issue applies to them personally. Be careful to allow them to answer voluntarily, not by force! (i.e., "How do we apply this to our personal lives?")

Handling talkative or silent members[1]

Research shows that people seated directly opposite the discussion leader are most likely to talk while those seated right next to the leader tend to be more quiet (due to the fact that it is harder to maintain eye contact with them).

Placing the silent member opposite the leader may help in drawing them into the conversation (or seating yourself next to a talkative member may deter "over-talkativeness"). Also, breaking eye contact with a more talkative member and redirecting it to the silent member may enable the conversation to shift.

Watch for opportunities to draw the quiet members into the group. Statements like "I'd like to hear from someone who hasn't spoken yet" may be helpful.

Also, watch for signs of interest on the face of the silent participant. At that point you may say "Sue, you look like you have something to add to this discussion."

Training resources:

When preparing for your responsibilities and for training others to be effective small group facilitators, read the following:

• Neal McBride, *How to Lead Small Groups.* (Colorado Springs: NavPress, 1990)
• Steve Sheely, *Leader's Handbook for Small Groups.* (Littleton, CO: Serendipity House, 1994).
• James Nyquist and Jack Kuhatschek, *Leading Bible Discussions.* (Colorado Springs: InterVarsity Press, 1985)

[1] Adapted from *How to Lead Small Groups* by Neal McBride, NavPress, 1990.

Speaker/Workshop Leaders Coordinator

Serves as a member of the Planning Team and reports to the Event Director.

KEY RESPONSIBILITIES

Coordinate the recruitment, selection, and confirmation of all speakers/workshop leaders for the event.

QUALIFICATIONS

Organized; has knowledge and experience in working with speakers/teachers; has a sense for the range of needs expected at the event; is resourceful; has a servant's heart.

RESPONSIBILITIES CHECKLIST

☐ During the early stages of planning, provide estimated cost per person to Budget Coordinator.

☐ With input and direction from the Planning Team, determine what type of speaker(s) are needed for the event. (Remember to consider your own pastor, a pastor from across town, or a key leader from your group. Of course, as the old saying goes, if the person is from more than 50 miles away, he or she is a pro!)

☐ Research possible speakers that fit your needs.

☐ The speaker should be a solid Christian (with rare exception) with strong professional credentials and the ability to speak intelligently and compassionately to single adults. Allow up to one year to acquire a well-known speaker.

☐ If you will be using teaching or small-group materials provided with the event, make sure the speaker is someone who can synthesize material and communicate the thoughts and ideas of the resources/books being referenced without reading them to the group. In addition, the leader must have the ability to adapt, supplement, and apply Scripture and personal illustrations to the suggested thoughts and ideas.

☐ Prepare a contract clearly outlining fees or honorarium and expectations you have for the speaker, including how many times he or she is expected to speak and when.

☐ Confirm that the speaker has received the contract and that everything is agreeable.

☐ See that any required deposit has been sent to and received by the speaker.

☐ Finalize topic/theme/Scriptures with the speaker.

☐ If you plan to tape the speaker's presentations, be sure to get a signed release form. This form should include:
  • Speaker's name, signature, date of signature
  • Event name, location, date
  • Permission to reproduce, distribute, and fill orders on taped talk/music (as applicable)

☐ Send the speaker a copy of all promotional material, event schedule, etc.

☐ Arrange for lodging, airport pickups (if applicable), and transportation to the event site. If lodging is needed, prepay the hotel.

☐ Have check(s) prepared to give the speaker(s) at the event. Include approved reimbursement of expenses for transportation costs, etc.

☐ When you need to get several speakers/workshop leaders, recruit a team of people who can help.

(Continued)

Process for Selecting a Speaker

Although many of the events in this book do not require a special guest speaker, if you decide to invite a speaker and/or workshop leaders for the program—and if you do not already have a speaker in mind—here is one possible selection process that involves the whole Planning Team:

☐ Request a Planning Team meeting to brainstorm ideas.
  • Ask each team member to bring the names of three potential main speakers, five workshop topics, and five potential workshop leaders for each of the following areas: (1) Spiritual growth; (2) Relational growth; (3) Personal growth.
  • Have all team members present their main speaker and workshop topics/leaders ideas.
  • After the meeting, compile all this information on a master list and duplicate enough copies for each team member.

☐ At the next Planning Team meeting choose the main speaker and workshop topics/leaders.
  • Distribute copies of the master list.
  • Have each person rate each suggested main speaker, each workshop topic, and each leader on a scale of 1-5 (1 being first choice and 5 being last).
  • Total the scores and rank each idea according to popularity.
  • From the top-rated speakers, topics, and workshop leaders, discuss and select those to be used for the event.
  • If needed, recruit help in contacting the various speakers.

Worship Coordinator

Serves as a member of the Planning Team and reports to the Event Director.

KEY RESPONSIBILITIES

Plan and lead the worship portions of the event.

QUALIFICATIONS

Spiritually mature; sensitive to the various levels of spiritual growth among the participants; has an ability to lead in communion and group worship and a servant's heart.

RESPONSIBILITIES CHECKLIST

☐ During the early stages of planning, provide estimated cost per person to Budget Coordinator.
☐ With input from the Planning Team, plan worship time(s) based on the theme of the event. Recruit people to help, as necessary.
☐ If Communion is to be served, ask a singles minister, director, or authorized lay person to work closely with you and the Event Director and Assistant Director to prepare and present a meaningful communion service.
☐ Where appropriate, be available throughout the weekend for people who may be struggling with personal issues or who are seeking a relationship with Christ.
☐ Determine and obtain supplies (worship music, elements for Communion, candles, worship cloth, flowers, etc.), if needed, through the church's worship committee.

Transportation Coordinator

Serves as a member of the Planning Team and reports to the Event Director.

KEY RESPONSIBILITIES

To coordinate, schedule, and organize all transportation to and from the event site.

QUALIFICATIONS

Organized, detail-oriented, responsible, dependable, and resourceful; has had personal experience with travel arrangements and/or tours; has a servant's heart.

RESPONSIBILITIES CHECKLIST

Note: Chartering a bus will add a substantial cost to your trip. Carpooling is less expensive, but may require more organization and planning.

☐ During the early stages of planning, provide estimated cost per person to Budget Coordinator.
☐ If needed, arrange for an extra vehicle to transport food, equipment, and supplies.
☐ Once transportation plans have been confirmed, inform the Registration Coordinator so he or she can include this information in the confirmation letter to all registrants.
☐ Where needed, obtain any necessary travel documentation/papers.
☐ If cars will be parked overnight at the departure location, secure permission from the church, police, or other appropriate authorities.
☐ If passenger pickup will be available at sites other than the main departure point, inform the Planning Team and drivers. (Also, make sure the Registration Coordinator communicates this to all participants in the final confirmation letter.)
☐ Obtain from the Event Site Coordinator a map to the event site. Provide a copy to the Event Materials Coordinator so copies can be provided to all participants as needed.
☐ Arrange for any insurance coverage or forms as may be required by your church.

If using commercial travel (air, chartered bus, rental vehicles, etc.):

☐ Confirm plans, dates, times, etc.
☐ See that any required deposit is paid.
☐ If travel by air is being considered, contact a travel agency or airline for arrangements and rates. (If traveling with ten or more people, ask for group fares.)
☐ Confirm with the travel agent and/or airline the number of participants expected.
☐ If chartered buses will be used, confirm their reservations now. Send a letter to the bus company with maps and instructions.

If using car pool or church van/bus:

☐ If church vehicles are to be used, complete the necessary requisition procedures and paperwork in the church office. Make sure vehicles (and qualified drivers) are scheduled and confirmed. Note it on the church calendar.
☐ If carpooling, determine available drivers and the number of persons they can each take.
☐ Select qualified and licensed drivers.
☐ Be sure all drivers have a map to the event location.
☐ Make carpool assignments (and a way to account for all participants).

Have each participant sign a liability release form for any event where risk is involved (white-water rafting, mountain climbing, etc.). Adapt the following sample for your own use, being sure to have your church's legal advisor check and approve it.

Liability Release Form (Sample)

Event Name _____ Event Date(s) _____

Sponsoring Church/Organization _____

EMERGENCY RELEASE FORM

Should an emergency arise, the leaders or supervisors of this event have my permission to obtain any necessary emergency medical care for me. I agree to defend and indemnify (name of sponsoring church/organization), its employees, and volunteers against any claim or action that might arise on behalf of myself other than for willful, wanton, or reckless misconduct of (name of sponsoring church/organization), its employees, or volunteers.

_____   _____
      signature   date

In case of an emergency please contact:

Name _____

Address _____

Phone (Day) (____)_____   (Evening) (____)_____

Relationship _____

Alternative Contact _____

Address _____

Phone (Day) (____)_____   (Evening) (____)_____

Relationship _____

Do you have any particular allergies or medical or physical conditions that we should be aware of? No ____ Yes ____ (please explain below)

Followup Guidelines
(Sample)

The event is not over until the follow-up is completed. Here is a checklist of items to consider doing after each event. Have the Planning Team meet for pizza some evening to handle all follow-up items. Adapt as needed to fit your specific needs and situation.

Note: The following should all be completed within two to four weeks after the event.

Planning Team—Evaluation and Reporting:

☐ Conduct an evaluation of the event. If evaluation forms were distributed to participants at the event, read and summarize them. In what ways was your event especially successful? What things could have been done better? What would you do differently if you held this event again? It is helpful to create a three-ring notebook with this evaluation summary and related notes to help with the planning of future events. The lessons learned each time ought to be passed on and remembered for future ministry (see sample "Evaluation Form" on page 255).

☐ Send a report on the event to the senior pastor (and other key leaders in the church). It is important to let them know how lives are being touched and what is being accomplished in your single adult ministry.

Budget Coordinator—Finances:

☐ If not already done, send honorariums to speakers/musicians, etc.
☐ Make sure all bills have been paid and out-of-pocket expenses reimbursed.
☐ Provide the Planning Team an account of all expenses and income.

Planning Team—Thank Yous:

☐ Send thank-you notes to all who played a key role in helping make this event happen.

Publicity Coordinator—Publicity and Public Relations:

☐ Send a final news release report, along with appropriate photos, to the media.
☐ With the help of the photographer, compile a photo album (and/or slides or video) of the event and present it to the Event Director. With the Event Director, set a date when all photos/slides/video could be shown at a newcomer's brunch or to the entire singles group. (This is not only a fun time, but it also helps create interest for your next event.)
☐ Create a photo display of the event on your singles ministry bulletin board.

Planning Team—Returning Borrowed Items:

☐ If any equipment, utensils, or supplies were borrowed for the event, see that they are returned promptly and in good condition.

Event Director and Ministry Leaders—Newcomers' Follow-Up:

☐ Special events are often an entry point for newcomers to your ministry. All first-time visitors should be contacted by a follow-up team with a telephone visit and an invitation to return.
☐ Have Small-Group Leaders send a letter or card to all those in their group to encourage them and to invite newcomers to another singles group function.

Evaluation Form
(Sample)

Evaluations are useful for planning our next event/retreat. They help the Planning Team take into account individual needs and interests. Remember: What you liked is just as important as what you didn't like.

How did you hear about this event? _____

Is this your first event with our group? ❐ Yes   ❐ No

A. Please rate the following aspects of <u>name of event</u> from 1 to 5. (1 = Didn't like at all; 5 = liked a lot.)

1 2 3 4 5	1. Publicity and pre-event information
1 2 3 4 5	2. Housing arrangements
1 2 3 4 5	3. Meals
1 2 3 4 5	4. Leisure-time activities
1 2 3 4 5	5. Study topic/theme
1 2 3 4 5	6. Study presentation
1 2 3 4 5	7. Leader/speaker's knowledge and information
1 2 3 4 5	8. Worship times
1 2 3 4 5	9. Music
1 2 3 4 5	10. Opportunity to make new friends

B. Please answer the following questions:

11. What one new thing did you learn from this event that will help you in your life?

12. What was the highlight of this event for you?

13. What was a disappointment to you?

14. If you were on the planning team, what one thing would you do differently next time?

15. What topic(s) would you like to see offered next year?

16. If you would be willing to be on the next event/retreat Planning Team, please write your name here or contact <u>name of Event Director</u>.

C. Additional Comments? Please write on back.

SINGLES
Ministry Resources

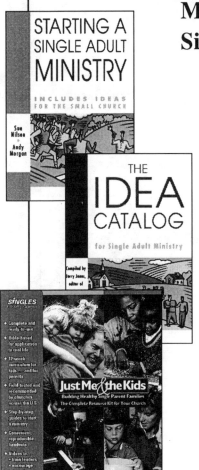

Materials available from Singles Ministry Resources:

Foundational Books

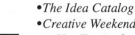

- *Starting a Single Adult Ministry*
- *Giving the Ministry Away:* Empowering Single Adults for Effective Leadership
- *Growing Your Single Adult Ministry*
- *Developing a Divorce Recovery Ministry:* A How-to-Manual
- *Helping Single Parents with Troubled Kids:* A Ministry Resource for Pastors & Youth Workers

Idea Books

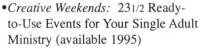

- *The Idea Catalog*
- *Creative Weekends:* 231/2 Ready-to-Use Events for Your Single Adult Ministry (available 1995)
- *Building Your Leadership Team:* Practical Ideas for Single Adult Ministry (available 1995)

Program Materials

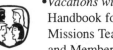

- *Just Me & the Kids:* Building Healthy Single-Parent Families
- *Vacations with a Purpose:* A Planning Handbook for Your Short-Term Missions Team (Leader's Manual and Member's Handbook)

Newsletter

- Single Adult Ministries (SAM) Journal

To receive more information about these and other quality singles ministry resources or to order, contact your local Christian bookstore

OR

SINGLES MINISTRY RESOURCES
P.O. Box 60430
Colorado Springs, Colorado 80960-0430

Or call (800) 323-7543
Canada (800) 387-5856
or (719) 635-6020

Singles Ministry Resources is a division of Cook Communications Ministries